U0409705

标记理论视角下闽南-闽东音系学研究

A Phonological Analysis of Southern Min and Eastern Min from the Perspective of Markedness

吴秀龙 著

苏州大学出版社

图书在版编目(CIP)数据

标记理论视角下闽南-闽东音系学研究 = A Phonological Analysis of Southern Min and Eastern Min from the Perspective of Markedness : 英文 / 吴秀龙著. --苏州: 苏州大学出版社, 2024.8. -- ISBN 978-7-5672-4794-9

Ⅰ. H177.2

中国国家版本馆 CIP 数据核字第 2024Q9A918 号

书　　名: 标记理论视角下闽南-闽东音系学研究
　　　　　A Phonological Analysis of Southern Min and Eastern Min from the Perspective of Markedness

---

著　　者: 吴秀龙
责任编辑: 汤定军
策划编辑: 汤定军
装帧设计: 刘　俊

出版发行: 苏州大学出版社(Soochow University Press)
社　　址: 苏州市十梓街 1 号　邮编: 215006
印　　装: 广东虎彩云印刷有限公司
网　　址: www.sudapress.com
邮　　箱: tangdingjun@suda.edu.cn
邮购热线: 0512-67480030
销售热线: 0512-67481020

开　　本: 700 mm × 1 000 mm　1/16　印张: 17.75　字数: 309 千
版　　次: 2024 年 8 月第 1 版
印　　次: 2024 年 8 月第 1 次印刷
书　　号: ISBN 978-7-5672-4794-9
定　　价: 68.00 元

Contents

Chapter 6 Similarities and Differences of the Finals Between Quanzhou and Fuzhou

Chapter 7 Tones of Quanzhou and Fuzhou

Chapter 8 Conclusion

Symbols and Abbreviations

// = Underlying form

[ ] = Surface form

> = More marked than

MoA = Manner of Articulation

PoM = Preservation of Markedness

PoA = Place of Articulation

SDA = Successive Division Algorithm

Chapter 1

Introduction

1.1 Background of the present study

There are mainly seven dialect groups in Chinese, which include the northern dialect group (represented by Mandarin regarded as Standard Chinese), the Wu dialect group, the Gan dialect group, the Min dialect group, the Xiang dialect group, the Yue dialect group and the Hakka dialect group (see Chao 1967). Due to the mutual intelligibility between the dialect groups, there exists controversy with regard to whether they should be regarded as different "dialects" as viewed from the perspective of political and psychological reasons and orthographic system, or as different "languages" in accordance with Western linguists (e. g. Bloomingfield 1933) on the basis of the criterion of mutual intelligibility for distinguishing between dialects and languages. This book follows our tradition and official concept that Chinese is a single language composed of several dialect groups including Min dialect which is the focus of this present study.

The Min dialect group, as one oldest dialect group in China, is noted for its conservative features, which may even data back to the 7th century B. C. with some respects even earlier than Ancient Chinese. In this sense, the Min dialect group is like a weather-beaten tower in Chinese. (Zhang 2011) Min dialects are spoken throughout Fujian Province except the southwest where Hakka is spoken, in Chaozhou of Guangdong Province, on Leizhou Penisula, on Hainan Island, in Zhongshan district south of Canton City, and also in parts of the provinces of Zhejiang, Jiangxi, Sichuan, and Guangxi. In Taiwan, the Southern Min dialect ("Amoy") is spoken by the majority of the population, referred to as "Taiwanese".

Despite the integrity of Min sub-dialects as discussed in Chen & Li (1983), the disparity between Southern Min and Northern Min① is so remarkable that the related academic research once divided the Min dialect group into two dialect groups such as Southern Min and Northern Min, parallel to the other six dialect groups of Chinese. For example, *Language Area Division Map* in *The New Map of The Republic of China* and *The New Map for Division of Provinces of China* divide dialect groups in China into eleven, which include the Northern Mandarin (represented by Standard Chinese), the Southwestern Mandarin, the Xiajiang Mandarin, the Xiang dialect group, the Gan dialect group, the Wu dialect group, the Hakka dialect group, the Yue dialect group, the Hui dialect group, Southern Min and Northern Min (Eastern Min). In the same year, *Mandarin Primer* by Chao (1948) divides the Min dialect group into Southern Min and Eastern Min. In order to highlight the discrepancy between the Min dialect group, Ding and Li proposed that Chinese dialects should be divided into eight groups, namely the Northern Mandarin, Wu, Xiang, Gang, Hakka, Yue, Southern Min and Eastern Min (Deng 2007: 1). As for the reasons for the division of Min into Southern Min and Eastern Min parallel to the other dialect groups in China, there has been little discussion. For example, the Central Research Institute marks the division of Southern Min and Eastern Min into parallel dialect groups in a map without literal illustration (Li Rong 1989). While some other researches which also divide Min into Southern Min and Eastern Min propose that such a division of Southern Min and Eastern Min is aimed at highlighting the phonetic discrepancy of Southern Min and Eastern

---

① Northern Min in the broad and old sense referred to the languages spoken in the northern part and eastern part of Fujian Province (Deng 2007). In a narrow sense, it is generally referred to the sub-dialects of Min centering on Fuzhou and is changed to be Eastern Min ever since (see Ding 1982). In this book, Northern Min is taken to mean what is labeled as Eastern Min nowadays in a narrow sense.

Min, for example, in Southern Min there are three nasal codas -m, -n, -ŋ and four obstruent codas -p, -t, -k, -ʔ, while in Eastern Min there is only one nasal coda and one stop coda such as -ŋ and -ʔ (Ding 1982: 169 – 170). What motivates so many proposals that initiate the division of Min into Southern Min and Eastern Min as parallel dialect groups? What factors account for such significant disparity of Southern Min and Eastern Min? These questions have been the concern of many scholars for a long time.

1.2 Brief introduction to Southern Min and Eastern Min

The Eastern Min dialect group is distributed along Min River as well as Jiaoxi River in Fujian Province. Historically, Fuzhou has acted as the center of Eastern Min, dominating about ten sub-dialects around it, which include Fuqing, Changle, Minhou, Lianjiang, Luoyuan, Minqing, Yongtai, Pingtan. *Chinese Language Maps Collection* divides Eastern Min dialects into three parts such as Houguan area, Funing area and Man dialect area (Yuan 2010: 10). The number of the people with Eastern Min dialects as their native language is about ten million.

Southern Min is not only distributed in the southern parts of Fuzhou, but also in Zhejiang, Guangdong, Hainan, Taiwan as well as the Southeast of Asia. In Fujian, Southern Min is mainly spoken in Quanzhou, Zhangzhou, Xiamen as well as Longyan, which is a combination of Hakka dialect and Southern Min dialect. In terms of the accents of Southern Min of Fujian Province, Quanzhou, Xiamen and Zhangzhou are three main representatives (Zhou 1986: 69). The number of the people with Southern Min as their native language is about seventy million.

In the related research of Southern Min and Eastern Min, it is widely accepted that the mutual intelligibility between Southern Min and Eastern Min is very low. But how low is the mutual intelligibility between Southern Min and Eastern Min? Is the mutual intelligibility between Southern Min and Eastern Min symmetrical for people of these two dialect areas? Is Eastern Min more difficult to understand than Southern Min or the reverse? In this book, a testing① on the intelligibility between Southern Min and Eastern Min in terms of phrases and sentences reveals the low intelligibility between these two dialects.

1.3 Literature review and research questions

1.3.1 Previous studies of Min dialects

Till now, there have been many researches on the sound systems of Min dialects from different perspectives. Some researches on the division of Min dialects such as Zhang (1985), Chen & Li (1983), Huang & Li (1998), Ding (1998), etc. provide the discussion on the division of Min dialect areas according to different criteria, either emphasizing similarities or differences of the related sub-dialects of Min. Some researches highlight the similarities of Min dialects. For example, Chen & Li (1983) emphasizes the unity of Min dialects. Ding (1998) also proposes to combine Southern Min and Northern Min within one large dialect area due to some shared features, though he also suggests that the great disparity of codas of Southern Min and Northern Min is enough to separate these two dialects into different dialect groups. Norman (2006) divides Chinese dialects into seven dialect areas, stressing the uniqueness of the lexicons of Min dialects.

Some researches on the single dialect of Min such as Cai (2006), Deng (2007), Zeng (2008), Nie (2012), Chen (2012), etc. are devoted to the analysis of the phonological systems of some sub-dialects of Min such as

---

① The testing on the intelligibility between Southern Min and Eastern Min in terms of phrases and sentences indicates as follows:

Dialects	Intelligibility (%) (Phrases)	Intelligibility (%) (Sentences)	Intelligibility (%) (A-value)
Southern Min	6 %	4 %	5 %
Eastern Min	5 %	2 %	3.5 %

The details of this intelligibility test will be discussed in the following pages.

Puxian, Northern Min, Central Min, Southern Min. For example, Cai (2006) analyzes Puxian dialect, focusing on the features that characterize Puxian dialect as a transitional dialect. Deng (2007) studies the phonetics of Northern Min and Central Min. Zeng (2008) conducts a phonological research of Dongtou Southern Min dialect in Southern Zhejiang Province. Nie (2012) analyzes the phonological system of Taining of Northern Min. Most of these researches tend to give a detailed description of the phonological systems of the related sub-dialects of Min.

There are some comparative researches as well as historical analysis of Min dialects by such as Norman (1973, 1979, 1981), Li Rulong (1985), Zhang Kun (1985, 1991), Zhang Guangyu (1996, 2011), Ding (1998), Chen Zhongmin (2012), Dai (2005), Wu (2002, 2009, 2010), Zhang Jingfen (2013), Zeng (2013), Lin (2013), Du (2013, 2014), which is devoted to the analysis of some remarkable finals, initials as well as codas of Min. For example, Li Rulong (1985) analyzes the evolution of the voiced initials of Min dialects in Middle Chinese. Chen Zhongmin (2012) gives a detailed analysis of the historical strata of Yu Rhyme in Quanzhou, Xiamen, as well as Zhangzhou. Zhang (2011) concentrates on the reservation and innovation of Min dialects. Zeng (2013) analyzes the similarities and differences of seventeen sub-dialects of Quanzhou before his reconstruction of early phonology of Quanzhou. Some researches employ Min dialects to probe into the historical development of Chinese. For example, Wu (2002) discusses the strata reflected in the literate and colloquial expressions within the framework of the fourth final. Wu Ruiwen (2009) focuses on the reconstruction of * y of common Min and the related questions. Lin (2013) analyzes the sound changes of the ancient nasal rhymes of Chaozhou from the perspectives of literature recording, dialect comparison and phonological structure. Besides, there is also some research on the formation of Min dialects, such as Zhang (1996) who discusses the formation of Min dialects with factors such as ages, areas and types taken into consideration.

There are some special researches of Eastern Min such as Wright (1983),

Chan (1985), Bao (1997), Chen Zeping (1998, 2003), Li (2000), Dai (2006, 2008, 2010), Chen Qin (2006), Yuan (2013) to give detailed analysis of finals, initials, tones, syllables, as well as related sound changes of Eastern Min. For example, Chen Zeping (1998) provides a comprehensive description of the phonological system of Fuzhou. Dai (2005) analyzes the historical strata of Min dialects with Puxian dialect as a starting point before taking some other Min dialects into consideration. Yuan (2010) gives a detailed analysis of the historic strata of Eastern Min dialect. Wu Qingran (2009) develops a theoretical analysis of tone and tone sandhi in disyllabic sequences in Fu'an dialect within OT. Yuan et al (2013) discuss the distribution areas as well as the evolutionary stages of categorical transformation of initials of Eastern Min, backed up with phonetic experiments.

Some special researches are devoted to Southern Min such as Chen (1987), Lin (1989), Hsu (2003), Hsieh (2005), Yang (1982), Zhang Zhenxing (1985), Zhou (1986), Zhang (1996), Lin (1993), Chung (1997), Hong (1999, 2003), Cai (2002), Du (2006), Dong (2006), Chen Shujuan (2010), Chen Baoxian (2010), Chen Xiaoqi (2010), Zheng (2012), Cao (2012), Zeng (2014). For these researches, some focus on the segmental phenomena. For example, Lin (1988) discusses the nasal segments in Taiwanese secret languages. Chung (1997) argues that the preglide of Southern Min of Taiwan belongs to rhyme on the basis of five phenomena. Hsu (2003) reexamines syllable contraction in Taiwanese Southern Min. Hong (2003) analyzes the breakdown of schwa of Taiwanese Southern Min from the perspective of markedness. Zheng Weina (2012) analyzes the distribution of stop codas as well as nasal codas and the possible reason for such distribution. Some concentrate on the suprasegmental perspective. For example, Chen (1987) analyzes the syntax of Xiamen tone sandhi with Mandarin tone sandhi as a contrast. Barries (2006) analyzes tone circles and contrast preservation of Xiamen in an OT framework. Guillaume (2008) provides an analysis of the Xiamen Tone Circle using extensions of OT.

The above researches are noted for their contribution to the description of some single Min dialects, or to the analysis of the diachronic evolution of Min dialects, or to the further understanding of some remarkable phonological phenomena from the synchronic perspective under the framework of modern phonological theories. Yet there is little discussion on the comparison of Southern Min and Eastern Min, despite the fact that they are deemed so different that it is even suggested that they should be divided into different dialect areas in the related literature. There is no attempt of comparison of the phonological differences between Southern Min and Eastern Min from the perspective of markedness. In this book, I will try to delve into the phonological systems of Southern Min and Eastern Min and find out the phonological differences between these two dialects and the possible motivation for such differences under the guidance of markedness theory and the theory of hierarchy of contrastive features.

1.3.2 Research questions

Based on the above discussion, this book is mainly concerned with the following hypotheses:

a. The dialects originated from the same Proto dialect group may manifest markedness difference due to the influence of the principles of markedness preservation, markedness reduction, and markedness conflation.

b. The systematic contrast shifts may result in differences of dialects.

c. The phonological differences of dialects can be reflected in the difference of hierarchies of contrastive features of the dialects.

To testify the three hypotheses mentioned above, this book is designed to take Quanzhou of Southern Min and Fuzhou of Eastern Min as the subjects of comparison, with characteristics of some other sub-dialects taken into consideration to analyze the phonological structures of Southern Min and Eastern Min systematically with an aim to answer the following questions:

a. Are the phonological differences between Southern Min and Eastern Min systematic or sporadic phenomena?

b. How are the phonological differences of Southern Min and Eastern Min manifested segmentally and suprasegmentally?

c. What forces may be responsible for having shaped the original dialects from the same Proto-Min in evolving into different directions?

d. What is the difference of markedness in the phonological structure of initial system, final system, tone system and syllable structure of Southern Min and Eastern Min?

e. Is it possible to relate the phonological differences of Southern Min and Eastern Min to the hierarchies of contrastive features of the dialects? Is there any difference in feature hierarchical structure between Southern Min and Eastern Min? And what are they, if any?

1.4 Significance of the study

This study is academically significant for a phonological study on the difference between Southern Min and Eastern Min under phonological feature theories, particularly the feature specification theory (Chomsky & Halle 1968), the theory of feature hierarchy (Dresher 2009) and the markedness theory (De Lacy 2002, 2006). More importantly, this study is trying to probe into the phonological motivation for the possible difference of Southern Min and Eastern Min to shed a light to the understanding of the disparity of Southern Min and Eastern Min.

The innovation of this study lies in the employment of modern phonological theories to discuss the phonological differences between Southern Min and Eastern Min. Furthermore, the related phonological processes in Southern Min and Eastern Min will be analyzed to discover the phonological characteristics and possible evolutionary tendencies of Southern Min and Eastern Min. Markedness theories, feature hierarchy theory and feature geometry theory will be employed to analyze the phonological structures and the hierarchies of the contrastive features of Southern Min and Eastern Min to explain why Southern Min and Eastern Min from the same Proto-Min are suggested to be divided into different dialect groups.

1.5 Framework of the book

This book presents a comparative analysis of the overall phonology of Quanzhou which is the representative of Southern Min and Fuzhou as the representative of Eastern Min from a synchronic perspective to work out the possible reasons for a number of notable suggestions for dividing Southern Min and Eastern Min into different dialect areas, with an aim to delve into the possible evolutionary tendencies of Southern Min and Eastern Min.

Chapter 1 first presents the background of the present study and provides the phonological information of Southern Min and Eastern Min. Then the literature review of the relevant studies and the significance of the study as well as the framework of the book are presented.

Chapter 2 introduces the theoretical framework, including the markedness theory which defines the concepts of markedness as well as the new development of markedness theory and introduces the dimensions of markedness, the hierarchies of markedness as well as the conflict of markedness. Then on the basis of the successive division algorithm, the hypothesis of this study as well as the method of this study is presented.

Chapter 3 presents phonological hierarchies of Quanzhou initial consonants after the relevant analysis of the related consonants as well as the related phonological processes is introduced. Then it gives the analysis of the categorical transformation of initials of Fuzhou under the guidance of feature geometry theory before the feature hierarchy of initial consonants of Fuzhou is established according to the related phonological processes.

Chapter 4 first analyzes the simplex finals of Quanzhou before the hierarchy of the contrastive features of simplex vowels in Quanzhou is established. Then the possible complex finals as well as possible phonological processes of Quanzhou are explored.

Chapter 5 focuses on the analysis of the distribution of simplex vowels in Fuzhou, before the hierarchy of the contrastive features of simplex vowels in

Fuzhou is established. Then the possible phonological changes of the finals in Fuzhou are discussed.

Chapter 6 provides a comparison of the phonological characteristics of the finals in Quanzhou and Fuzhou in terms of the markedness of simplex final inventories as well as the hierarchies of contrastive features of simplex vowels in Quanzhou and Fuzhou. Then the syllable markedness contrast reflected in the finals comparison of Quanzhou and Fuzhou is made. Moreover, the phonological processes of the finals in Quanzhou and Fuzhou are compared, followed by the analysis of the possible motivation for the difference between Quanzhou and Fuzhou.

Chapter 7 focuses on the tone system of Quanzhou including tone specification and tone sandhi before the markedness analysis is presented. On the basis of the analysis of the tone system of Fuzhou dialect, including tone sandhi of Fuzhou, the internal structure of tones of Fuzhou, markedness of tone and tone sandhi, the characteristics of Fuzhou tone sandhi are revealed.

Chapter 8 presents a summary of the book and makes some suggestions for future research.

Chapter 2

Theoretical Framework and Methodology

The contemporary phonological theories will help provide an explicit explanation to many issues in this book. In this book, markedness theories (Rice 2007; De Lacy 2002, 2006) and contrast theories (De Lacy 2002, 2006) will help shed light on the phonological changes of initials, finals and tones in Southern Min and Eastern Min. The feature geometry theory (Clements 1985) will help unveil the motivation for the categorical transformation of the initial consonants of Eastern Min. Theories of syllable will help offer an analysis of the syllable structure of both dialects.

2.1 Markedness theory

Many linguistic phenomena display a bias towards certain elements. Certain structures are often avoided while others are generated, which very much likely results from markedness. There have been quite many studies on markedness, including Trubetzkoy (1969), Jakobson (1949, 1978), Greenberg (1966, 1975, 1978), Stampe (1972), Kean (1975), Kiparsky (1982) and Archangeli (1984, 1988). The previous studies of markedness often center on the markedness of language behavior, such as the frequencies of some segments (Greenberg 1966, 1975; Kean 1975; Paradis & Prunet 1991). This section will present a brief picture of markedness theory.

2.1.1 Concepts of markedness

The term "markedness" is used in phonology to capture the central observation that not all elements in a phonological system are of equal status. Markedness was first introduced by Trubetzkoy (1969) to refer to relations between elements of a phonological class (e. g. place of articulation, phonation types) on a language-particular basis (Rice 2007). Unmarked elements can be the sole output of processes, fail to trigger alternations and undergo processes alone. In addition, unmarked elements are more common, have simpler structures and are acquired earlier in children's acquisition. In contrast, marked elements are rarely the output, are often the only triggering elements, and are often exempt from undergoing processes (De Lacy 2006). Cross-linguistically, languages tend to choose more unmarked elements, avoiding more marked elements. For example, in choosing epenthetic consonants, the preferable segments tend to be coronal consonants or glottal stops, instead of labial consonants or dorsal consonants. Similarly, the neutralization of consonants tend to be glottal consonants or coronal consonants, instead of labial consonants or dorsal consonants. Such tendency lies in the fact that the glottal and the coronal are more unmarked than the labial and the dorsal in terms of place of articulation (PoA). In the same vein, the nuclear prefers more sonorant elements while fewer sonorant elements are preferable in the position of initials.

2.1.2 New development of markedness theory

De Lacy (2002, 2006) proposes that markedness is part of language faculty, influenced by three conflicting principles, namely preservation of the marked (PoM), reduction of markedness, and conflation of markedness. The conflation of markedness refers to that the markedness of segments can be conflated. For example, the dorsal is more marked than the coronal, hence some languages prefer to choose the coronal instead of the dorsal while some other languages may treat the dorsal and the coronal as the same marked categories as a result of which the markedness conflation may lead to fewer marked segments or more marked segments. For example, in Pali, the conflation of /bh/ and /t/ results in [dh], preserving the less marked coronal place, while the conflation of /k/ and /ʃ/ leads to [kh]. However, the hierarchies of markedness can never be reversed, implying that no languages may choose the dorsal without choosing the coronal.

De Lacy (2006: 28) proposes six valid diagnostics to judge markedness. Whether the phonological processes are sensitive to markedness or not can refer to the six following diagnostics:

(1) Valid markedness diagnostics

a. Neutralization: output

If /α/ and /β/ go through structurally conditioned neutralization and result in output [α], then there is some markedness hierarchy in which [β] is more marked than [α].

b. Deletion

Suppose /β/ undergoes structurally conditioned deletion, which is not found in the case of /α/, then there is some markedness hierarchy in which [β] is more marked than [α].

c. Consonant epenthesis

If consonant [α] is chosen as the epenthetic consonant instead of [β], then there is some markedness hierarchy in which [β] is more marked than [α].

d. Assimilation: triggers

If /γ/ assimilates to /β/ with respect of some feature F, but /γ/ does not assimilate to /α/ in terms of F-value, then there is some markedness hierarchy in which [β] is more marked than [α].

e. Prosodification: mutual influence

If some prosodic constituent P attracts or is attracted to [α] instead of [β], there is some markedness hierarchy in which [β] in constituent P is more marked than [α] in constituent P.

f. Inventory structure

Suppose the presence of [α] in a segmental inventory always has implication for the presence of [β] but not vice versa, then there is some markedness hierarchy in which [β] is more marked than [α].

All the markedness hierarchies are not always consistent, which means that the markedness of one hierarchy does not imply the markedness of another hierarchy. In terms of PoA, the glottal is the least marked, while the other markedness hierarchies may tend to choose non-glottal segments. Whether the glottal or the coronal is more unmarked is language-specific, depending on the markedness hierarchies.

2.1.2.1 Hierarchy of markedness

There are many markedness dimensions, including voice markedness, sonority markedness, PoA markedness, manner of articulation (MoA) markedness, etc. Markedness relations between prosodic structures have also been identified.

There are three common markedness hierarchies centering on PoA, Sonority, as well as MoA, which are presented as follows:

(2) PoA markedness hierarchy

dorsal > labial > coronal > glottal

According to this hierarchy, dorsal is the most marked place of articulation, followed by labial which is more marked than coronal and glottal. While this PoA markedness hierarchy is related to the position of syllable, as the hierarchy of initial position is different from the hierarchy of coda position.

(3) Sonority markedness hierarchy

a. Consonant: voiceless obstruent > voiced obstruent > voiceless fricative > voiced fricative > nasal > lateral > glide > glottal

b. vowel: ɨ ʉ > ə > i y u > e o > ɛ ɔ > a ɑ ɒ

In accordance with (3) a, voiceless obsrtuent is the least sonorant of all consonants while glottal is the most sonorant consonant in contrast with the other consonants in terms of sonority. With respect of the sonority of vowels, the low vowels are the most sonorant vowels while the central vowels are the least sonorant.

De Lacy (2006: 62 – 68) divides the syllable nucleus and syllable non-nucleus into DTE (the Designated Terminal Element), specified as $\Delta\sigma$ and non-DTE, indicated as -$\Delta\sigma$. DTE prefers more sonorant elements while non-DTE tends to have fewer sonorant elements. The ranking of DTE is as follows:

(4) Ranking of DTE

a. *$\Delta\sigma\leqslant$T(voiceless obstruent), *$\Delta\sigma\leqslant$D, *$\Delta\sigma\leqslant$S, *$\Delta\sigma\leqslant$Z, *$\Delta\sigma\leqslant$N, *$\Delta\sigma\leqslant$L, *$\Delta\sigma\leqslant$ʔ/, *$\Delta\sigma\leqslant${ɨ ʉ}, *$\Delta\sigma\leqslant${ə}, *$\Delta\sigma\leqslant${i u}, *$\Delta\sigma\leqslant${e o}, *$\Delta\sigma\leqslant${ɛ ɔ}, *$\Delta\sigma\leqslant${a ɑ}

b. *-$\Delta\sigma\geqslant$a, *-$\Delta\sigma\geqslant${ɛ ɔ}, *-$\Delta\sigma\geqslant${e o}, *-$\Delta\sigma\geqslant${i u}, *-$\Delta\sigma\geqslant$ə, *-$\Delta\sigma\geqslant$ɨ ʉ, *-$\Delta\sigma\geqslant$ʔ, *-$\Delta\sigma\geqslant$L, *-$\Delta\sigma\geqslant$N, *-$\Delta\sigma\geqslant$Z, *-$\Delta\sigma\geqslant$S, *-$\Delta\sigma\geqslant$D, *-$\Delta\sigma\geqslant$T

In line with (4)a, the voiceless obstruent is the most dispreferable as the nuclear of syllable due to its lowest sonority while the low vowel is the best candidate as the syllable nuclear as it incurs the least violation. Such ranking finds its reverse counterpart when it comes to the non-nuclear position.

There is also manner of articulation (MoA) markedness. De Lacy (2006) does not discuss MoA in a specific chapter, but only mentions the preservation of MoA indicated with the constraints such as IDENT [±continuant], IDENT [±nasal], IDENT [±lateral] and IDENT [±voice]. The ranking of these constraints is language-specific.

2.1.2.2 Conflict of markedness

Markedness hierarchies may conflict: one hierarchy may prefer x to y, while another favors y rather than x. The different dimensions of markedness have no implication for each other, namely there is no meta-restriction that all markedness hierarchies be consistent at the segmental level (De Lacy 2006). So while glottal is the least-marked in terms of PoA, other markedness hierarchies prefer non-glottals over glottals. Whether glottals or coronals are treated as least marked is language-specific, depending on which markedness hierarchy is in the dominant position. Furthermore, quite a number of markedness hierarchies vary with prosodic context, which results in variation in terms of what may be the least-marked segment in a particular language, even though the variation is limited. For the variation of markedness hiearchy with prosodic context, a widely cited example is the sonority hierarchy. As indicated by De Lacy (2006: 69), the hierarchies combine with DTEs and non-DTEs in different ways, which means that the traditional notion of "markedness" does not apply directly to certain hierarchies. For example, it is not valid to say the sonority category "low vowel" is unmarked, since markedness of prosodic hierarchies is dependent on the structural element with which they combine. Therefore, in this case, "low vowel" is the most marked for non-DTEs, though it is the least marked category with respect of DTEs. Also voiceless stops are the least marked margins but the most marked syllable peaks (Prince & Smolensky 2004; De Lacy 2006: 66). Therefore, markedness hierarchy conflict is responsible for the variation seen in phenomena that are sensitive to markedness (Waugh 1979: 157; De Lacy 2006: 25).

2.2 Feature geometry

So far, the assumption has been that the representation of a segment is an unstructured list of features. In the model of feature geometry, it is assumed that the segment is not a single constituent, but has internal structure, which is represented by means of a tree diagram. The development of feature trees (or feature geometry) is mainly due to Clements (1985), Sagey (1986) and McCarthy (1988). In this model, the grouping of features is solved by representing segments as trees, in which the nodes represent features and feature groups (Gussenhoven & Haike 2011: 185). In the model of feature geometry, the node that dominates the place features is called the PLACE node, which dominates four articulator nodes corresponding to the univalent features [LABIAL], [CORONAL], [DORSAL], [RADICAL]. Each of these four nodes also has its relevant subconstituent features dominated under their nodes. In this way, the [LABIAL] node has two subconstituents such as [round] and [distr], the [CORONAL] dominates [ant] and [distr] and the [DORSAL] has [back], [high] and [low] included as its subconstituents. The representation of the PLACE node is as follows:

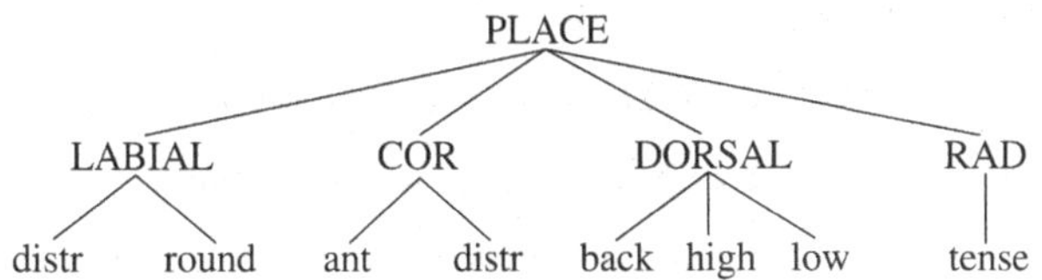

Diagram 2-1 Feature geometry configuration

In this feature geometry, Gussenhoven assumes that the position of [tense] is under [RAD], assuming it is equivalent to [ATR] (Gussenhoven & Haike 2011). For the classification of [tense]/[ATR], there are different views in the related literature. In Halle (1995), ATR as well as RTR are included under the node of [Tongue Root] which is included under the node of [Guttural] parallel to the node of [Place].

The main advantage of the autosegmentalized representation of feature geometry is that features or particular groups of features can spread to neighboring segments, which greatly improves the description of assimilation processes (Gussenhoven & Haike 2011: 185). It is found that assimilation tends to show a non-arbitrary relationship between the structural description and the structural change. Commonly, the same groups of features appear to be transferred from one segment to the next. For example, many languages have processes that transfer the features specifying a consonant's place of articulation to a preceding nasal consonant. Since the features in the traditional matrix are unstructured, it is impossible to assert that the feature groupings in the assimilation processes of many languages are in fact natural groups of features. Besides, in the traditional unstructured matrix some unnatural feature groups may be expressed as a natural one (Gussenhoven & Haike 2011: 186). To avoid the problems mentioned above, feature geometry as a different approach solves the problem of the grouping of features by representing segments as trees with the nodes representing features and feature groups. In this way, the assimilation problem is solved by assuming that a single node may be part of more than one tree.

2.3 Successive division algorithm

For a given phoneme in a particular language, it is not obvious to decide which of its features are contrastive or not. One approach used to be employed widely is the pairwise approach that is based on comparing fully specified phonemes with special attention to minimal pairs, which identifies as contrastive only specifications that are not logically redundant (Dresher 2009: 35). Due to its basis on full specifications, Dresher argues that the pairwise approach has severe logical problems. As an entirely different approach, contrastive specification by feature ordering can be seen as early as in Jakobson and Lotz (1949) although they themselves did not make their method explicit. In this feature ordering approach, all the potential distinctive features are put into an ordered list and the inventory is divided successively on the basis of this list until every segment has received a distinct representation. In this method of deriving contrastive specifications, the ordering makes a difference. Take the contrastive specifications for French bilabial stops as an example (Jakobson & Lotz 1949; Dresher 2009: 15). The ordering of [nasal] > [voiced] applied to /p, b, m/ will yield the following form of tree:

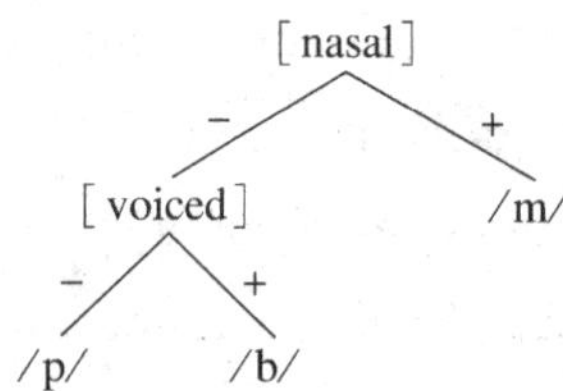

Diagram 2-2 Ordering of contrastive features: [nasal > [voiced]

In Diagram 2-2, /m/ is the only nasal consonant, and so is already distinct from the others. The remaining two non-nasal consonants need to be distinguished by the feature [voiced]. However, with the reverse of the ordering of the two features [voiced] and [nasal], the result is different, as follows:

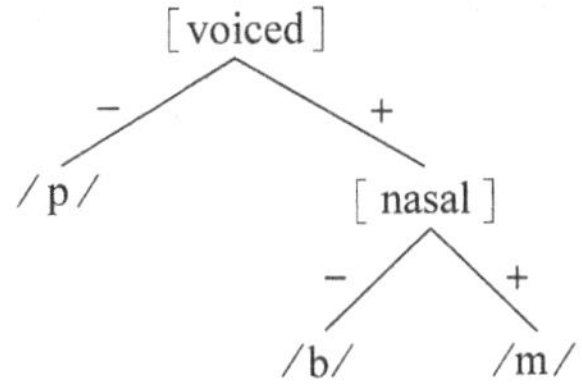

Diagram 2-3 Ordering of contrastive features: [voiced] > [nasal]

In Diagram 2-3, /p/ is the only voiceless consonant, and this feature suffices to set it apart from the other consonants, and the rest two voiced consonants need to be distinguished by the feature [nasal].

According to this method, contrastive specifications are determined by splitting the inventory by means of successive divisions, which is governed by an ordering of features (Jakobson & Halle 1956; Halle 1959). Corresponding to this idea, an algorithm, namely the Successive Division Algorithm (SDA) is proposed in Dresher (2003) based on the work of Jakobson and his collaborators.

2.3.1 Core ideas of SDA

SDA is a very general formulation for defining contrast and redundancy for members of an inventory. It designates feature values as being contrastive or redundant in terms of an ordering of features called a contrast hierarchy. In contrast with pairwise comparison which always leads to the same answer, feature ordering can present more than one answer, depending on the ordering of the features. Accordingly, in this approach, contrast is a matter of relative scope or ordering of contrastive features (Dresher 2009: 16). SDA proposed in Dresher (1998, 2003) works as follows (Dresher 2009: 16 – 17):

(a) Begin with no feature specifications: assume all sounds are allophones of a single undifferentiated phoneme.

(b) If the set is found to consist of more than one contrasting member, select a feature and divide the set into as many as subsets as the feature allows for.

(c) Repeat step (b) in each subset: keep dividing up the inventory into sets, applying successive features in turn, until every set has only one member.

Zhang Xi (1996) employs SDA to establish the hierarchy of the vowel system of Classical Manchu, as follows (Dresher 2009: 182):

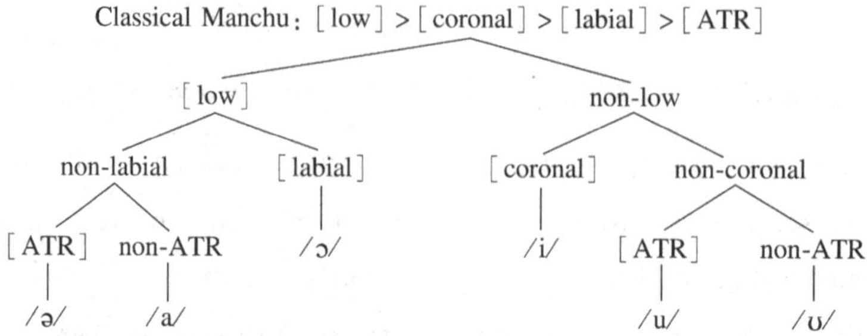

Diagram 2-4 Contrastive hierarchy of classical Manchu language

This hierarchy is a good indication that [ATR] does not extend to /i/ despite that it is phonetically [ATR]. Furthermore, /u/ and /ʊ/ are not under the scope of the feature [labial] which indicates that they are not specified with this contrastive feature, which is in line with the observation that these two vowels though phonetically [labial] do not trigger labial harmony. Such construction is a good reflection of the related phonological processes in this language.

2.3.2 Contrastive features and markedness

The hierarchy of contrastive hypothesis adopts the Contrastivist Hypothesis which holds that phonology computes only contrastive features, and only the contrastive features in a language are the triggers of related phonological processes. For example, in most Inuit dialects, there is a process of palatalization of a consonant following the vowel i, as follows:

(5) Barrow Inupiad palatalization after strong i (Kaplan 1981: 82; Dresher 2009: 166)

Stem	Gloss	"and a N"	"N plural"	"like a N"
a. iglu	"house"	iglulu	iglunik	iglutun
b. iki	"wound"	ikiʎu	ikiɲik	ikisun
c. ini	"place"	inilu	ininik	initun

However, such palatalization does not happen in all the cases of i. In fact, some contemporary dialects distinguish between two kinds of *i*: strong *i* which descends from */i/ and weak *i*, which comes from */ə/, and the weak *i* does not trigger palatalization. Dresher (2009) proposes that the contrastive marked values of /i/ account for the fact that strong [i] can account for the fact of palatalization. In contrast, the weak [i] which is found to be schwa underlyingly does not have such relevant contrastive feature, which is responsible for not triggering palatalization.

Dresher and Rice further analyze Markedness and the Contrastive Hierarchy in Phonology and put forward MSC (Modified Contrastive Specification). Starting from a focus on complexity in phonology (Avery & Rice 1989) and evolving to focus on markedness and contrast, MSC proposes that complexity in representation is motivated by contrast and markedness and only marked features count toward complexity under the assumption that each feature has a marked and unmarked value. In this way, segments with fewer marked features are less complex than those with more marked features (De Lacy 2009). The relationship between markedness and contrast can be seen in the following example. In a vowel inventory which contains a front and back vowel such as /i,a,u/, either /i/ and /u/ may pattern as marked in terms of phonological activity, since only one contrast is needed to distinguish back rounded vowel from unrounded front vowel. With a central vowel added to the system, it is predicted that both the back and front vowels may pattern as marked relating to the central vowel, which follows an empirically-supported prediction that the central vowel is more unmarked. Accordingly, a more marked representation is permitted only if it is necessary to establish a contrast with a less marked one. The theory of MSC leads to an expectation of a relation between the amount of segmental markedness a system allows and the number and nature of contrasts it has (Dresher 2009: 164).

2.4 Method of the study

This book is devoted to the analysis of the phonological differences of Quanzhou and Fuzhou, especially the markedness differences. Starting out from the question why some related research put forward the division of dividing Southern Min and Eastern Min into different dialect groups, the book tries to figure out the possible phonological motivation for such proposal of dividing Southern Min and Eastern Min into different dialect groups. In this book, Quanzhou as the representative of Southern Min and Fuzhou as the representative of Eastern Min will be chosen for the comparison of the phonological differences. Such comparison of the phonological systems of Quanzhou and Fuzhou is composed of three parts: firstly, the inventories of initial consonants, the distribution and the phonological processes of these initial consonants as well as the hierarchies of the contrastive features of these initial consonants will be analyzed; secondly, the inventories of finals, including the inventories of simplex vowels, the distribution and the phonological processes of these simplex vowels as well as the hierarchies of the contrastive features of these simplex vowels will be analyzed, after which the syllable markedness contrast reflected in the comparison of the complex finals will be made; thirdly, the tone systems of Quanzhou and Fuzhou, especially the tone sandhi processes and the typological differences observed sychronically will be discussed. The book is trying to figure out the phonological differences as well as markedness differences of these two dialects.

Chapter 3

Initials of Quanzhou and Fuzhou

This chapter provides an analytic description of the initials of Quanzhou and Fuzhou. Since the differences of the initial consonants of these two dialects are not so remarkable as those of the finals of these two dialects, the initial consonants of Quanzhou and Fuzhou are discussed within this chapter. Before analyzing the distinct initial consonants and their phonological features, it will describe the overall numbers and forms of the initial consonants of Quanzhou and Fuzhou. In this chapter, both markedness theory and feature hierarchy theory are applied to the analysis. After presenting an analysis of the distribution of initial consonants, a feature hierarchy of distinctive initial consonants of Quanzhou and Fuzhou will be developed based on the phonological behavior of these initial consonants, before a comparison of the initials of Quanzhou and Fuzhou is conducted.

3.1 Initials of Quanzhou

In this chapter, syllable-initial consonants are referred to as "initials". Quanzhou has a relatively simple initial consonant inventory like the other sub-dialects of Min, which includes the following consonants:

(1)	p	p^h	b(m)	
	t	t^h	l(n)	
	ts	ts^h		s
	k	k^h	g(ŋ)	
	ø			h

It is indicated in (1) that there are fourteen initial consonants in Quanzhou. The most remarkable characteristics of the Quanzhou initials (compared with Mandarin and other Chinese dialects) is the fact that Quanzhou still retains the merged state of stops and fricatives, which is said to be a characteristic that can even date back beyond Middle Chinese (Lin 1993). The following subsections will discuss all classes of possible Quanzhou initial consonants: oral stops, fricatives/affricates, and sonorants.

3.1.1 Stops

The oral stops of Quanzhou are very common as syllable initials. Totally, there are eight oral stops in Quanzhou which include three voiceless unaspirated stops, three voiceless aspirated stops and two voiced unaspirated stops, as listed in (1):

(2) a.	pu^{24}	"roast"	b.	p^hu^{24}	"float"	c.	bu^{24}	"no"
	tu^{24}	"kitchen"		t^hu^{24}	"dawdle"		(lu^{24})	("wriggle")
	ku^{24}	"qu" (surname)		k^hu^{24}	"foot"		gu^{24}	"cow"

In the examples above, the syllables in (2)a all have voiceless unaspirated stops; those in (2)b have voiceless aspirated stops; (2)c have voiced unaspirated stops. The examples show that in (2)c there is no voiced coronal stop, which is replaced by a lateral. All these oral stops in (2) are all in contrastive distribution.

The initial stops of Quanzhou are distinguished from those of Mandarin and other Chinese dialects that have already split into different categories, hence increasing more contrast in consonants. The preservation of the old initial system in Quanzhou dialect is mainly reflected in the following three aspects. Firstly, in terms of initial coronal stops, the coronal stops of Mandarin are noted to have two sub-types, one of which is still coronal stop, such as [ti] "bottom", the other of which has evolved into the retroflex fricative, while the stops of Quanzhou still contain contrasts embodied in these two categories. Here are some examples:

(3) Quanzhou	Mandarin	Meaning
[ti]	[ti]	底 "base"
[di]	[tʂi]	蜘 "spider"
[tu]	[tʂʰu]	厨 "kitchen"

Secondly, the initial labial stops of Quanzhou contain one contrast, which corresponds to two contrasts in the labial consonants of Mandarin which include labial stops and labio-dental fricatives, for example,

(4) Quanzhou	Mandarin	Meaning
[pi]	[pi]	比 "than"
[pu]	[fu]	妇 "woman"
[pui]	[fei]	肥 "fat"

Thirdly, in Quanzhou the initial dorsal stops find their correspondence in the contrasts of dorsal stop, retroflex fricative, alveolopalatal fricative, as well as the glottal fricative in Mandarin, as follows:

(5) Quanzhou	Mandarin	Meaning
[ki]	[tɕi]	基 "base"
[kʰa]	[tɕiao]	骑 "ride"
[ki]	[tʂi]	枝 "twig"
[kʰɔ]	[hɔ]	叫 "call"

Here is a summary of contrasts embodied in the stops of Quanzhou dialect and their counterparts in Mandarin:

(6)

Quanzhou Dialect	Mandarin
bilabial stop /p/	bilabial stop: /p/
	labio-dental fricative: /f/
coronal stop /t/	coronal stop: /t/
	coronal retroflex fricative: /tʂ/
dorsal stop /k/	dorsal stop: /k/
	alvoelopalatal fricative: /tɕ/
	retroflex fricative: /tʂ/
	glottal fricative: /h/

It is clear that compared with the variety of contrasts embodied in the initial consonants in Mandarin, the initial consonants in Quanzhou are noted for far fewer contrasts. Here is an interesting question as to whether the initial consonants in Mandarin have split to have more contrasts or whether the initial consonants in Quanzhou have merged to have fewer contrasts. Zhang (2011) presents a comparison of some cognates of Xiamen and Qieyun, which can shed a light to this question. Since the focus of this book is Quanzhou, we replace the examples of Xiamen with those of Quanzhou (Zhang 2011: 99).

(7)

Example	指	齿	痣	支	柿	星	醒	生	鼠
Quanzhou	ki	k^{h}i	ki	ki	k^{h}i	ts^{h}ĩ	ts^{h}ĩ	ts^{h}ĩ	ts^{h}ɯ
Qieyun	tɕ-	tɕ^{h}	tɕ-	tɕ-	dʒ-	s-	s-	ʃ-	ɕ-

It is clear that what are classified as fricatives and affricates in Qieyun are classified as affricates and stops in Quanzhou. The experiences of historical linguistics indicate that lenition is more often than fortition in the evolution of languages, which proves the conservative quality of the initial consonants of Quanzhou (Zhang 2011).

3.1.2 Sonorants

Besides eight obstruents in Quanzhou as discussed above, there are also four initial sonorant consonants in Quanzhou. All these four initial sonorant consonants can all appear in syllable initial position. In the following section, all these initial sonorant consonants will be discussed according to their natural classes such as nasals and non-nasal sonorants.

3.1.2.1 Nasals

In this subsection, I will first briefly introduce three initial sonorant nasals: bilabial nasal, coronal nasal and velar nasal, all of which can appear in syllable initial positions, and can form minimal contrastive pairs, as follows:

(8)	ĩ	ã	ɔ̃
	mĩ^{24} 棉 "cotton"	mã^{55} 马 "horse"	mɔ̃^{42} 毛 "fur"
	nĩ^{24} 年 "year"	nã^{22} 挪 "move"	nɔ̃^{42} 怒 "anger"
	ŋĩ^{22} 硬 "hard"	ŋɔ̃^{55} 雅 "elegant"	ŋɔ̃^{24} 鹅 "goose"

As indicated, all the three initial nasal consonants can surface with three different vowels, which implies that three nasal initials can be contrastive with each other. What is interesting for these nasals is that they can not occur before the oral vowels, which will be discussed in the following section.

3.1.2.2 Initial non-nasal sonorants

Apart from these three initial nasal sonorants, there is still one more initial sonorant consonant, namely lateral. The lateral in Quanzhou is mainly distributed in two cases. Lin (1993) proposes that the [l] in Quanzhou is in fact a flap and occurs with the other two voiced obstruents as the alternants of three initial nasals in the case of being followed by oral vowels, as follows (Du 2014: 381):

(9)

Cognates	Southern Min			Eastern Min		Northern Min	
	Quanzhou	Zhangzhou	Chenghai	Fuqing	Gutian	Shipo	Jianyang
	n/l	n/l	n/l	n	n	n	n
让 "let"	niũ	niõ	niẽ	nyoŋ	nyøŋ	nioŋ	
染 "dye"	nĩ	nĩ	nĩ	nieŋ		niŋ	nieiŋ
软 "soft"	nŋ	nuĩ	nəŋ	nuoŋ	nuoŋ	nyiŋ	nyeiŋ
韧 "tough"	lun	lun	lun	noŋ		nyiŋ	nyeiŋ
闰 "intercalary"	lun	lun	zuŋ	noŋ	nuŋ	ɦueiŋ	ɦeiŋ

As shown, when the nasal initials are followed by the oral vowel, the nasal initials turn to be lateral, which is just the case as discussed above.

Secondly, the lateral in Quanzhou finds its counterpart in Eastern Min and Northern Min in zero initial or the voiced glottal fricative, as follows (Du 2013:381):

(10)

Cognates	Southern Min			Eastern Min			Northern Min	
	Quanzhou	Zhangzhou	Chenghai	Fuqing	Gutian	Zherong	Shipo	Jianyang
	l	dz	z	ø	ø	ø	ɦ/ø	ɦ/ø
儿 "kid"	li	dzi	zi	i	i		ɦi	ɦi
扰 "bother"	liau	dziau	ziou	ieu	iau	iau	iau	
柔 "soft"	liu	liu	ziu	iu	iu	iu	ɦiu	iu
人 "man"	lin	dzin	ziŋ	iŋ	iŋ	iŋ		ɦiŋ

As indicated, the ancient Chinese forms of all these cognates had nasal initials (Zhengzhang 2003), which correspond to laterals in Quanzhou and voiced affricates as well voiced fricatives in Zhangzhou and Chenghai of Southern Min. What is responsible for such alternation of a lateral? Is such replacement of the voiced alveolar stop by a lateral typologically attested? In fact, the mutual replacement of laterals and voiced alveolar stops is also found in other languages, such as Baima Tibetan, in which laterals and voiced alveolar stops are interchangeable before the vowel [i]. However, when [l] is used in place of [d] as the consonant patterned with the other two voiced stops in the Quanzhou dialect, it has no such requirement.

3.2 Sound changes of the initial consonants of Quanzhou

It is generally considered that there are not so many remarkable sound changes of the initial consonants in Quanzhou as in Fuzhou. Yet there is still some brief description of some sound changes of the initial consonants of Quanzhou in the related research such as Lin (1993), Lin (1988: 63), etc.

3.2.1 Denasalization of Quanzhou

The oral stops of Quanzhou are noted for their three-divison distribution which includes voiceless unaspirated stops, voiceless aspirated stops and voiced unaspirated stops. As for the voiced stops in Chinese, Chao (1928) believes that the voiced stops are typical of the Wu dialects. For example, Shaoxing Wu dialect has the voiced obstruents that come from Middle Chinese (Zhang Jisheng 2006: 19). Modern Chinese (Mandarin) and the other five Chinese language families have lost all the voiced obstruents from Middle Chinese. In this sense, the voiced stops of Quanzhou dialect are not the same as those of Shaoxing which are from Middle Chinese. Then, how did these voiced stops come into being?

In the related literature about Quanzhou, it is indicated that the oral vowels and nasalized vowels are in contrastive distribution when following the voiceless initials, as follows (Lin 1993: 3625, 3647 - 3648):

(11) a. pi^{33} "beer" c. $p\tilde{i}^{33}$ "strip"

b. p^hi^{33} "wrap" d. $p^h\tilde{i}^{33}$ "bully"

As shown above, the oral vowels and nasalized vowels are in contrast when their initials are voiceless initials of either aspiration or unaspiration. As a contrast, the voiced stops in Quanzhou are followed by oral vowels while nasal initials are followed by nasalized vowels (Lin 1993; Du 2014), as follows:

(12) a. li^{24} "separate" d. nĩ^{24} "year"
b. gi^{55} "ant" e. ŋĩ^{22} "hard"
c. bi^{33} "smile" f. mĩ^{24} "cotton"

It is observable that the voiced stops and nasals are in complementary distribution depending on whether they are followed by the oral vowels or the nasalized vowels. But which are the underlying forms, the voiced stops or the nasals? There are three principles which have to be taken into consideration in determining the underlying segment inventory of a language (according to Maddieson 1984: 163 and Zhang Jisheng 2006: 75): (a) which allophone has the widest distribution; (b) which allophone most appropriately represents the phonetic range of variation of all allophones; (c) which allophone is the one from which other allophones can be most simply and naturally derived (Maddieson 1984: 163; Zhang Jisheng 2006: 75). Lin (1988: 68) holds that the initial nasals in Taiwanese are the result of assimilation from nasalized vowels. Taiwan Southern Min has its origin in Quanzhou dialect. So this nasal assimilation for initial system also seems to be true for Quanzhou dialect. Here are some examples about nasal assimilation in Quanzhou (Lin 1988: 63) as follows:

(13) a. /bĩ/—[mĩ] "noodle" /bi/—[bi] "rice"
b. /lĩ/—[nĩ] "year" /li/—[li] "you"
c. /gẽ/—[ŋẽ] "hard" /ge/—[ge] "tooth"
d. /bŋ/—[mŋ] "door"
e. /lŋ/—[nŋ] "egg"

In this way, the underlying forms are the voiced stops, and the nasals are the result of application of the nasal assimilation of the nasalized vowels. Under such an approach, the inventory of the initial consonants of Quanzhou dialect would be an inventory that lacks nasal consonants. However, according to Professor Stuart Davis (by personal communication 2017), an inventory that lacks nasals is quite rare from a typological perspective. Snohomish, an

American Indian language of the Pacific Northwest, may be one of the few languages that have no nasal consonant phonemes. So it seems not reasonable to stipulate an inventory of the initial consonants of Quanzhou with some voiced stops but no nasal consonants.

Hu (2005) claims in his phonetic experiment that the voiced stops of Xiamen are in fact [^{m}b, ^{ŋ}g, ^{n}d] instead of voiced oral stops in the common sense. He points out that [^{m}b, ^{ŋ}g, ^{n}d] come from the nasal initials of Middle Chinese, and it is preferable to say that the voiced stops in Xiamen are from the nasal stops, then when these nasal stops are followed by oral vowels, the following oral vowels trigger denasalization of the preceding nasal initials, which results in the voiced stops. Since the Quanzhou dialect and the Xiamen dialect are so closely related in terms of origin, the result of Hufang for voiced stops in Xiamen also seems to hold true for those of the Quanzhou dialect. While if Hu's analysis is correct, there is a regressive denasalization triggered by the following oral vowels. Although typologically speaking, the phonological change from [+nasal][-nasal] to [-nasal][-nasal] is not so common, there are still some denasalization cases. For example, there are some cases of historical or allophonic denasalization that have produced oral stops. In some languages with nasal vowels, such as Paicĩ, nasal consonants may only occur before nasal vowels; but before oral vowels, prenasalized stops are found. This allophonic variation is likely to be from a historical process of partial denasalization. Similarly, in several languages around Puget, sound underwent a process of denasalization about one century ago: except in special speech registers, such as baby talk, the nasals [m, n] became the voiced stops [b, d]. It appears from historical records that there was an intermediate stage when stops were prenasalized stops [^{m}b, ^{n}d] or poststopped nasals [m^{b}, n^{d}]. Something similar also occurs to word-initial nasals in Korean: in some contexts, [m] and [n] are denasalized to [b] and [d]. In this sense, it is typologically plausible to suppose the voiced stops of Quanzhou come as the result of denasalization of nasal initials.

In fact, it can be found that the same cognates in the other sub-dialects are nasal initials in contrast with the voiced stops in Quanzhou dialect. Some examples are given as follows (Hong 2001):

(14) Cognates	Quanzhou	Xiamen	Zhangzhou	Chaozhou	Haikou
买 "buy"	bue	bue	be	boi	boi
糜 "porridge"	bə	be	muẽ	muẽ	mue
贸 "trade"	bio	bɔ	bɔ	mou	mou

In fact, the similar cases can also be found in Wu (2002), as follows:

(15) Cognates	Fuzhou	Quanzhou	Xiamen	Jieyang	Chaoyang
粘 "sticky"	nieŋ	liam	liam	niam	
念 "read"	nieŋ	liam	liam	niam	
眠 "sleep"	miŋ	bin	bin	mi	
尧 "a king"	ŋieu	giau			ŋiau

The examples provided in Wu (2002) indicate that the voiced stops in Quanzhou find their counterparts in nasals in other sub-dialects of Min. According to Zeng (2013), the cognates with the voiced stop initials of Quanzhou mostly date back to the cognates of nasal initials, as follows:

(16) Cognates	AC	MC	Quanzhou Dialect
微 "slight"	mɯl	m^{w}ɨi	bi^{14}
无 "no"	ma	mio	bo^{14}
网 "web"	mlaŋʔ	m^{w}iɐŋ	baŋ^{22}
万 "ten thousand"	mlans	m^{w}iɐn	ban^{41}
磨 "grind"	maːls	muɑ	bo^{41}
米 "rice"	miːʔ	mei	bi^{55}
慢 "slow"	mroːns	mɯan	ban^{41}

Therefore, it is proposed in this book that the voiced stops in the Quanzhou dialect are the result of denasalization.

3.2.2 Debuccalization of Quanzhou

Indo-European languages usually have eight or more fricatives, while most Southeast Asian languages have relatively few fricatives. Mandarin has five fricatives, which are all voiceless; Cantonese has four fricatives; Thai, Korean and Taba① have three fricatives (Zhang Jisheng 2006: 29). In Quanzhou dialect, there are only two fricatives: /s/ and /h/, which is quite a small number in comparison with other Chinese dialects such as Wu dialect with eight fricatives. Both of these two fricatives are underlying segments, as they exist in contrast with each other, as follows:

(17)	[s]	su^{55} 黍 "millet"	[h]	hu^{55} 腐 "rotten"
	[s]	sɯ^{33} 师 "teacher"	[h]	hɯ^{33} 吁 "pant"
	[s]	sa^{24} 傻 "stupid"	[h]	ha^{24} 虾 "shrimp"

Although these two fricatives can combine with the same rhymes in some cases, there is an obvious asymmetric distribution with respect to their combination with rhymes, as follows:

(18)	hiauʔ^{5}	举止轻浮	"frivolous"
	hmʔ^{24}	默	"silent"
	hɔ̃^{55}	火	"fire"
	hãiʔ^{5}	后悔	"regret"
	hẽʔ^{55}	用力过度	"excessive"
	hiũʔ^{24}	心里痒痒	"eager"
	hiuʔ^{5}	血(管)	"vessel"
	sŋʔ^{5}	勒紧绳子	"tighten"
	siʔ^{5}	闪	"shine"
	seʔ^{5}	掉落	"drop"

① Taba is an Austronesian language spoken in the northern Maluku Province, Indonesia.

As shown, it is obvious that the glottal fricative has more frequent distribution than the coronal fricative, especially in the combination with the nasalized vowels. Why does the glottal fricative have such frequent combination with nasalized vowels?

Zhang (2011: 100) points out that some nasal initials of Middle Chinese (MC) find their correspondence in the glottal fricative [h] in the Quanzhou dialect. For example:

(19) QZ 鱼 hi 砚 hĩ 瓦 hia 额 hiaʔ 艾 hiʔ 岸 huã 耳 hi 燃 hiã

In Middle Chinese, the initial consonants of all these example words belonged to the category of nasal initials (*m-, *n-, *ŋ-, *ȵ), and now the most of these words are initialless or keep the nasal initials, such as [mao] "spear" (茅) in Mandarin; in contrast, all these words have the glottal fricative [h] as their initials in the Quanzhou dialect. What is the motivation for nasals to be transformed to be glottal fricative?

Dai (2007) cites an example of Pingnan, a subdialect of Southern Min, in which these words have devoicing velar nasal as their initial consonants in contrast with glottal fricative in the Quanzhou dialect, as follows:

(20)

Example	艾 "mugwort"	岸 "bank"	燃 "burn"	兄 "elder brother"
Zhangzhou	hiã	huã	hiã	hiã
Pingnan	ŋ̊ia	ŋ̊ua	ŋ̊ia	ŋ̊ia
Quanzhou	hiã	huã	hiã	hiã

Dai (2007) makes a reconstruction of the consonant transformation from the glottal fricative to the voiceless nasal initials, due to the influence of the following nasalized vowel. But as stated, the initial consonants of these words in Middle Chinese were nasals. According to to Dai's analysis, it seems a bit weird why the nasal initial consonants in Middle Chinese would go through the process of debuccalization to be [h] before it reemerged as a nasal. Hence, in this book, it is suggested that the voiceless nasal is the transitional point from the nasal initials to the glottal fricative initial. In fact, this is also in alliance with the cross-linguistic observation. For example, such transformation from nasal initials to fricatives can also be found in Tibetan. Wang (2012: 52) gives some examples of some cognates of Tibetan dialect, which reflects the transformation from nasals to fricatives, as follows:

(21)

Tibetan	Seda	Daofu	Luhuo	Gande	RangTang	Banma	Cognates
sɲ̥iŋ	s̥ɲ̥aŋ	s̥ɲ̥aŋ	s̥ɲ̥aŋ	s̥ɲ̥aŋ	s̥ɲ̥aŋ	s̥saŋ	“heart”
sna	s̥na	s̥na	s̥na	s̥na	s̥na	s̥sa	“nose”
sŋon po	s̥ŋon bo	s̥ŋon bo	s̥ŋon bo	s̥ŋon bo	s̥ŋon bo	s̥son bo	“blue”

As shown in (21), the nasal in the traditional Tibetan /sɲ̥iŋ/ is transformed to the fricative [s̥saŋ] in Banam. What will come about if the coronal fricative undergoes the further reduction? O'Brien gives some typological examples of reduction of fricatives as follows:

(22)

Proto-Greek (Sommerstein 1973)	s > h before V
Ukrainian (Czaplicki 2006)	ɣ > ɦ in onset position
Proto-Indo-European (Lass 1976)	s > h Iranian
	s > h Brythonic Celtic h

Such process in which a sound with supralaryngeal articulation is realized at a later historical stage as a laryngeal sound is usually referred to as a debuccalization (Fallon 2002). From a feature geometry perspective, debuccalization involves delinking some node (usually Place), while retaining the features associated with laryngeal specification (McCarthy 1988, who cites Clements 1985). Iverson (1989) argues that fricatives debuccalize to [h], because what is left is the Laryngeal node and [+continuant]. What is concerned in Quanzhou is the debuccalization of the nasal initials to be glottal fricatives. Cross-linguistically speaking, the glottal fricative often behaves as if it is phonologically placeless (Steriade 1987a). De Lacy (2006: 2) points out that the glottal fricative is the most unmarked in terms of the place of articulation. Hence, the debuccalization from nasal initials to glottal fricatives in the Quanzhou dialect is a process of markedness reduction.

3.2.3 Regressive assimilation of Quanzhou

Assimilation involves a sound becoming more like a nearby sound with respect to one or more properties (Gordon 2016: 123). There are many types of assimilatory processes that can be characterized along several dimensions: whether consonants or vowels serve as triggers or targets of assimilation, the features that assimilate, the directionality of assimilation, etc (Gordon 2016: 124). Lin (1993: 59) puts forward that Quanzhou is observed to have an assimilation process in which the coronal nasal coda of the preceding syllable is assimilated by the labial initial consonants of the following syllable, as follows:

(23)	kan^{33}	pue^{41}	→	kam^{33}	pue^{41}	"dried scallop"	干贝
	sin^{33}	pu^{22}	→	sim^{33}	pu^{22}	"daughter-in-law"	新妇(媳妇)
	sin^{33}	bun^{14}	→	sim^{33}	bun^{14}	"news"	新闻

This assimilation process in Quanzhou is noted for its regressive direction. In fact, such phonological assimilation change is also prevalent in the other Southern Min dialects, such as Taiwan as described in Zhang (1983) and Bao (2000):

(24)	sin pu	→	sim pu	"new bride"
	sin bun	→	sim bun	"news"
	lam t'an	→	lan t'an	"southern play"
	sat bu	→	sap bu	"gnat"
	pak tɔ	→	pat tɔ	"belly"
	bak tsiu	→	bat tsiu	"eyeball"
	k'in pian	→	k'im pian	"convenient"
	kan pue	→	kam pue	"scallop"

This regressive assimilation is noted for the fact that it not only targets the nasals, but also targets the stops. Assimilation is typically motivated by considerations of articulatory ease, although directionality asymmetries in assimilatory patterns appear to reflect perceptual considerations (Gordon 2016: 123). It will be demonstrated that this assimilation of Quanzhou is different from the assimilation of Fuzhou not only in terms of direction but also in targets.

3.3 Contrastive hierarchy of the consonant system of Quanzhou dialect

It has long been assumed that phonological criteria for determining markedness relations can be found in the asymmetrical patterning of features (or sounds) in inventories and phonological processes (Trubetzkoy 1969; Archangeli 1984; Kiparsky 1985). In fact, in Rice's evaluation of markedness criteria, she proposes that the strongest and most compelling arguments come from phonological processes. When features are compared within a class, one feature may pattern asymmetrically with respect to others; it is this feature that is deemed the unmarked member of the relation. Consider an example from Yoruba. There are three tones in the language's tonal inventory (High, Middle, Low). The middle tone, unlike H and L, never appears in the structural descriptions or changes of phonological rules. The middle tone thus patterns asymmetrically with respect to other members of the tonal class and, as a result, is often considered the unmarked member (Akinlabi 1985; Hume 2003).

Any structure of any kind of complexity presupposes some form of hierarchy (Halle 1970). The theory of the contrastive feature hierarchy makes two empirical claims. The first claim is that distinctive features in each language are organized into a hierarchy. The second claim is that this hierarchy determines which feature values are contrastive in a given language (De Lacy 2006: 170). De Lacy (2006: 25) points out that hierarchy conflicts account for the variation seen in phenomena that are sensitive to markedness, a point made previously by Waugh (1979: 157), Dressler (1989: 118) and Battistella

(1990: 54ff.). Exactly which segment is favored in which environment in a particular language depends on which markedness hierarchy dominates in that language. For example, in German the obstruent voicing hierarchy has sway over the sonority hierarchy, so /g/→[k] in codas (i.e. /ta:g/→[ta:k] "day", cf. [ta:g-ə]). However, in Dakota the sonority hierarchy takes precedence, so that /k/ becomes the more sonorous [g] in codas: e.g. /ʃok/ →[ʃog] "thick, solid", cf. [ʃok-a] (Zhu 2013: 37). Since several feature orderings may be possible for the same surface inventory, there must be ways to determine which ordering is used in a given language. Dresher proposes that the order of the hierarchy can be determined by assuming what Hall (2007) calls the "Contrastivist Hypothesis" (Hall 2007: 20). According to this theory, the phonological component of a language L operates only on those features which are necessary to distinguish the phonemes of L from one another. If the phonology cannot reference non-contrastive features, then the contrastive feature specifications of a given phoneme can be determined by how it patterns together (and fails to pattern together) with other members of the inventory in phonological processes. Thus, for example, if a language shows a vowel triggered backing process which involves the feature [+back], then only vowels with a contrastive specifcation for [+back] can act as triggers. If /a/ and /u/ together serve as triggers of such a process, then [±back] must be ordered before [±low]. However, if only /u/ behaves as a back vowel to the exclusion of /a/, then [±low] must be ordered before [±back].

In terms of how to decide contrastive features, Dresher (2009) assumes that features are only present underlyingly where they are used to distinguish members of the inventory from each other. Contrastive features are assigned by a procedure known as the Successive Division Algorithm (SDA), which divides the inventory in a series of binary cuts one feature at a time until all phonemes of the language are distinguished from each other. Crucially, the order in which features are used to divide the inventory is language-specific. This means that languages with phonetically identical inventories may assign different phonological features to what would otherwise appear to be the "same" phoneme. In fact, Dresher (2009: 174) puts forward that there is evidence that different dialects with similar-looking inventories actually differ in their feature ordering, and hence in the relative scopes of contrastive features. For example, for both Anywa (Reh 1996) and Luo (Tucker 1994), related Nilotic languages have a dental/alveolar contrast in the coronal stops; in both languages, the alveolar nasal /n/ has no dental nasal partner. What is the patterning of /n/ in both dialects? Mackenzie (2005, 2009) argues that the two languages adopt different solutions to this question: in Anywa /n/ acts as if it is contrastively alveolar, in Luo it acts neutrally with respect to the contrast, as follows:

Nilotic dental/alveolar contrast (Mackenzie 2005):

(25)

<table>
<tr><th colspan="2">Anywa</th><th colspan="2">Luo</th></tr>
<tr><td>Dental</td><td>Alveolar</td><td>Dental</td><td>Alveolar</td></tr>
<tr><td>t̪</td><td>t</td><td>t̪</td><td>t</td></tr>
<tr><td>d̪</td><td>d</td><td>d̪</td><td>d</td></tr>
<tr><td></td><td>n</td><td colspan="2">n</td></tr>
</table>

3.3.1 Laryngeal features

It is assumed that segments consist of two main parts: the laryngeal and the supralaryngeal constituent. Under the laryngeal node, there are three features such as [spread], [voice], and [constricted] (Gussenhoven & Haike 2011: 189 – 190), as follows:

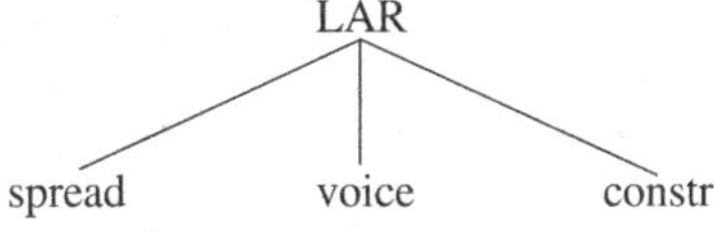

As discussed above, the voiced obstruents in Quanzhou are only surface segments; therefore, [voice] feature is unnecessary in building the hierarchy of Quanzhou. What is concerned in Quanzhou is the feature of [spread glottis] ([sg]), which ensures the consonants with [+sg] feature form minimal contrastive pairs with the consonants with [-sg] feature, as follows:

(26)	pi^{33}	"tomb"	pu^{24}	"toast"
	p^hi^{33}	"wrap"	p^hu^{24}	"float"
	ti^{33}	"know"	tu^{24}	"kitchen"
	t^hi^{33}	"whip"	t^hu^{24}	"loaf"
	ki^{33}	"twig"	ku^{33}	"pony"
	k^hi^{33}	"bully"	k^hu^{33}	"body"

It is observable that aspirated consonants of three places of articulation are distinguished from the unaspirated consonants of three places of articulation. It is suggested to use the feature [spread] to distinguish these aspirated consonants and unaspirated consonants, as follows:

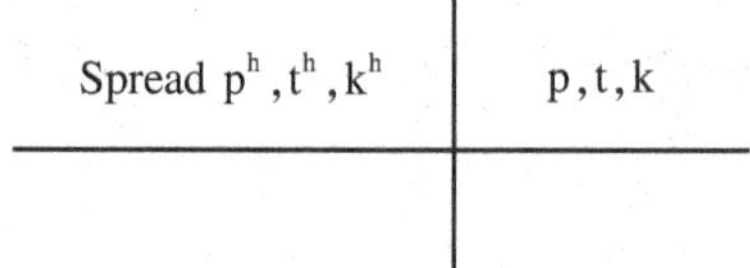

Diagram 3-1 Division of the aspirated obstruents and unaspirated obstruents

3.3.2 Manner features

According to De Lacy (2006), different markedness hierarchies may conflict; in different languages, different hierarchies have priority: in some languages, the PoA may take precedence over manner, but in some other languages manner may come before the PoA. Which markedness hierarchy is more dominant in Quanzhou dialect? De Lacy (2006: 162) points out that in keeping with the Contrastivist Hypothesis, phonological activity serves as the chief heuristic for determining what the feature hierarchy is for a given language.

In Quanzhou dialect, the [nasal] manner of consonants prefers to be maintained in the phonological changes. As discussed, there is a phonological regressive assimilation which is prevalent in Southern Min dialects, including the Quanzhou dialect (Bao 2000; Zhang 1983; Lin 1993)

(27)			
	sin pu →	sim pu	"new bride"
	sin bun →	sim bun	"news"
	lam t'an →	lan t'an	"southern play"
	sat bu →	sap bu	"gnat"
	pak tɔ →	pat tɔ	"belly"
	bak tsiu →	bat tsiu	"eyeball"
	k'in pian →	k'im pian	"convenient"
	kan pue →	kam pue	"scallop"

This regressive assimilation is noted for that it not only targets the nasals, but also targets the stops. Jun (1995, 1996, 2004) explores the impact of these asymmetries on the typology of place assimilation and finds certain implicational scales governing the trigger and target of place assimilation. Jun finds that different manners of articulation show different degrees of susceptibility to place assimilation: nasals are found to be most likely to be targeted for assimilation followed by plosives; the least likely to assimilate are continuants. Thus, some languages (e. g. Diola Fogny, Lithuanian) assimilate only nasals, while in others (e. g. Korean, Malay, Thai) both nasals and stops undergo assimilation (Gordon 2016). As revealed in (27), the place feature of the initial of the second syllable always trigger the assimilation of the nasal codas as well as stop codas of the first syllable. In this process of assimilation, the manner of the coda consonants of the first syllable is maintained in the phonological change such as the change from "sin pu" to "sim pu" does not change the nasal manner of [n] of the first syllable, while the place of the coda consonants of the first syllable is changed as in the case from [n] to [m]. When comparing members of a feature class in assimilation, it is commonly assumed that "the unmarked pole of an opposition is lost or obscured, with the marked pole remaining ... In assimilation, the marked features within a class are active ... the unmarked features, on the other hand, are passive, or inert ... overridden by other features" (Hume 2003). According to this phonological process, it is found that the manner of consonant is maintained while the place feature of consonants is changed. Hence, it is proposed that the manner of consonants takes precedence over the PoA in the Quanzhou dialect, which can be indicated as follows:

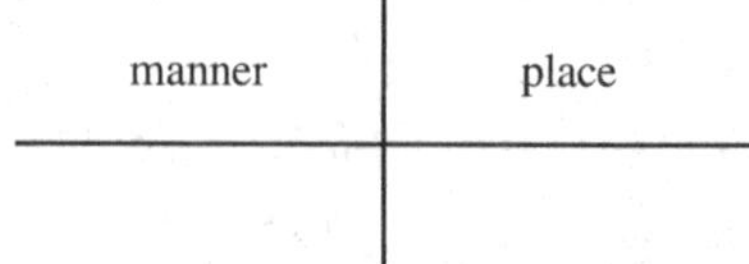

Diagram 3-2 Division of manner and place of the consonants of Quanzhou

3.3.2.1 Nasal feature

For the contrastive initial consonants of Quanzhou, there are different manner dimensions such as nasal, strident, continuant. The feature [nasal] can differentiate the nasal consonants from the non-nasal consonants. The feature [strident] and [continuant] can separate fricatives from obstruents. Which manners are necessary in the construction of the feature hierarchy of Quanzhou is dependent on the phonological processes of the related consonants. The Quanzhou dialect is remarkable in having some voiced obstruents, which can not be found in other sub-dialects of Min. As mentioned, there is a complementary distribution between the nasals and the voiced obstruents, the underlying segments of which are the nasals instead of the voiced stops. These nasals surface up when the following vowels are nasal vowels; when the following vowels are oral vowels, the nasal initials are denasalized under the influence of oral vowels to be the voiced stops. Accordingly, this process differentiates nasals from non-nasal consonants which can pattern both with oral vowels and nasalized vowels, indicated as follows:

(28)	ba^{24}	"cat"	sa^{33}	"sand"	pi^{33}	"beer"	pʰi^{33}	"wrap"
	la^{33}	"pull"	tsa^{41}	"explode"	ti^{33}	"know"	tʰi^{33}	"sticky"
	ga^{24}	"tooth"	ha^{22}	"rainbow"	ki^{33}	"twig"	kʰi^{33}	"strange"
	mã^{24}	"mother"	sã^{33}	"three"	pĩ^{33}	"whip"	pʰĩ^{33}	"bully"
	nã^{24}	"basket"	tsã^{55}	"chop"	tĩ^{33}	"sweet"	tʰĩ^{33}	"sky"
	ŋã^{24}	"rock"	hã^{22}	"seam"	kĩ^{33}	"knit"	kʰĩ^{33}	"ravine"

Hence, in the construction of hierarchy of Quanzhou [nasal] feature has precedence over all the other manner features. Therefore, the first step of constructing the feature hierarchy of initial consonants in Quanzhou is indicated as follows:

[nasal] m, n, ŋ	p, p^h; t, t^h; k, k^h ts, s, h

Diagram 3-3 Division of nasal and non-nasal consonants

In terms of the further division of nasal consonants, the coronal nasal can be separated from the labial nasal and the velar nasal due to the fact that the labial nasal and the velar nasal can be the independent syllabic consonants while the coronal nasal can not in the Quanzhou dialect, indicated as follows:

(29) /m/		/ŋ/	
m^{24}	"waxberry"	$pŋ^{33}$	"help"
m^{55}	"aunt"	$tŋ^{24}$	"long"
m^{42}	"no"	$kŋ^{33}$	"change"

The further independent evidence of the unmarked status of the coronal nasal will be further provided in the following section. So the above hierarchy tree can be further formulated as follows:

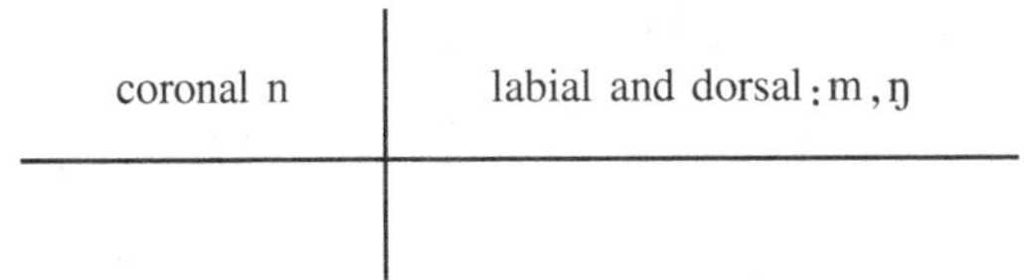

Diagram 3-4 Sub-division of nasal consonants

As seen in this step of division of the consonants of Quanzhou, the manner feature dominates the place features; of all the manner features the feature [nasal] is dominant over all the other manner features due to their distinct behavior from all the other segments, which are further divided according to the different phonological behavior of different places of nasals.

3.3.2.2 Strident & continuant features

For the non-nasal segments, which features are necessary in further division? In Quanzhou dialect, it is obvious that [-nasal] consonants are made up of stops, fricatives and affricates. In terms of the classification of natural classes, the fricatives and affricates tend to pattern together as a natural group for their similar phonological behavior. Natural classes should be able to assimilate, dissimilate, and otherwise participate in phonological processes (De Lacy 2006: 44). The motivation for the catergorization of the fricatives and affricates of Quanzhou together can find evidence in the same role in patterning as the initial of some words which are initialless in Mandarin. For example,

(30)	Quanzhou	Mandarin	Meaning
	hɔ	yu	"rain"
	hun	yun	"cloud"
	tsiũ	yang	"itch"
	sĩ	yan	"salt"

Besides such similar phonological behavior, fricatives and affricates are also found to be the only initials of rhyme /əm/ which is the only rhyme of the central vowel with a nasal coda in Quanzhou, as follows:

(31)	/əm/	Meaning
	tsəm^{33}	"needle"
	tsəm^{55}	"what"
	tsəm^{33}	"ragged"
	səm^{33}	"woods"
	səm^{41}	"filter"
	həm^{33}	"prosperous"

Based on this similar patterning, fricatives and affricates can be separated from stops in Quanzhou. But what features are needed in separating fricatives and affricates from stops? As noted above, there are two fricatives /s/ and /h/ and one affricate /ts/. For these non-stops, the features of [continuant] and [strident] may be concerned. It is interesting to note that while two fricatives /s/ and /h/ share the feature [continuant], the affricate /ts/ has both [-continuant] and [+continuant]; yet while the coronal fricative /s/ and affricate /ts/ are also called "sibilant" rendering that they can be classified under the feature of [strident]. Hall (2008: 221) points out that segments marked with [+strident] include not only the sibilant fricatives /s/ but also all affricates (LaCharité 1993; Rubach 1994; Clements 1999; Kehrein 2002), the glottal fricative can not be included in the sibilant fricative class. Therefore, for the features [continuant] and [strident], which will come first in the further division of the non-stops? In the classification of natural classes, which group is more natural in the Quanzhou dialect depends on their phonological behavior. Chen Zhongmin (2012) points out Yu rhyme ("鱼"韵)① of Quanzhou dialect has different allomorphs following two kinds of initials. Following the coronal fricative and the coronal affricate, the rhyme turns to be [ɔ], while the rhyme is [u] when it follows the other initials as follows:

(32)	Yu Rhyme	Initials: fricative and affricate	The other initials
	/u/	[ɔ]	[u]

With respect of the similar patterning of coronal fricative and affricate, here is one more evidence from the comparison of sub-dialects of Southern Min, which is indicated as follows (Du 2014: 183):

① In Middle Chinese, Yu rhyme is reconstructed to be [io].

(33)

Examples with Liu Rhyme①	Initials in Southern Min dialect	Nan'an	Quanzhou	Zhangzhou
贸 "trade"	b	bio	bio	mɔ
斗 "contest"	t	tio	tio	tɔ
偷 "steal"	t^h	t^hio	t^hio	t^hɔ
陋 "ugly"	l	lio	lio	lɔ
叟 "old man"	s		so	sɔ
奏 "play"	ts	tsio	tso	tsɔ
构 "construct"	k	kio	kio	kɔ
寇 "bandit"	k^h	k^hio	k^hio	k^hɔ
后 "behind"	h	hio	hio	hɔ

As shown, in Nan'an the rhyme following all initials is [io], in Zhangzhou the rhyme after all initials is [ɔ], but in Quanzhou dialect there are two allophones: [o] which follows coronal fricative and coronal affricate, and [io] which comes after the rest initials including the glottal fricative /h/. The presence or absence of the glide [j] following the initials sets the coronal fricative and affricate from the other initials, including the glottal fricative.

Here is one further case that can embolden the classification of coronal fricative and affricate as a natural class. The rhyme /əm/ can be found in Quanzhou and Jinjiang which is sub-city of Quanzhou. As is mentioned above, the rhyme /əm/ can only have coronal affricate, coronal fricative and glottal fricative as its initial in the Quanzhou dialect. But for the same rhyme in the Jinjiang dialect, the glottal fricative initial first disappears while the coronal affricate and fricative remain.

(34) Quanzhou /əm/

a. tsəm^{33} "admonish"

b. səm^{33} "woods"

c. həm^{33} "prosperous"

Jinjiang /əm/

d. tsəm^{33} "admonish"

e. səm^{33} "woods"

f. ×

① Liu Rhyme is consisted of 侯 əu, 尤 ĭəu, 幽 iəu in Middle Chinese.

Hence, in the further division of two fricatives and one affricate into sub-groups, it is preferable to divide the coronal fricative and the coronal affricate into one group, and the glottal fricative into the other group. For this division, the feature [strident] can be used, as follows:

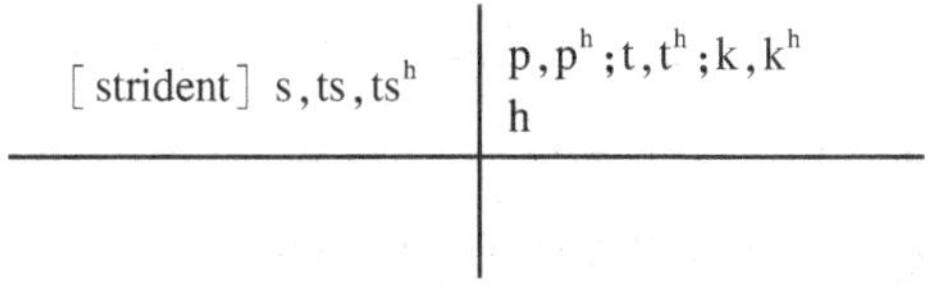

Diagram 3-5 Sub-division of fricatives and affricates

Apart from the nasal and strident segments, the rest segments /p, p^h; t, t^h; k, k^h; h/ obviously include two natural groups, namely the obstruents /p, p^h; t, t^h; k, k^h/ and the fricative /h/. To separate the obstruents and the glottal fricative /h/, the feature [continuant] is enough. Therefore, the manner-first approach of the division of the initial consonants of Quanzhou can be seen as follows:

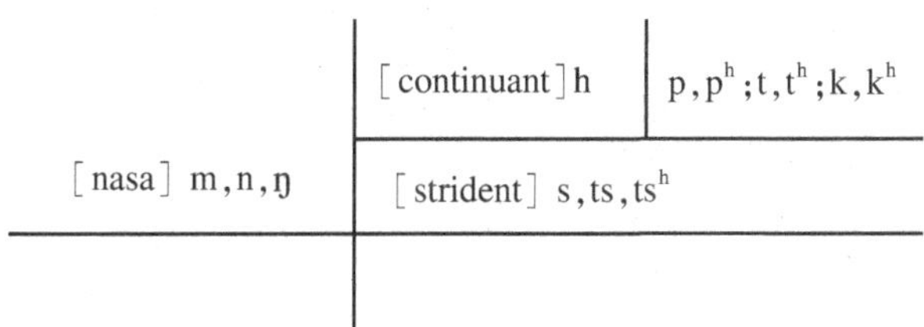

Diagram 3-6 Last division of manners of consonants of Quanzhou

3.3.3 Place features

Alongside with the manner features, another important dimension of consonants is the place feature. According to Lombardi (2002), De Lacy (2002, 2006: 35) puts forward that the main places of articulation include [LABIAL], [CORONAL], [DORSAL], [GLOTTAL], the ranking of which is as follows: [DORSAL] > [LABIAL] > [CORONAL] > [GLOTTAL], namely [GLOTTAL] is the most unmarked followed by [CORONAL] while [DORSAL] and [LABIAL] are more marked. Are the place features of Quanzhou also in accord with such observation? What observation can be made about the markedness of the place features of the consonants of Quanzhou?

3.3.3.1 Coronals

Many studies in the past two decades have argued that coronal stops like /t, t^h/ have properties that differentiate them from labial stops like /p, p^h/ and dorsal stops like /k, k^h/ (e.g. Paradis & Prunet 1991b). For example, in many languages coronals are the only sounds that undergo place assimilation or epenthesis. Likewise, the sound like /t/ is often the outcome of rules neutralizing place contrasts (Hall 2011). Do coronals in the Quanzhou dialect also have some distinct features that differentiate them from labials and dorsals? In Wu's (2014) analysis of Qi Rhyme, he points out that the first stratum of this rhyme only occur following the coronal initials, as follows:

(35)

Cognates	Southern Min					
	Quanzhou	Yongchun	Dongshan	Zhangzhou	Shantou	Jieyang
脐 "navel"	tsai	tsai	tsai	tsai	tsai	tsai
荔 "lychee"	lãi		lãi	lãi		
西 "west"	sai	sai	sai	sai	sai	sai
犀 "rhinoceros"	sai	sai	sai	sai	sai	sai
婿 "son-in-law"	sai	sai	sai	sai	sai	sai

For the cognates of this stratum, it seems that all the cognates have no initials of the other places of articulation, except coronals. Wu (2014) points out that it appears weird that the first stratum only has the coronal fricative, affricate and lateral as initials. In the further analysis, he adds that for this stratum, there are also some cognates with coronal stops as initials such as (1) tai ui^"底位" "indicating direction", (2) tai siŋ^"第先" "indicating order", (3) t^hai^"算了" "let it be". According to Wu (2014: 63 – 64), the cognates of the other strata can have different places of articulation as initials.

The unmarked status of coronal can also be found in the related Southern Min dialect in Taiwan which has its origin in the Quanzhou dialect. Bao Zhiming (2000: 106) mentions a language game named La-pi in Taiwanese Southern Min, which has been the subject of a number of studies (Li, Paul Jen-

Kui 1985; Lin 1989; Bao 1990; Duanmu 1990)

(36)				
a.	be	→	le bi	"buy"
b.	kam	→	lam kin	"sweet"
c.	tsin	→	lin tsin	"very"
d.	aŋ	→	laŋ in	"red"
e.	tsap	→	lap tsit	"ten"
f.	t'at	→	lat t'it	"kick"
g.	pak	→	lak pit	"peel"

There are some observations about these data: firstly, the first consonant of the first syllable surfaces as l, and the vowel of the second syllable surfaces as i in the results of La-pi game; secondly, the rhyme structure of the source syllable remains intact in the first syllable; thirdly, dorsal and labial codas become coronal in the second syllable. The observation relevant to the discussion here is the first observation that the coronal lateral is chosen as the default initial consonant in insertion and the third observation that the labial or dorsal coda of the source syllable turns to be the coronal coda as the result of the language game. Why is the coronal chosen as the default initial consonant of the first syllable and the default coda of the second syllable? Lombardi (2002: 237) points out that [n] is a default epenthetic consonant in a language game in Fula, which appears to be the only situation where epenthetic [n] appears in the language (Bagemihl 1989). Although it is clear that this is a highly restricted situation, since language games can be taken into account in constructing the theory of phonology, and thus fits the generalization. Therefore, it is proposed that in Quanzhou, coronal is more unmarked than labial as well as dorsal.

Then what feature can separate coronals from labials and dorsals? Avery & Rice (1989: 195) place [LABIAL] and [DORSAL] under the node of [peripheral] as follows:

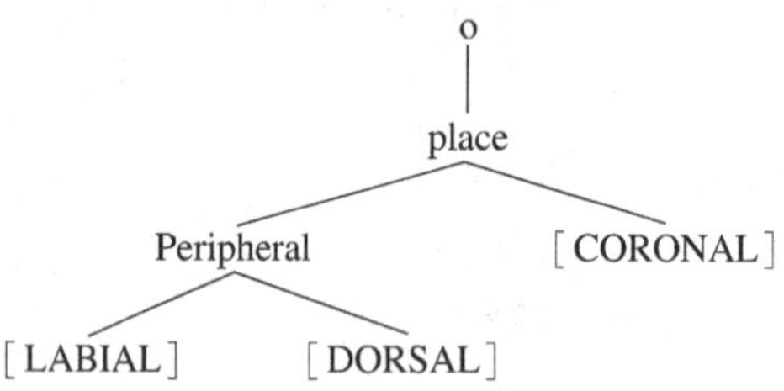

Diagram 3-7 Places of articulation (Avery & Rice 1989)

The peripheral (or Grave) node is an extra layer of structure to the Place node introduced in Avery & Rice (1989) as a sister node to the Coronal node. Based on this, it is proposed to use feature [peripheral] to divide coronals from labials and dorsals, as indicated as follows:

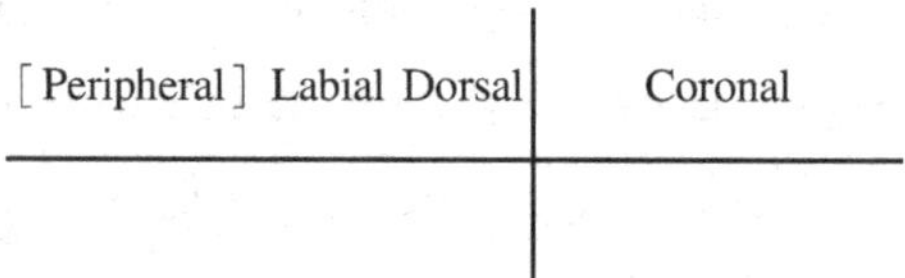

Diagram 3-8 The first division of main PoA

3.3.3.2 Labial vs dorsal

As to the separation of labials and dorsals, there is one obvious labial co-occurrence restriction in the Quanzhou dialect, which can separate dorsals from labials. According to De Lacy (2007: 80), the marked segment is more specific and appears in less grammar. In the Quanzhou dialect, the labial consonant is subject to more restriction in phonotactics constraints, indicated as follows:

(37)	* pim	* pam	* piam	* pip	* pap	* piap
	tin	tan	tian	tit	tat	tiat
	kiŋ	kaŋ	kiaŋ		kak	kiak

As shown, the labial initial consonant has high restriction in its phonotactics, but the coronal and dorsal initial consonant has no such restraints. In the Quanzhou dialect, more than one labial segment is restrained from occurring in the same syllable. Given the representation within the standard theory of feature geometry (Clements 1985; Sagey 1986), labials are adjacent on the labial tier, although they may not be string-adjacent. Bao (2000) formulates the labial co-occurrence restriction as follows:

*[... Labial ... Labial ...] syl

Due to the restraints on the labial phonotactics, it seems reasonable to say that the labial consonant is more marked. But is there further evidence of phonological behavior that can prove the special status of the labial consonant? As indicated, there is a special final which consists of schwa and a labial nasal coda in Quanzhou. The final consisting of schwa with velar nasal coda can no longer be found in Quanzhou. Luckily, this final still exists in Nan'an, a county of Quanzhou. The combination of the initial consonants with this schwa final can give a hint about the phonological behavior of the initial consonants. The following gives a list of the combination of the initial consonants and the schwa finals.

(38)

	p	t	k	ts	s	h
əm				√	√	√
əŋ		√	√	√	√	√

There are some observations about (38). Firstly, the combination of the initial consonants with the final [əm] in Nan'an is the same as that of Quanzhou. Secondly, with respect of the combination of the initial consonants with the final [əŋ], the first initial consonant that disappears is labial stop. Is this a system gap? But as the following indicates, the labial stop can combine with the schwa final.

(39)

	p	t	k	ts	s	h
ə	√	√	√	√	√	√

Hence, such phonotactic characteristics further separates the labial stop from the dorsal stop. It is commonly assumed that unmarked segments (or features) should have a wider distribution and occur more frequently within a language, which implies the relatively narrow distribution of the marked segment (e. g. Trubetzkoy 1969; Greenberg 1966; Battistella 1990). For the stops of Quanzhou dialect, labials are the most marked one which has the narrowest distribution compared with dorsals and coronals. With respect to the unmarkedness of dorsals and coronals, despite the unmarkedness of coronals, there is argument about the unmarkedness of dorsals (e. g. Trigo 1988) and coronals (e. g. Paradis & Prunet 1991a; Mohanan 1993; Prince & Smolensky 2004; Hume 1996; Wilson 2001). However, in the Quanzhou dialect, coronals are obviously more unmarked compared with dorsals. De Lacy (2006: 27) points out that /k/ neutralizes to [t] in a Taiwanese reduplication, /k/ and /t/'s value for PoA is different, so dorsals must be more marked than coronals on some hierarchy. De Lacy (2006: 44) provides a sub-hierarchy like | dorsal, labial > coronal, glottal | which implies that dorsals and labials form a natural class, and coronals and glottals form a natural class. In the initial consonant inventory of Quanzhou dialect, there is no phonemic glottal stop, hence this hierarchy can be reformalized as | dorsal, labial > coronal |.

On the basis of the above analysis, the feature hierarchy of Quanzhou consonants is constructed as follows:

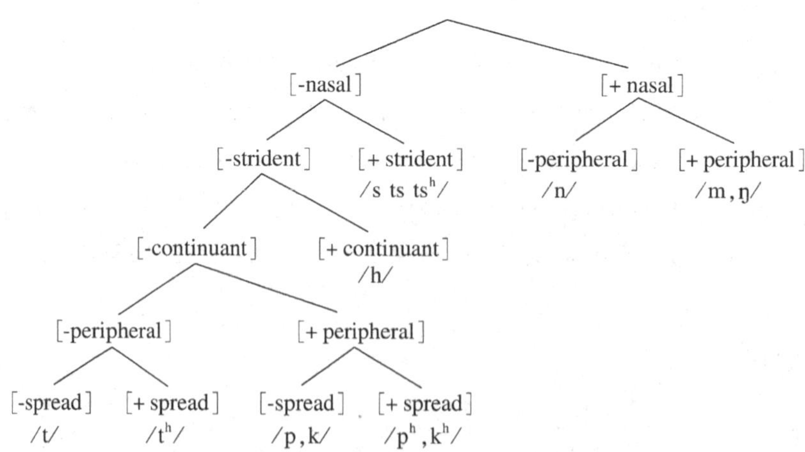

Diagram 3-9 Hierarchy of the contrastive features of consonants in Quanzhou

3.4 Initials of Fuzhou

This section will first be devoted to the detailed description of initial consonants in Fuzhou. Following the related description, a most famous phonological process of Fuzhou, namely the categorical transformation of the consonants will be analyzed under the framework of feature geometry before the feature hierarchy of the initial consonants of Fuzhou is established according to the synchronic and diachronic sound changes of these initial consonants under the guidance of the markedness theory and feature hierarchy theory.

As the representative of Eastern Min, Fuzhou is noted to have the following initial consonant inventory (Chen Zeping 1998: 7):

(40)	p	p^h	m	
	t	t^h	n(l)	
	ts	ts^h		s
	k	k^h	ŋ	x
	ø			

Obviously, in (40), Fuzhou also has fourteen initials, quite similar to those of Quanzhou.

3.4.1 Categorical transformation of initial consonants of Fuzhou

Fuzhou dialect is noted for its remarkable systematic categorical transformation of initial consonants, although some similar sporadic phenomena are reported in some other Chinese dialects such as the Yiyang dialect of the Xiang dialect group. The categorical transformation of initials in Fuzhou refers to the systematic transformation of the initials of the second syllable under the influence of the final segment of the preceding syllable in the domain of prosodic words. Such categorical transformation of initials is largely dependent on the final system of the first syllable of prosodic words. The final system of Fuzhou retains the three-division state of Middle Chinese which includes finals ending with a vowel or syllabic ending①, finals ending with nasal codas, and those ending with glottal stop codas. Such different endings play a key role in the categorical transformation of initials in Fuzhou (for detailed discussions see Chen Zeping 1998: 9 – 10). Based on the different codas of the first syllable of prosodic words, the categorical transformation of initials can be divided into the following two parts: the categorical transformation triggered by a syllabic ending of vowel and the categorical transformation triggered by a nasal coda.

3.4.1.1 Categorical transformation triggered by a vowel or syllabic ending of vowel

The different initials of the non-initial syllables in the domain of prosodic words undergo the categorical transformation with respect to vowel or syllabic ending of vowel of the preceding syllables.

Firstly, the labial initial will turn to be [β] when following a vowel or syllabic ending of vowel, as follows:

(41)	菜包 "vegetable bun"	ts^hai pau	→	ts^hai βau
	茶杯 "cup"	ta pui	→	ta βui
	大炮 "cannon"	tuai p^hau	→	tuai βau

Secondly, the coronal initials /t/, /t^h/ and /s/ will turn to /l/② when they follow a vowel or syllabic ending of vowel, as follows:

(42)	花店 "flower store"	xua taiŋ	→	xua laiŋ
	戏台 "stage"	xie tai	→	xie lai
	雨伞 "umbrella"	y saŋ	→	y laŋ

Thirdly, the affricate initials /ts/ and /ts^h/ will be transformed into [z]

① In Fuzhou, there are three kinds of codas, namely the syllabic ending of vowel which include /i/, /u/ and /y/ in cases such as /ai/, /uai/, /au/, the stop coda including /ʔ/, and the nasal coda such as /ŋ/.

② Chen Zeping (2013) proposes that [l] transcribed here is not the real lateral. It is better to transcribe it as [ɾ]. The reason for treating it as [l] is that such transcription can better describe its alternantion with [n].

when following a vowel or syllabic ending of vowel. The transformation results of these two consonants are noted for the relaxed articulation and the weak restriction upon airstream. They will be strengthened to be [z] or [ʒ] in emphasis and will turn to a semi-vowel in the state of extreme relaxation.

(43)	粗纸 "coarse paper"	ts^{h}u tsai	→	tsu zai
	祖宗 "ancestor"	tsu tsuŋ	→	tsu zuŋ
	花彩 "money"	xua tsai	→	hua zai

Fourthly, the dorsal initials /k/,/k^h/ and /x/ will be deleted when following a vowel or syllabic ending of vowel, as follows:

(44)	西瓜 "watermelon"	sɛ kua	→	sɛ ua
	提琴 "violin"	t^{h}i k^{h}iŋ	→	ti iŋ
	水鸡 "frog"	tsui kie	→	tsui ie
	布扣 "button"	puo k^{h}au	→	puo au

Fifthly, when the preceding syllable ends with a glottal stop, the initial of the following syllable usually does not undergo the categorical transformation. In some cases, the initial of the following syllable will go through the categorical transformation when the glottal stop of the preceding syllable is not so steady, as follows:

(45)	石板 "slate"	suoʔ peiŋ→suo βeiŋ	合倍 "double"	haʔ pui→haʔ pui
	烛斗 "candle"	tsuoʔ tau→tsuo lau	泼水 "splash"	p^{h}uaʔ tsui→p^{h}uaʔ tsui
	石狮 "city name"	suoʔ sai→suo lai	拾起 "pick up"	k^{h}aʔ-k^{h}i→k^{h}aʔ-k^{h}i

The categorical transformation in Fuzhou is so intricate that not only stops may turn to fricatives, to laterals, or be deleted, but fricatives may also turn to laterals and affricates may surface as fricatives.

3.4.1.2 Categorical transformation triggered by a nasal coda

When the first syllable ends with a nasal coda, the initial of the following syllable will also undergo the categorical transformation. The following examples indicate different transformation results when the first syllable ends with a nasal coda (the data come from Chen Zeping 2013: 113)

(46)

汤房 "bathroom"	t^{h}ouŋ puŋ→t^{h}ouŋ muŋ	痰盆 "phlegm basin"	t^{h}aŋ puoŋ→t^{h}aŋ muoŋ
铜片 "copper slip"	tøyŋ p^{h}ieŋ→tøyŋ mieŋ	传票 "summons"	tuoŋ p^{h}ieu→tuoŋ mieu
饭店 "restaurant"	puoŋ taiŋ→puoŋ naiŋ	钢钉 "steel pin"	kouŋ tiŋ→kouŋ niŋ
冬天 "winter"	tøyŋ t^{h}ieŋ→tøyŋ nieŋ	风头 "wind"	xuŋ t^{h}au→xuŋ nau
电光 "light"	tieŋ kuoŋ→tieŋ ŋuoŋ	唱机 "record player"	ts^{h}uoŋ ki→ts^{h}uoŋ ŋi
银行 "bank"	ŋyŋ ouŋ→ŋyŋ ŋouŋ	中医 "TCM"	tyŋ i→tyŋ ŋi
红枣 "date"	øyŋ tso→øyŋ nzo	番钱 "silver dollar"	xuaŋ tseiŋ→xuaŋ nzieŋ
甘草 "licorice"	kaŋ ts^{h}o→kaŋ nzo	砖墙 "brick wall"	tsuoŋ tsuo→tsuoŋ nzuoŋ

The above data reveal three cases of categorical transformation of the initials of the following syllables when preceded by a nasal coda.

The systematic categorical transformation of Fuzhou is so complicated as to rende it difficult to summarize with the explicit transformation rules. This may be the reason why such a phenomenon is always a hot topic in the related research.

3.4.2 Categorical transformation under the framework of feature geometry

According to the feature geometry theory (Clements 1985: 225 - 252), the distinctive features comprising different segments are distributed within the geometrical configuration; features with different properties are located under the nodes of different layers, each having its independent phonotactics restriction and its own dimensional structure, as follows:

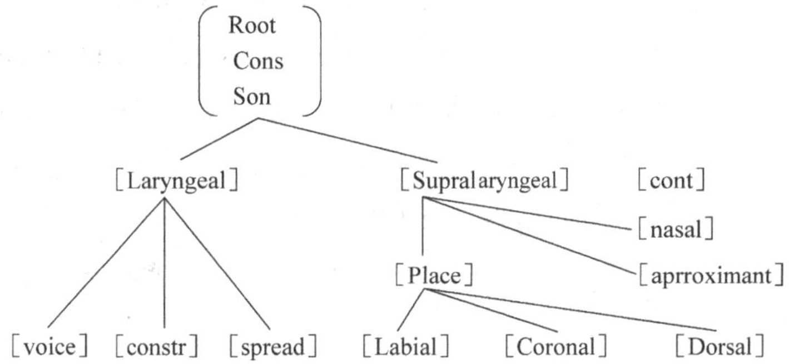

Diagram 3-10 Feature geometry (**Gussenhoven & Jacobs 2011: 190**)

The feature geometry based on the properties and functions of features has correlation with the physiological structure: the features that go through changes under the same environment often belong to the same articulator or the neighbouring organs; those that do not share similar changes do not have such relation. Under the framework of feature geometry, a lot of research (Halle & Vergnaud 1980; Clements 1985) describe the phonetic assimilation as one or several features on one layer spread to the adjacent layers. The dimensional approach of feature geometry provides a vivid approach to describe the synchronic relation of features (Clements 1985: 225 – 252).

3.4.2.1 Feature geometry of the categorical transformation triggered by a vowel or syllabic ending

It is noted that the categorical transformation of Fuzhou is not only dependent on the final segment of the first syllable but also closely related to the places of articulation of initials of the following syllables in the domain of prosodic words. According to the data mentioned above, in the categorical transformation of Fuzhou, the labial obstruent /p/ and /p^h/ are realized as [β] when preceded by a vowel or a syllabic ending of vowel. /β/, /p/ and /p^h/ which though are of the same place of articulation are different in such features as [voice] and [continuant]. Under the framework of feature geometry, it is reasonable to understand the categorical transformation as a process in which the features such as [+ voice] and [+ cont] of the syllabic ending of vowel of the preceding syllable spread to the initial of the following syllable, which leads to the delinking of [-cont] and [-voice] of the original initial of the second syllable. With the labial feature of the initial of the second syllable retained, the initial of the second syllable with added [+ voice] and [+ cont] features is realized as the voiced bilabial fricative, namely [β]. The contrast between aspiration and unaspiration of the initial of the second syllable is neutralized in this process. The feature geometry representation of its phonological rules is represented as follows:

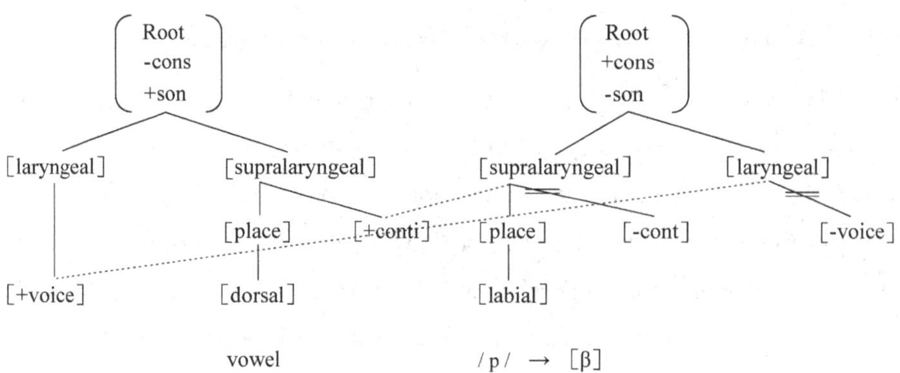

Diagram 3-11 Categorical transformation of bilabial initials

Note: In Diagram 3-11, the dotted lines indicate the spreading of features; " = " stands for the delinking of features. These symbols hold for the following pictures.

Different from the labial consonants which have only two obstruents besides the nasal /m/, the coronal consonants also include obstruents, fricative and even affricate, besides the nasal /n/. In the categorical transformation, the coronal consonants such as /t/, /t^h/ and /s/ are realized as [l] when the first syllable ends with a vowel. Chen Zeping (2013: 109) puts forward that the transformation result of coronal obstruent and fricative following a syllabic ending of vowel is not a typical lateral, but rhotic or tap like the flapping "t" in American English "water". In fact, whether the transformation result is realized as either [l] or [r] can be accounted in the same way, since these two segments are classified under the category of approximant in phonology

(Gussenhoven & Haike 2001: 69). Under the framework of feature geometry, the reason why /t/, /t^h/ and /s/ are realized as [l] following a syllabic ending of vowel is related to the spreading of the feature [approximant] from the vowel ending of the preceding syllable to the initial of the second syllable, which changes the manner of the consonants and turns them to approximants of the same place of articulation. In this transformation, the spreading of [approximant] implies the spreading of [voice] and [cont], represented as follows:

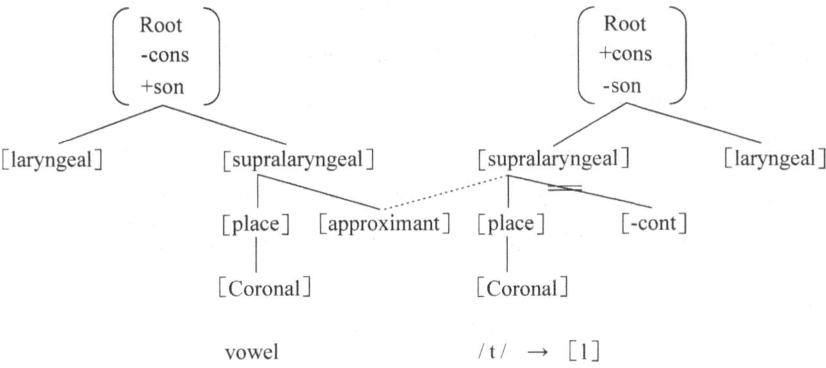

Diagram 3-12 Categorical transformation of coronal obstruents

Here is an observation about the features of the root of the following consonant. Different from the change from /p/ to [β] in which the features at the root of the following consonant are [+cons, -sonorant], in the change from /t/ to [l], the features at the root of the following consonant are [+cons, +sonorant], the difference of the specification of [son] lies in the quality of the following consonants. According to Gussenhoven & Haike (2011: 77), [+son] segments are produced with a constriction in the vocal tract which allows the air pressure behind it and in front of it to be relatively equal, and [+son] are all vowels, glides, liquids and nasals. In this case, it is the transfer of [+approximant] from the proceeding vowel to the following consontnat. [+approximant] segments are those segments which have a constriction in the vocal tract which allows a free (frictionless) escape of air, while for [-approx] segments this is not the case (Ladefoged 1971). (The term "lateral" is used for any l-type sound, while the term "rhotic" refers to any r-type sound; laterals and rhotics are often referred to as "liquids".) Accordingly, the change from /t/ to [l] is not only reflected in the changes of the subordinated nodes but also in the root.

A most distinct difference among the coronal consonants is the change of affricates /ts/ and /ts^h/ in the categorical transformation. Unlike the coronal obstruents, fricatives, as well as nasals, the affricates /ts/ and /ts^h/ in Fuzhou are realized as [z] in the categorical transformation. The affricates /ts/ and /ts^h/ are noted for having two opposite features such as [-cont] as well as [+cont] at the same time. In the feature geometry, this transformation process can be understood as the spreading of [+voice] and [+cont] of the syllabic ending of vowel of the preceding syllable to the initial of the following syllable, resulting in the acquisition of [+voice] and [+cont] in the second syllable, which is realized as [z] with the retained place [coronal], indicated as follows:

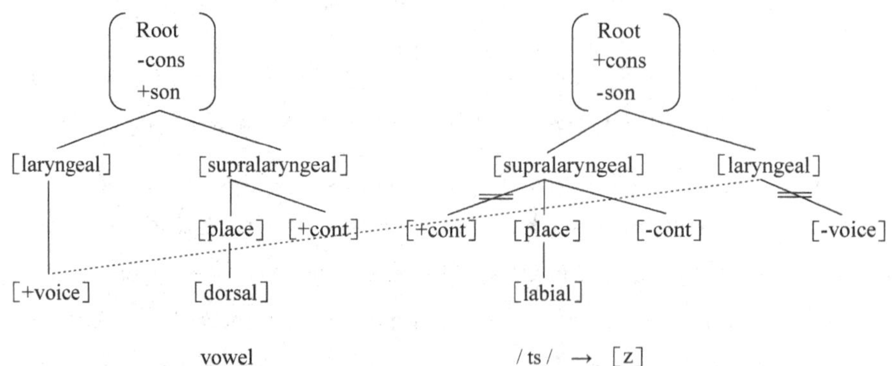

Diagram 3-13 Categorical transformation of coronal affricates

The biggest change in the categorical transformation in Fuzhou is the case of the dorsal consonants /k, k^h, x/ which disappear when following a syllabic ending of vowel, leading to the initialless state of the following syllable. Under the framework of feature geometry, this can be understood as the dorsal node of the second syllable is deleted when the features [+cont] and [voice] spread from the ending of the preceding syllable, which results in no phonetic realization of the initial of the second syllable.

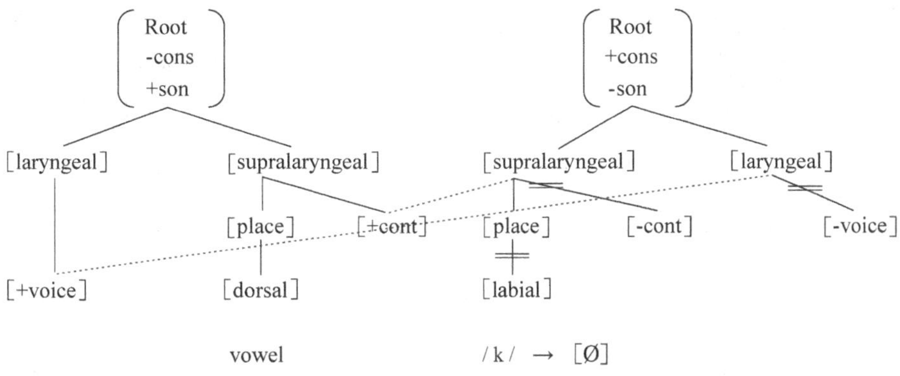

Diagram 3-14 Categorical transformation of dorsal obstruents

From the perspective of the phonetic coherence, the categorical transformation of initials in Fuzhou can be deemed as a requirement imposed by the prosodic words upon the morphonemic boundary of Fuzhou. To achieve more coherent effect within prosodic words, the initial consonant of the second syllable is modeled in terms of feature to become more aligned with the adjacent vowel segments. To put it in a more specific way, the initials of the second syllable receive the manner features spread from the coda of the first syllable (either vowel or nasal), with their own place of articulation retained, to bring about more coherent pronunciation.

3.4.2.2 Feature geometry of the categorical transformation triggered by a nasal coda

As indicated before, if the first syllable ends with a nasal coda, the initial of the following syllable will also undergo the categorical transformation. Different from the nasal codas of Southern Min which retain the three division of nasal codas including /m, n, ŋ/, the nasal codas of Fuzhou have coalesced to be the velar nasal /ŋ/. The categorical transformation involving the nasal coda includes three cases, as follows:

Firstly, when the first syllable ends with a nasal coda, and the initial of the following syllable is the labial obstruent, the coronal obstruent, or the velar obstruent, the initial of the following syllable will receive the nasal manner of the preceding syllable and turn to the nasal initial of the same place, as follows:

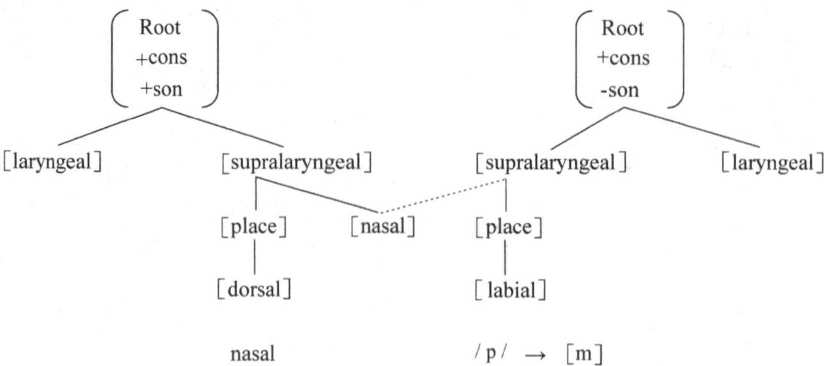

Diagram 3-15 Categorical transformation of obstruents triggered by nasal coda

Secondly, when the first syllable ends with a nasal coda, and the second syllable is initialless, the second syllable will surface with a velar nasal initial. Chen Zeping (2013: 114) holds that the initialless syllables in Fuzhou bear an unspecified glottal stop initial. Phonologically, the glottal stop bears no suprasegmental feature. Hence the initial of the following syllable will receive the nasal feature of the nasal coda of the first syllable, as follows:

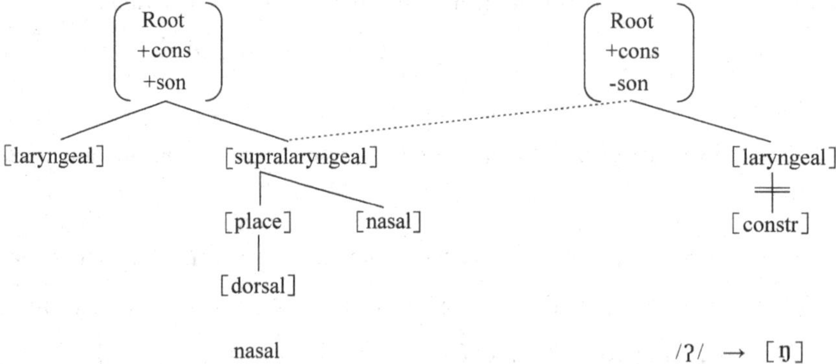

Diagram 3-16 Categorical transformation triggered by nasal coda in the initialless case

Thirdly, when the initial of the second syllable is /ts/ and the coda of the first syllable is nasal, /ts/ will be turned to [nz]. This is indicated as follows:

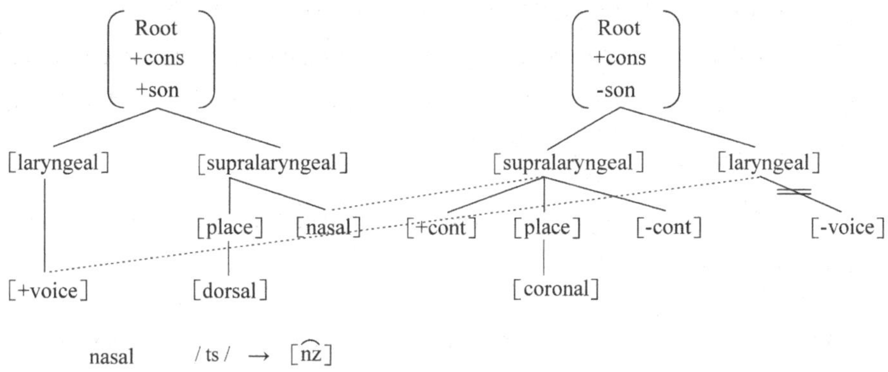

Diagram 3-17 Categorical transformation of affricates triggered by nasal coda

As indicated in Diagram 3-17, [nasal] is under the supralaryngeal node and [voice] is under the laryngeal node. The initial of the following syllable /ts/ which bears [-cont] and [+cont] will turn to [n͡z] when [+nasal] and [+voice] of the first syllable spread. Such voiced fricative with the feature of [nasal] can better satisfy the phonetic coherence requirement. It is well-proved (Zhang Jisheng 2007: 291 - 297), there is no clear distinction between vowels and consonants, which forms a gradual progression from the strongest occlusion to the weakest occlusion such as obstruent > affricate > fricative > lateral, nasal > semi-vowel > high vowel > low vowel. This indicates that the obstruents are the strongest in terms of consonantality while the low vowel is the most vocalic. Hence the consonantality is reduced from affricate to fricative, or from obstruent to nasal, to reduce the distance between two adjacent segments in the first syllable and the second syllable to meet the requirement of co-articulation.

Chen Zeping (2013: 112) proposes that the autosegmental approach can not account for why the transformation result is not a vowel when the features of obstruents are replaced by the features of adjacent vowels. It is proposed here that as indicated in the above analysis, the feature [consonantal] is under the root node and many evidences reveal that the node features such as [consonantal] and [sonorant] generally do not spread. Hence the consonant in VCV sequence can get closer to the neighbouring vowels in terms of the agreement of features but do not turn to vowels.

What triggers such categorical transformation? Why is the dorsal initial completely deleted in this process? Why do the coronal consonants have different transformation results such as the lateral and voiced coronal fricative? This will be discussed in the following sections.

3.4.3 Hierarchy of contrastive features of initial consonants in Fuzhou

In the following part, the feature hierarchy of consonants of Fuzhou will be established according to the phonological behaviors of consonants in Fuzhou under the framework of SDA and markedness theory.

Chomsky & Halle (1968) argue that, for every feature in every possible environment, one value will be unmarked (Trask 1996). The more marked feature, the more unnatural; the more natural, the more unmarked (Chomskey & Halle 1968: 400 – 435). Markedness has different tendencies such as reduction, preservation or integration. Zhang Jisheng (2006: 152) points out that in markedness theory, there are at least two separate markedness hierarchies that play a role in phonological processes such as assimilation, epenthesis, lenition and deletion (Torre 2003). As indicated in the above analysis, the consonants in Fuzhou can be divided into obstruents, fricatives, affricates, nasals according to the manner of articulation; they can also be classified as coronal consonants, labial consonants and dorsal consonants based on the place of articulation. In the markedness theory, the hierarchy of the place of articulation (PoA) and the hierarchy of the manner of articulation (MoA) both play important roles in phonological processes. The hierarchy which ranks higher is language-specific. In the Wenzhou dialect and the Wujiang dialect, PoA outranks MoA (Zhu 2013: 71, 149). In the Quanzhou dialect, MoA ranks higher than PoA. Then in the Fuzhou dialect, which hierarchy is more dominant? For the establishment of hierarchy, it is a good criterion to refer to the phonological behaviors of consonants.

3.4.3.1 Dorsal vs non-dorsal

De Lacy (2006: 2) puts forward the hierarchy for major place of articulation built on work by Lombardi (1991, 2002) and others as follows: dorsal > labial > coronal > glottal. In many cross-linguistic data, the dorsal consonant is either deleted for markedness reduction or is retained for markedness preservation due to its most marked place of articulation (De Lacy 2006: 23). Christopher et al. (2014: 522) propose that the deletion of dorsal consonants between identical vowels in Colloquial Bamana is not a typologically uncommon process. For example, in Bamana, words of the shape C1V1C2V1, where C2 is a dorsal stop, manifest the endpoint of a more general diachronic progression of lenition (i. e., k-g-ɣ-h-Ø) that yields total segmental loss of the dorsal consonantal and subsequent derivation of a long vowel. In the same vein, the similar schemes of dorsal consonant deletion (VCD) have also been noted cross-linguistically, as in Turkish (Sezer 1981), Kranichfeld German (Glover 2009), Kwasio (Duke & Martin 2009). In the synchronic categorical transformation of Fuzhou dialect, the dorsal initial is deleted between two different vowels in the domain of phonological words, which is in contrast with the change of coronal consonants, some of which turn to the approximant and some turn to the voiced fricative, as well as the change of the labial consonants which turn to the voiced fricative of the same place of articulation. Such change of the dorsal consonants in Fuzhou is unlike those of Xianyou dialect, another subdialect of Middle Min in whose categorical transformation the dorsal initials turn to the fricatives of the same place of articulation by receiving the related features of the preceding vowel. In the diachronic sound changes, some markedness reduction is more obvious while some other markedness reduction is not so distinct. From the perspective of effort-saving, the pronunciation of an obstruent between two vowels is the most strenuous for a smooth transition compared with that of fricatives or laterals, hence the most marked. The change of the dorsal from an independent segment to the complete deletion in the categorical transformation of Fuzhou is in a sense the greatest markedness reduction. The unique performance of dorsal consonants is compatible with the markedness about dorsal consonants made in De Lacy (2006) which proposes that the dorsal is the most marked in terms of PoA and the observation made in

Rice (2007: 80) which puts forward that marked elements are less stable. Accordingly, it is suggested that the consonants of Fuzhou are first divided into dorsal and non-dorsal consonants according to the place of articulation.

Furthermore, the dorsal initial in Fuzhou is the only initial that is allowed preceding the preglide [y], which is underlyingly [i], as follows:

(47)

Final	p,p^h,m	t,t^h,n	ts,ts^h,s	$k,k^h,ŋ,x,0$
yoŋ	×	×	×	√
yoʔ	×	×	×	√

Hence it is suggested to first divide consonants into dorsal and non-dorsal, as follows:

POA	[LABIAL] [CORONAL]	[DORSAL]

Diagram 3-18 Division of dorsal consonants and non-dorsal consonants

Sagey (1986: 274) proposes such feature as [DORSAL] which includes /k/, /g/, and /ŋ/. The subordinate features of [DORSAL] include [high], [low] and [back], as follows:

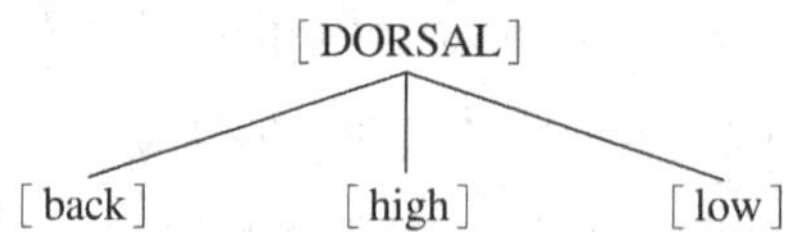

Diagram 3-19 Feature geometry on the subordinate features of [DORSAL] (Sagey 1986)

For the separation of the dorsal from the coronal and the labial, the feature [back] will be employed in the division of consonants. This division means that in Fuzhou the place of articulation outranks the manner of articulation, which is different from that in Quanzhou in which the manner of articulation ranks first.

In dividing dorsal consonants further, the phonological behavior difference is an important criterion. The velar nasal /ŋ/ can be the syllabic consonant besides being initial. Hence the distinctive feature [nasal] can be employed to further divide the dorsal consonants, as follows:

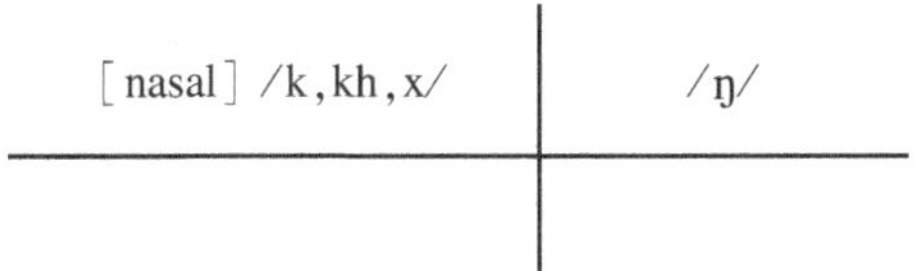

Diagram 3-20 Sub-division of dorsal consonants

3.4.3.2 Coronal vs non-coronal

Numerous studies in the past two decades have argued that coronals like /t/ and /n/ have properties that differentiate them from labials like /p/ and /m/ and dorsals like /k/ and /ŋ/ (e.g. Paradis & Prunet 1991b). The coronal place of articulation is proposed as the unmarked place with respect to labial and dorsal places of articulation for some reasons. Especially, there are some phonological reasons, with coronal consonants patterning as asymmetrically to other place of articulation. For instance, coronals are different from labials and dorsals in that they may be epenthetic and may result from neutralization, while labials and dorsals are argued not to show such patterning; in addition, coronals may be the target of asymmetrical assimilation while labials and dorsals are triggers rather than targets. De Lacy (2006: 23 – 27) proposes that markedness hierarchies are universally consistent, although in different languages, coronals may show different phonological behavior, for example in the Wujiang dialect of Chinese, the coronal consonants are different from the labial and dorsal in that the rounded glide following the coronal initial disappeared first (Zhu 2013: 142). For the coronal consonants in Fuzhou, their phonological behavior in the categorical transformation may first provide some clues for their unmarkedness. For the smooth transition within prosodic words, the transformation from an obstruent to a consonant not so strong in terms of consonantality will bring the consonant C in V_1CV_2 closer to neighboring vowels with respect of sharing features. In the categorical transformation of Fuzhou, the coronal consonants undergo the change from obstruents to laterals, which, according to sonority hierarchy, is within the closest distance with vowels except rhotic (Burquest & Payne 1993).

(48)

	Low vowel	Middle V	High V	Rhotic	Lateral	Nasal	Voiced Fricative	Voive-less F	Voiced Obstruent	Voice-less O	Complex
sonority	11	10	9	8	7	6	5	4	3	2	1

Hence the change from the coronal to the lateral in the categorical transformation can be deemed as the greatest markedness reduction, except the complete reduction like the dorsal. In fact, the umarkedness of the lateral can also get evidence from the phonological process of splitting words in Fuzhou in which the second syllable in the word splitting results usually chooses the most sonorant consonant /l/ as its initial, indicated as follows (Chen Zeping 1998: 114).

(49) Word splitting process of Fuzhou

吊 tau^{214}-ta^{21} lau^{214}	卷 $kuoŋ^{33}$-kuo^{33} $luoŋ^{33}$
塌 $t^ha?^{24}$-t^ha^{21} $la?^{24}$	缠 $tieŋ^{53}$-tie^{33} $lieŋ^{53}$
腆 $t^hiaŋ^{214}$-t^ha^{21} $laiŋ^{213}$	跳 t^hiu^{213}-t^hiu^{21} liu^{213}

As indicated, in this popular process of word splitting in Fuzhou, the lateral is chosen as the initial of the second syllable, since /l/ is almost within the closest distance to vowels in terms of features except rhotic. Accordingly, the most unmarked segment in light of effort saving is in the domain of prosodic phrases. The change of the coronal which is different from the case of the dorsal whose deletion is due to its most markedness is the result of its unmarkedness.

What sets the coronal apart from the dorsal and labial also lies in its relationship with the following rhymes. Zhu (2013: 141) makes an observation that the coronal in the Wujiang dialect and the Wenzhou dialect in Zhejiang Province behave in a similar way in that the finals following the coronal initial are not so steady as following the labial and dorsal initials that the finals following the coronal initials tends to change first. Is there any other phonological behavior that sets the coronal consonant from the labial and the dorsal consonant in Fuzhou? Yuan proposes that [uɔ] and [ɔ] are in complementary distribution in that [uɔ] follow the labial and dorsal initials while [ɔ] comes behind the coronal initials, which can be glimpsed through the comparison of sub-dialects of Eastern Min, as follows (Yuan 2010: 36 – 37).

Table 3-1 Complementary distribution of [uɔ] and [ɔ] following initials

Ge Final of Guo She (rounded preglide)					
Area	Labial	Coronal	Coronal Fri /Affr	Dorsal	Initialless
Fuzhou	uɔ	ɔ	ɔ	uɔ	uɔ
Fuqing	uɔ	o	o	uo	uo
Gutian	uo	o	o	uo	uo
Zherong	ɔ	ɔ	ɔ	uɔ	uɔ

Table 3-1 indicates the differences of the finals following the labial as well as the dorsal initials and the coronal initials in Fuzhou. It is interesting that the case of Zherong is a little bit different from that of Fuzhou in that [uɔ] only occurs following the dorsal initials instead of following the labial as well as the dorsal initials. What is responsible for such a difference? Which form is older, [uɔ] or [ɔ]? Yuan proposes that [uɔ] is a strata older than [ɔ]. Hence, it is suggested that [uɔ] is reduced to [ɔ] first following the coronal initials while this rounded preglide is reserved in following the labial and dorsal initials. Du (2014: 195 – 196) also offers the following data from which it can be observed that the preglide *y* preceding the nuclear vowel *o* in Fuzhou will turn to *u* when following the coronal initials, as follows:

(50)

Cognates	Eastern Min		
	Fuzhou	Fuqing	Zherong
	yoŋ/uoŋ	yoŋ	yøŋ
两 "two"	nuoŋ	lyoŋ	lyøŋ
张 "surname"	tuoŋ	tyoŋ	tyøŋ
胀 "dwell"	tuoŋ	tyoŋ	tyøŋ
伤 "hurt"	suoŋ	syoŋ	syøŋ
章 "surname"	tsuoŋ	tsyoŋ	tsyøŋ
让 "let"	yoŋ	yoŋ	yøŋ
疆 "border"	kyoŋ	kyoŋ	kyøŋ
香 "fragrant"	xyoŋ	hyoŋ	xyøŋ

Such change can be summarized with a rule presented as follows:

(51) -y- > -u-/{t, ts}_o

According to this rule, the preglide *y* will turn to *u* when following the coronal initials. Accordingly, for the non-dorsal consonants, the coronal can be separated from the labial due to its unmarkness. Avery & Rice (1989: 195) includes [LABIAL] in the category of peripheral segments, according to which the feature [peripheral] can be employed to separate the coronal and the labial. This is indicated as follows:

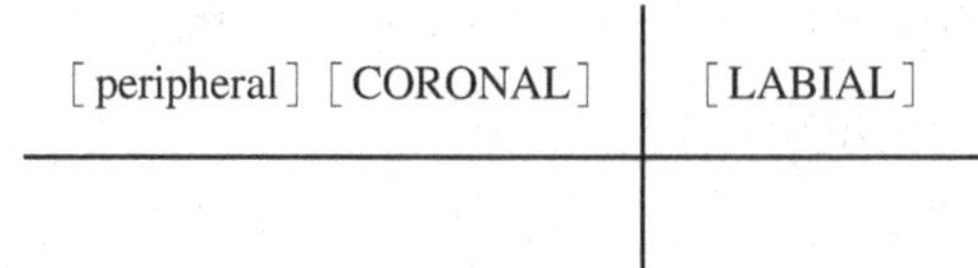

Diagram 3-21 Division of coronal consonants and labial consonants

3.4.3.2.1 Coronal nasal vs coronal non-nasal

In Fuzhou dialect, there are five coronal consonants /t, t^h, s, n, ts/, which can be divided into obstruents, fricatives, affricates, and nasals according to the manner of articulation. For these coronal consonants, at the first sight the affricates /ts, ts^h/ seem to be different from the other coronal consonants such as /t, t^h, s, n/ which are the same way in being converted to be lateral in the categorical transformation when following a syllabic ending, while the affricates turn to the voiced coronal fricative, as indicated in the following examples (Chen Zeping 1998: 8):

(52)

Original intials	Initials in the categorical transformation	
	Following a syllabic ending of vowel	Following a nasal coda
p, p^h	β	m
t, t^h, s, n	l	n
ts, ts^h	z	nz
k, k^h, x	0	ŋ
m, ŋ	unchanged	unchanged

Based on this phonological behavior, it seems that affricates should be separated from the other coronal consonants. In this way, the coronal consonants would be divided into two groups such as /ts, ts^h/ vs /t, t^h, s, n/. This division, in spite of conforming to the phonological behavior in the categorical transformation, seems quite awkward, from the perspective of natural classification, since it contains stops, fricatives and nasals in a group. If the coronal consonants are not divided in this way, how do we account for the behavior of affricates different from the other coronal consonants in the categorical transformation? A comparison of the same phenomenon in other subdialects of Eastern Min will shed a light to this discrepancy. In the Xianyou dialect which is adjacent to Fuzhou in Central Min, the coronal affricates, like the other coronal consonants, turn to the approximant of the same place of articulation in the similar categorical transformation; in the Gutian dialect which is also a subdialect of Eastern Min adjacent to Fuzhou, the affricates are deleted in the categorical transformation. The sound change result of the affricates in Fuzhou stands between Xianyou and Gutian in this phonological process. It is suggested here that the difference of affricates from the other coronal consonants lies in the degree of reduction. It is likely that the reduction of affricates stopped before this process can continue to reduce to lateral like the other coronal consonants. In fact, a similar case can also be found in Zi rime change discussed in Yang (2015), in which the affricate initials became stop/fricative, lateral and finally deleted in lenition. In different places, the lenition results may stop at different stages, namely in some places the affricate initials stop at the stage of lateral, in some other places affricates are deleted completely. Therefore, the difference between affricates and the other coronal consonants is just the degree of reduction. It is not reasonable to divide the coronal consonants into /ts, ts^h/ and /t, t^h, s, n/. Within the coronal consonants, it is suggested to separate nasal consonants from non-nasal consonants, which is in accord with the phonological behavior of these consonants as natural classes, indicated as follows:

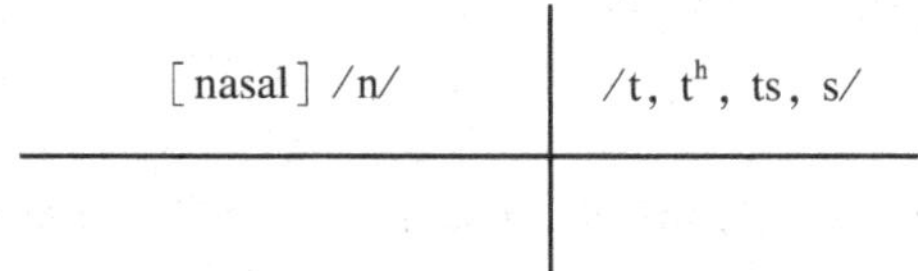

Diagram 3-22 Division of coronal nasal and coronal non-nasal consonants

3.4.3.2.2 Coronal fricative

For the coronal consonants except nasals, they can be further divided according to the manner features such as [strident] and [continuant], as follows:

(53)

Features	Obstruent	Fricative	Affricate
	t, t^h	s,	ts, ts^h
CORONAL	√	√	√
[continuant]	-	+	-
[strident]	-	+	+

It is observable that fricatives can be separated from the other consonants with the features such as [continuant] and [strident], affricates can be divided from the other consonants with the feature [strident], while fricatives and affricates share the feature [strident]. Is it likely to separate fricatives and affricates which can form a natural group with the feature [strident] from the other consonants? It is pointed out that some cognates which have affricate initials in Southern Min and Northern Min find their counterparts in fricative initials in Eastern Min, including Fuzhou, as follows (Lin 1993):

(54)

Cognates	Eastern Min Fuzhou	Southern Min Quanzhou
坐 "sit"	$sɔy^{242}$	tsue
蛇 "snake"	sie^{53}	$tsua^{24}$
晴 "sunny"	$saŋ^{53}$	$tsiŋ^{24}$

Chen Zhongmin (2013) puts forward that for these cognates, the affricate initial belongs to the colloquial stratum, which is older than the fricative initial which belongs to the literate stratum. For the special phonological behavior of affricate and fricative of Fuzhou, Yuan (2010: 52 – 53) also suggests that both in Yu Final 鱼韵 and Yu Final 虞韵 of Fuzhou, the complementary relations triggered by the initials accounts for the alternation of y/øy and u/ou as follows:

Yu Final(虞韵): y(øy) > y(øy)/the other initials

> u(ou)/affricate, fricative

Owing to such alternation between fricatives and affricates, it is suggested to further divide the coronal consonants except nasals into consonants with [+ strident] feature such as /s, ts/ and consonants with [-strident] features such as /t, t^h/, as follows:

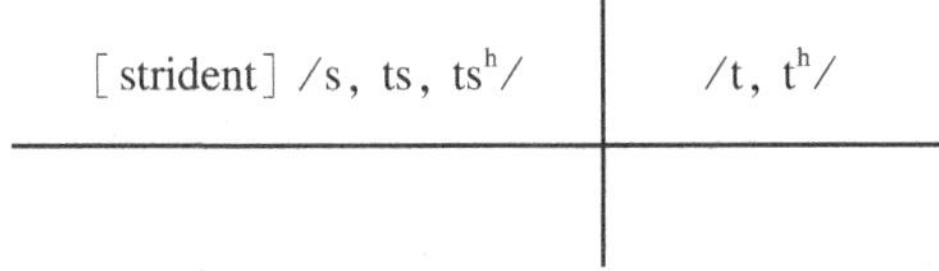

Diagram 3-23 Sub-division of coronal non-nasal consonants

For the further division of strident consonants such as /s, ts, ts^h/, the feature [continuant] is enough, owing to the different behavior of fricatives and affricates in the categorical transformation of initial consonants in Fuzhou. Therefore, it is reasonable to further divide strident consonants into /s/ which is specified with the feature [+ continuant] and /ts, ts^h/ which also bear the feature [-continuant].

3.4.3.3 Labial

In the Fuzhou dialect, there are only three labial consonants, including two obstruents and one nasal: /p, p^h; m/. The specification of the place of articulation and manner of articulation of these consonants is as follows:

(55)

Features	Obstruent	Nasal
	p, p^h	m
LABIAL	√	√
[sonorant]-	+	

The first noticeable difference between the labial initial and the coronal as well as the dorsal lies in its reduction degree in the categorical transformation in Fuzhou, in which the labial is transformed to be the labial fricative, unlike the coronal which is changed to be the coronal approximant or the dorsal which is deleted in the transformation. In terms of markedness reduction, the change of the labial in the transformation process is of the least degree. What is more interesting is that the rounded preglide [w] remains intact following the labial initial in Fuzhou when it has been deleted following the labial initial in Mandarin, which can be seen in the following example:

(56)

Example	Fuzhou	Mandarin
杯 "cup"	pui	pei
背 "back"	pui	pei
梅 "berry"	mui	mei
妹 "sister"	mui	mei

Accordingly, it is clear that the labial consonants in Fuzhou have distinct phonological behavior that distinguishes them from the coronal and dorsal consonants. Within the labial consonants in Fuzhou, there are both obstruents and nasals. Is it necessary to divide the labial consonants further into nasal consonants and non-nasal consonants? As indicated, the labial nasal does not undergo the categorical transformation like the labial consonant. Therefore, the labial consonants can be further divided as follows:

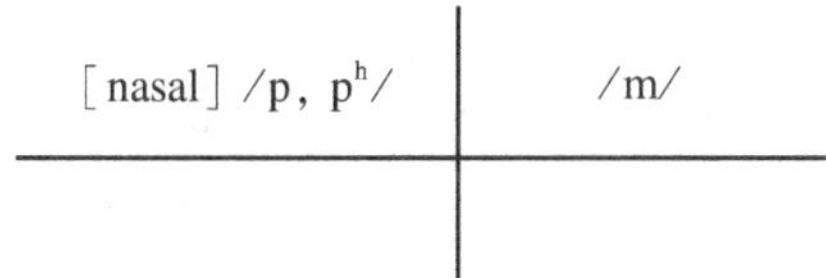

Diagram 3-24 Sub-division of labial consonants

3.4.3.4 Feature hierarchy of consonants in Fuzhou

On the basis of the phonological behavior of consonants in Fuzhou as well as their patterning, the contrastive features of consonants in Fuzhou include the following two categories:

PoA: [CORONAL], [LABIAL], [DORSAL]

MoA: [nasal], [strident], [continuant]

The ranking of these features are as follows:

- PoA > > MoA
- MoA: [nasal] >> [strident] >> [continuant]

The feature hierarchy of contrastive features of consonants in Fuzhou can be as follows:

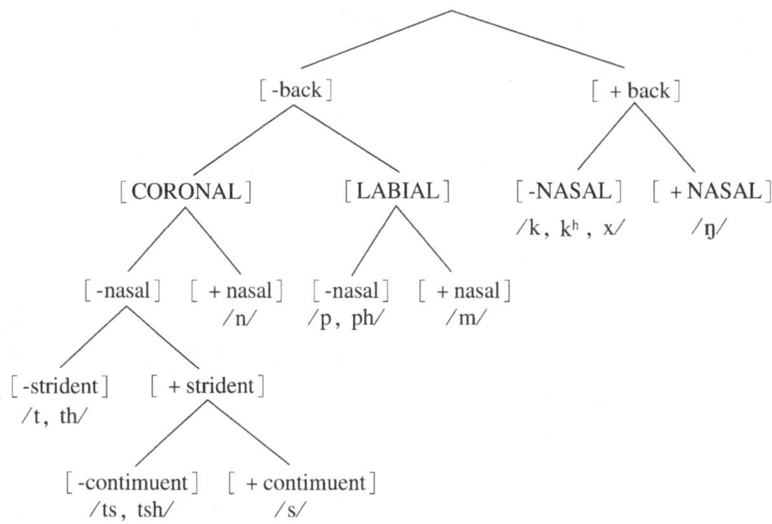

Diagram 3-25 Hierarchy of contrastive features of consonants in Fuzhou

3.5 Markedness of consonant inventories

Markedness, first proposed as a linguistic term by Trubetzkoy (1969), has come to occupy a position of considerable importance in phonology and other areas of linguistics (Hume 2003). Markedness is an important property of languages. The new markedness theory in De Lacy (2002, 2006) focuses on the markedness of segments. The core idea of De Lacy is that there are many markedness feature hierarchies which conflict with each other, as a result of which, many segments which may be deemed as the most marked in some hierarchies may turn to be unmarked in some other hierarchies. Therefore, the glottal is the least-marked place of articulation, while some other markedness hierarchies may favor non-glottals over glottals. Whether glottals or coronals are treated as least marked in a language depends on which markedness hierarchy dominates.

The markedness hierarchies of consonants mainly include PoA and MoA. PoA can be divided into the main places of articulation and the secondary places of articulation. According to Lombardi (2002, 2003), De Lacy (2002, 2006: 35) puts forward that the main places of articulation include [LABIAL], [CORONAL], [DORSAL], [GLOTTAL], the ranking of which can be presented as follows:

(57) Markedness ranking of the articulatory places (De Lacy 2006: 35)

[DORSAL] > [LABIAL] > [CORONAL] > [GLOTTAL]

The ranking here indicates that [GLOTTAL] is the most unmarked followed by [CORONAL] while [DORSAL] is the most marked and is followed by [LABIAL]. "Unmarked" elements can be the sole output of processes, fail to trigger alternations, and undergo processes alone. In contrast, "marked" elements are rarely the output, are often the only triggering elements, and are often exempt from undergoing processes (De Lacy 2006: 4). For example, consonants are often inserted to meet prosodic requirements. Such epenthetic consonants always have coronal or glottal place of articulation (e. g.

[t ʔ h] and so on); they are never dorsals (e. g. [k g x ŋ] or labials (e. g. [p b m]). Other phenomena like neutralization also produce glottals and coronals, but never labials and dorsals. As a contrast, the highly marked elements can be prevented from being eliminated in phonological phenomena like neutralization and assimilation (De Lacy 2006).

Alongside with the PoA, another important markedness hierarchy for consonants is MoA hierarchy. There are different dimensions of MoA, such as [voice], [nasal], [continuant]. According to Maddieson (1984), cross-linguistically, the obstruents are most common. Jakobson & Halle (1956: 42) argue that the obstruents occur in all the known languages, due to which the markedness of the obstruents is the lowest. Obstruents are usually divided into voiceless and voiced ones, and it is often said that voiceless obstruents are unmarked with respect to voiced obstruents (e. g. Lombardi 1991). Compared with obstruents, nasals are more marked, yet they are more unmarked with respect to other sonorants (Rice & Avery 1991; Rice 2007).

3.5.1 Comparison of markedness of consonant inventories in Quanzhou and Fuzhou

This section will make a comparative analysis of the consonant inventories of Quanzhou and Fuzhou from the perspective of PoA and MoA. According to the main PoA and the secondary PoA, the consonant inventories of Quanzhou and Fuzhou are listed as follows:

Table 3-2 Classification of consonants of Quanzhou and Fuzhou

Main PoA	Secondary PoA	Quanzhou	Fuzhou
Labial	bilabial	p p^h m	p p^h m
Coronal	dental	ts ts^h s	ts ts^h s
	alvoelar	t t^h n l	t t^h n l
Dorsal	velar	k k^h ŋ	k k^h ŋ
			x
Glottal	pharyngeal	h	

According to Table 3-2, the Quanzhou and Fuzhou dialects are found to be similar in terms of the distribution of surface consonants. It is observable that both Quanzhou and Fuzhou share six obstruents, two affricates as well as two fricatives which are different in their places of articulation. Moreover, both Quanzhou and Fuzhou are found to have one lateral, three nasals /m, n, ŋ/. Such cases of Quanzhou and Fuzhou are in line with the observation made in Maddieson (1984:12) which proposes that languages are most likely to have between five and eleven stops including affricates, and one to four fricatives, about 58% of languages; from two to four nasals (91% of languages), and two vocoid approximants (41% and 72% respectively). It is noted that the obstruents and affricates in both Quanzhou and Fuzhou have no contrast in voicing and voicelessness but are instead divided into aspiration and non-aspiration. A language which contrasts only 2 series of stops typically has a plain voiceless/voiced contrast, which is so for 117 of the 162 languages concerned (72.2%); while a further 27 have a contrast between plain voiceless and aspirated voiceless, or of plain voiced and aspirated voiceless (Maddieson 1984: 28). It is clear that the cases of the consonants in Quanzhou and Fuzhou belong to the more marked case as is indicated in the minor category listed in Maddieson (1984).

Despite the similarity in the surface inventory in two dialects, the consonants of Quanzhou and Fuzhou are remarkably different in the related phonological processes and changes brought about by these phonological processes. As discussed above, the consonants of Quanzhou do not undergo the categorical transformation, while the consonants of Fuzhou are all involved in the categorical transformation, which causes the consonants of the coronal and the labial to be lateral or fricative of the same place of articulation and the consonants of the dorsal to be deleted. This phonological process of Fuzhou reduces the contrasts of consonants of non-first syllable in the domain of prosodic words, but brings about new contrasts. Take the initials of the second syllable in the domain of a prosodic word as an example:

Table 3-3 Forms of the second syllable of Quanzhou and Fuzhou

The Underlying 2nd Syllable	The Surface 2nd Syllable		
	Quanzhou	Fuzhou	
t, t^h	t, t^h	l	m, n, ŋ
p, p^h	p, p^h	β	
k, k^h	k, k^h	ø	
s	s	l	
ts, ts^h	ts, ts^h	z	
n, m, ŋ	n, m, ŋ	n, m, ŋ	

As indicated, in Quanzhou the contrasts of consonants are kept intact. In contrast, in Fuzhou the original contrasts of the second syllable in the domain of a prosodic word are replaced by the new contextually-dependent contrasts which do not contain the plosive contrasts but only the contrasts between fricatives and laterals when the first syllable ends with a vowel; when the first syllable ends with a nasal coda, the contrasts of initials of the second syllable disregarding the plosives or fricatives or affricates all turn to the nasal contrasts, as discussed. In a word, the categorical transformation of Fuzhou results in completely new contrasts for the initials of the non-initial syllable. The consonants of Quanzhou, though due to denasalization, also experiences the increase of contrasts, yet the newly created contrasts do not influence the original contrasts of Quanzhou consonant system, but the contrasts of plosives are enlarged. The effects of the related phonological processes upon the consonant system of Quanzhou and Fuzhou can be summarized as follows:

Table 3-4 New contrasts of consonants of Quanzhou and Fuzhou

Fuzhou		Quanzhou
l	n	t, t^h
		s
z		ts, ts^h
β	m	p, p^h
ø	ŋ	k, k^h
m, n, ŋ		m, n, ŋ (b, l, g)

The categorical transformation of Fuzhou results in segments such as lateral and fricative as the initials of the non-first syllables whose higher sonority renders a more smooth transition between two vowels as in the domain "V. CV", due to which such categorical transformation process can be deemed as a lenition in the domain of prosodic words. Yet the higher sonority of laterals and fricatives as the newly created results of the categorical transformation may also mean more marked consonants in the position of initial which in fact prefers consonants of lower sonority.

In addition, Quanzhou and Fuzhou are also different in their patterning of segments as natural classes. In Fuzhou, the fricatives are found to be included within the same natural classes with the obstruents of the same place of articulation in the categorical transformation, added to which is the nasal which is also found to have the same transformation with the obstruents, indicated as follows:

Table 3-5 Different patterning of segments as natural classes in Quanzhou and Fuzhou

<table>
<tr><td colspan="3">Fuzhou: Categorical Transformation</td><td>Quanzhou</td></tr>
<tr><td></td><td>V#_</td><td>N#_</td><td>#_</td></tr>
<tr><td>p, p^h</td><td>β</td><td>m</td><td rowspan="2">p, p^h; t, t^h; k, k^h</td></tr>
<tr><td>t, t^h, s, n</td><td>l</td><td>n</td></tr>
<tr><td>ts, ts^h</td><td>z</td><td>nz</td><td>ts, ts^h, s, h</td></tr>
<tr><td>k, k^h, x</td><td>ø</td><td>ŋ</td><td>m, n, ŋ</td></tr>
</table>

This indicates that the manner of articulation is second to the place of articulation in the categorical transformation of Fuzhou. Contrary to the case in Fuzhou, the fricatives and affricate in Quanzhou pattern as a natural class in the related phonological process as discussed. What is more, unlike the dorsal fricative of Fuzhou which has some similar patterning with the obstruents, the glottal fricative of Quanzhou is attested to be distinctive markedness reduction result, as indicated in the debuccalization of the nasal initial.

On the basis of the different phonological behavior of consonants in Quanzhou and Fuzhou, it is proposed in this book that the major difference of consonants of Quanzhou and Fuzhou lies in the fact that the consonants of

Fuzhou manifests more markedness preservation while the consonants of Quanzhou shows more markedness reduction.

3.5.2 PoA first or MoA first

For the determination of the markedness of segments, Rice (1999, 2007), Causley (1999) and Dresher (2009) suggest that the markedness of segments is dependent on the contrastiveness of segments. Dresher (2003, 2009) highlights the importance of "contrastiveness" in the phonological research, and proposes that only the contrastive features are phonologically active. Jakobson, Fant, and Halle propose an approach about utilizing the Contrastive Hierarchy, which means that the related phonological processes can only be triggered if the related feature is a contrastive feature (Dreshera, Harveya & Oxford 2014).

According to the related phonological changes in Quanzhou, the hierarchy of contrastive features of consonants in Quanzhou can be constructed as follows:

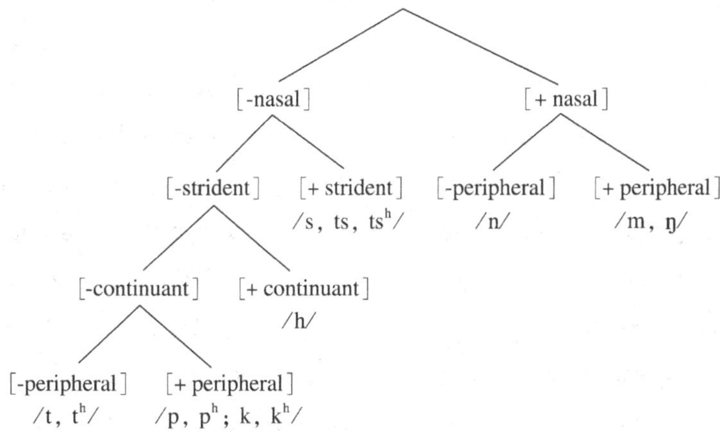

Diagram 3-26 Hierarchy of contrastive features of initial consonants in Quanzhou

Based on the categorical transformation as well as the other related phonological processes, the hierarchy of contrastive features of consonants in Fuzhou is established as follows:

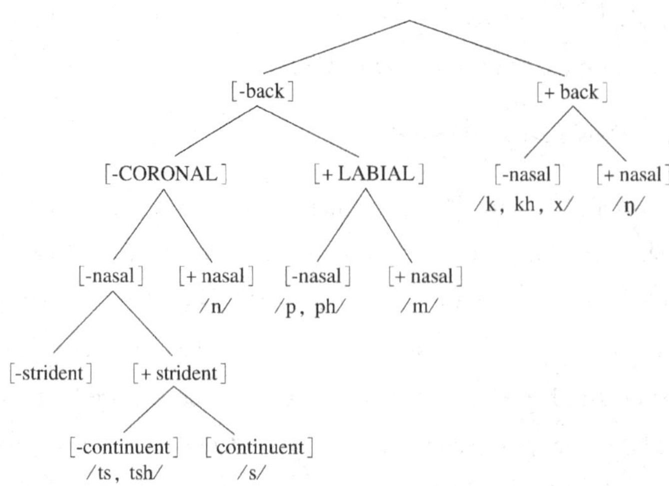

Diagram 3-27 Hierarchy of contrastive features of initial consonants in Fuzhou

It is noted that Quanzhou and Fuzhou are different in the specification of some contrastive features such as [peripheral] in Quanzhou and [back] in Fuzhou. More importantly, Fuzhou is found to have more specification of contrastive features, in contrast with Quanzhou. Zhu (2013: 218) puts forward that the number of the contrastive features is of great importance to the phonological system of a language. The more contrastive features, the more sound changes are likely triggered, which may lead to more varieties of phonological processes in the related language, although at the same time, not all contrastive features will trigger sound changes. Such difference of the specification of contrastive features accounts for the absence or presence of related phonological processes in Fuzhou and Quanzhou.

For the hierarchies of Quanzhou and Fuzhou, the most remarkable difference between them lies in the ordering of hierarchies. Quanzhou and Fuzhou are different not only in the rankings of main categories but also in the ranking of subcategories, as follows:

Table 3-6 Hierarchies of contrastive features of consonants in Quanzhou and Fuzhou

Quanzhou		Fuzhou	
I MoA	[nasal] > [strident] > [continuant]	I PoA	[Dorsal] > [Labial] > [Coronal]
II PoA	[Labial], [Dorsal] > [Coronal]	IIMoA	[nasal] > [strident] > [continuant]

As revealed, different hierarchical relations among features attest to different phonological patterning of segments in two dialects: In Quanzhou, the manner features dominate the place features while in Fuzhou the place features have wider scope than the manner features. Such a difference in the dominance of PoA or MoA in the hierarchies of two dialects is a reflection of different priority of PoA and MoA in the related phonological processes of two dialects such as the categorical transformation of Fuzhou and denasalization process of Quanzhou.

Furthermore, the different rankings in sub-categories of Quanzhou and Fuzhou indicate the different markedness embodied in these two dialects. In the hierarchy of Fuzhou dialect, the dorsal is under an independent node apart from the coronal and labial, which is in accord with the observation about the dorsal that is completely deleted in the categorical transformation in contrast with the reduction of certain degree of both coronal and labial. Dorsals and labials in Quanzhou are under the sister node apart from coronals, which is in alliance with the hypothesis that the segments under the same sister node can trigger similar phonological processes, as discussed. What is implied in such different hierarchies of the contrastive features of Quanzhou and Fuzhou?

3.5.3 Contrast shifts

Since the contrastive hierarchy has an important role in phonological patterning, Dreshera, Harveya & Oxford (2014) propose that a change in the hierarchy—a contrast shift—can have far-reaching effects on the phonology of a language. That is, contrast shift itself emerges as an important type of diachronic phonological change. Southern Min and Eastern Min were from the same ancestor of Proto-Min and should have manifested the similar hierarchies of the contrastive features if they were still of the same typological language. Yet now they have displayed the systematic typological differences. It is suggested that these phonological changes are brought about by the contrast shifts in the diachronic process. The contrast shifts have reshaped the phonological systems of related languages and brought about different typological characteristics. As for the verification of such hypothesis, it is necessary to take the vowel systems as well as the other related phonological respects of two dialects into consideration.

✻ 3.6 Summary

This chapter provides a detailed analysis of the initial consonants of Quanzhou and Fuzhou. The initial consonants of Quanzhou and Fuzhou are found to have the following characteristics:

a. The Quanzhou and Fuzhou dialects are found to be similar in terms of the distribution of the surface consonants, including six obstruents, two affricates as well as two fricatives, one lateral, three nasals /m, n, ŋ/.

b. The consonants of Quanzhou and Fuzhou are remarkably different in the related phonological processes and changes brought about by these phonological processes. The consonants of Quanzhou do not undergo the categorical transformation, while the consonants of Fuzhou are all involved in the categorical transformation. In addition, Quanzhou and Fuzhou are also different in their patterning of segments as natural classes. In Fuzhou, the fricatives are found to be included within the same natural classes with the obstruents of the same place of articulation in the categorical transformation, followed by the nasal which is also found to have the same transformation with the obstruents. The categorical transformation reduces the contrasts of consonants of the non-first syllable in the domain of prosodic words, but brings about new contrasts such as the contrasts between fricatives and laterals. The consonants of Quanzhou, due to denasalization, also experiences the increase of contrasts, yet the newly created contrasts do not influence the original contrasts of Quanzhou consonant system, but the contrasts of plosives are enlarged.

c. Quanzhou and Fuzhou are different in the specification of some contrastive features such as [peripheral] in Quanzhou and [back] in Fuzhou. More importantly, Fuzhou is found to have more specification of contrastive features, in contrast with Quanzhou. As for the hierarchy of contrastive features, in Quanzhou the manner features dominate the place features while in Fuzhou the place features have a wider scope than the manner features. Besides, Quanzhou and Fuzhou are different not only in the ranking of main categories but also in the ranking of subcategories.

Chapter 4

Phonological Characteristics of the Quanzhou Finals

Similar to the finals of other Chinese dialects, the finals of Min are more complicated and unstable than the initials. Since the finals of Quanzhou and Fuzhou are remarkably complicated, the finals of Quanzhou and Fuzhou will be discussed in two separate chapters. This chapter provides an analytic description of the characteristics in phonology of Quanzhou finals. It will describe the overall numbers and forms of the Quanzhou finals, after which a phonological feature hierarchy of simplex final vowels of Quanzhou will be shown based on their phonological behavior. Besides, the complex finals of Quanzhou will be analyzed from the perspective of phonological structure, and the phonological processes of Quanzhou will be presented.

4.1 Simplex oral finals

"Finals" in Chinese syllable structure refer to all material following syllable-initial consonants (Zhang Jisheng 2006: 38). The finals of Quanzhou are divided into three types, namely the finals ending with a vowel, the finals ending with a nasal, and the finals ending with stops. The exact inventory of finals in Quanzhou is an issue with little controversion. The inventory of the finals of Quanzhou based on Lin (1993) is summarized in the following table:

Table 4-1 Finals of Quanzhou

	Kaikouhu	Qichihu	Hekouhu	Cuokouhu
In open syllables		i	u	
	e		ue	
	a	ia, iau	ua, uai	
	o	io		
	ɔ			
	ə			
	ɨ			
		iu	ui	
	ai			
	au			
With nasal codas	am, im, əm	iam		
	an, in, un, ən	ian	uan	
	aŋ, iŋ, ɔŋ	iaŋ, iɔŋ	uaŋ	
With stop codas			uʔ	
		iʔ	uiʔ	
	aʔ, ɔʔ, oʔ, əʔ, eʔ, ɨʔ, auʔ	iaʔ, ioʔ, iuʔ, iauʔ	uaʔ	
			ueʔ	
	ŋʔ,mʔ			
		ip		
	ap	iap		
		it	ut	
	at	iat	uat	
	ak	iak		
	ɔk	iɔk		
With nasalized vowels	ã, ãi,ãʔ, ãiʔ, ãuʔ	iã, iãʔ,iãu, iãuʔ	uã,uãi	
	ĩ,ĩʔ		uĩ, uĩʔ	
	ɔ̃, ɔ̃ʔ			
	ẽ, ẽʔ			
		iũʔ		
Syllabic consonants	ŋ, m			

The finals of Quanzhou presented here include 18 finals ending with a vowel, 16 finals ending with a nasal, 30 finals ending with a stop, 20 nasalized vowels, and two syllabic consonants. It is observable in Table 4-1 that there are no Cuokouhu finals, namely the finals with preglide [y] in Quanzhou.

With respect to the finals ending with a vowel, they can be further divided into simplex finals and complex finals. The simplex finals refer to the finals with one vowel as the nuclear of syllable, while the complex finals are such finals as GV, VG, or GVG.

In this subsection, the author will discuss what vowels are used as simplex finals in Quanzhou, focusing on their different distributions and their phonological processes. In Quanzhou, there are eight simplex final vowels which serve as finals in syllables. They are presented as a simplex final vowel inventory in the following vowel diagram:

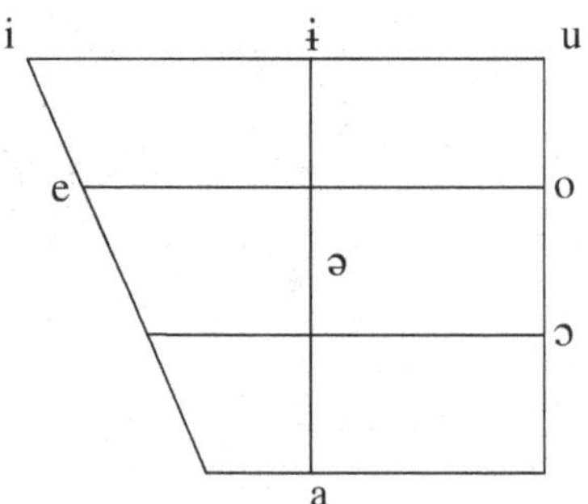

Diagram 4-1 Single vowel inventory of Quanzhou

It is noted in Diagram 4-1 that there are eight simplex final vowels /a, i, u, e, o, ɔ, ə, ɨ/ in the inventory of Quanzhou, including three high vowels, four middle vowels and one low vowel, which are symmetrically distributed in the diagram in terms of both height and backness. In the following subsection, all these single vowels will be discussed with respect to their distribution and their phonological processes. For the single vowel ɨ, Lin (1993) as well as Li (1998) transcribes this segment in his Quanzhou dialect dictionary as ɨ. But Hong (2001) transcribes this segment as ɨ for the symmetry of the system. Maddieson (1984: 147) puts forward an investigation of the acoustic, perceptual and auditory quality of the vowel /ɯ/ and suggests that this vowel is in fact quite centralized, verging on the quality of central /ɨ/. This book takes the transcription of Hong (2001), which can help describe the vowel system of Quanzhou in a more unified way.

4.1.1 Non-peripheral vowels

There are two non-peripheral vowels in the simplex final inventory of the Quanzhou dialect which are two typical central vowels, namely /ə/ and /ɨ/. Gordon (2016) summarizes most common vowel inventories of different sizes compared with those of the same size predicted to occur by Lijencrants & Lindbom (1972). In the inventories of Gordon (2016) and Lijencrants & Lindbom (1972), the central vowel occurs in the six-vowel inventory, but there is no case of co-existence of /ə/ and /ɨ/ in their examples. According to the vowel survey of 140 Chinese dialects in Ye (2011), the frequency of /ə/ is 50.7%, but the frequency of /ɨ/ is only 1.4%. Do these two central vowels in the Quanzhou dialect also have some asymmetric pattern? The present analysis will first focus on schwa, which is a more common central vowel.

4.1.1.1 Schwa

Schwa is noted for its dual status in its being both marked and prone to deletion and also unmarked and optimal for epenthesis (Gouskova 2003: 191). Phonologically speaking, schwa is able to serve three linguistic functions in the world's languages (Oostendorp et al., 2011). The first phonological process that schwa can undergo is epenthesis. The second phonological process that schwa can undergo is reduction or, in more extreme cases, deletion. The third possible articulation of schwa is the stable schwa (Oostendorp et al., 2011). This is when the schwa is unaffected by neither epenthesis nor reduction. The stable schwa is the default pronunciation of schwa as the mid-central vowel. For example, in languages like British English, schwa may carry stress and also display properties that are expected of its more peripheral middle vowel counterparts (Gordon 2016: 4). According to Ye (2011: 44), schwa is a relatively high frequent vowel in Chinese dialects, besides those typical peripheral vowels. But in different dialects, schwa has different phonological behavior. In Mandarin, schwa is the underlying segment of the middle vowels, which undergoes assimilation and results in different middle vowels on the surface (Lin, Yen-Hwei 2002). In the Shaoxing dialect, schwa can never constitute a final when standing on its own after initials so that it can never contrast with the proposed six phonemic vowels. In the Wenzhou dialect, schwa, parallel to the other middle vowels, can be final independently and has a stable performance in this language. How about the schwa in the Quanzhou dialect? Can schwa in Quanzhou be an independent final on its own? In fact, the schwa in Quanzhou has a quite wide distribution as follows:.

(1) a.	$pə^{33}$	"fly"	$tsə^{33}$	"plague"
	$p^hə^{33}$	"embryo"	$sə^{42}$	"tax
	$bə^{33}$	"gentle"	$kə^{55}$	"cake"
	$tə^{33}$	"pancake"	$k^hə^{33}$	"subject"
	$t^hə^{33}$	"shirk"	$hə^{33}$	"grey"
	$lə^{55}$	"puppet"	$ə^{33}$	"disaster"
b.	$bəʔ^{24}$	"socks"	$tsəʔ^{24}$	"extinct"
	$təʔ^{24}$	"seize"	$səʔ^{24}$	"circle"
c. /ə/:	$pə^{24}$	"compensate"	$kə^{55}$	"cake"
/e/:	pe^{24}	"climb"	ke^{55}	"fake"
/o/:	po^{24}	"grandma"	ko^{55}	"draft"

The examples in (1) show that schwa in Quanzhou can not only stand alone as an independent final following all the initials as in (1)a, but also can occur with glottal stops, as in (1) b, which will be discussed in the following section. Furthermore, schwa can also form minimal contrastive pairs with the other two middle vowels under the same tone, as in (1) c. Why is schwa so active in Quanzhou? Is it also active in the other sub-dialects of Southern Min? Does it have a similar distribution with the other single vowel final? Before answering this question, a comparison of cognates between Southern-Min may provide some clues (Hong 2001):

(2)

	Kaikouhu		Qichihu		Hekouhu		Cuokouhu	
Example	袋 "bag"	胎 "fetus"	被 "quilt"	糜 "porriage"	过 "pass"	螺 "snail"	说 "say"	雪 "snow"
Quanzhou	tə	t^hə	p^hə	bə	kə	lə	səʔ	səʔ
Xiamen	te	t^he	p^he	be	ke	le	seʔ	seʔ
Zhangzhou	te	t^he	p^hue	muẽ	kue	le	sueʔ	seʔ
Chaozhou	to	t^ho	p^hue	muẽ	kue	le	sueʔ	seʔ
Haikou	ɗe	hai	fue	mue	kue	le	te	toiʔ

Zeng (2013: 91) also provides some patterning of schwa in Southern Min, as follows:

(3)

Example	Southern Min			
	Quanzhou	Shishi	Xiamen	Quangang
髓 "pith"	ə	e	e	ue
吹 "blow"	ə	e	e	ue

As is seen in (2) and (3), the schwa in the Quanzhou dialect corresponds to the middle vowel e/ɛ in other sub-dialects of Southern Min, such as Zhangzhou, Xiamen, and it finds its counterpart as o in another sub-dialect of Southern Min such as Chaozhou. These examples indicate the schwa has a similar patterning with the other middle vowels in Southern Min. For the correspondence between the schwa in Quanzhou and the middle vowels in the other Southern Min dialects, it is unclear whether the schwa in Quanzhou is the reduction result of corresponding rhyme or an underlying segment that evolves to the middle vowels in the other sub-dialects of Southern Min.

Central vowels are noted for their double markedness status: on the one hand, they are relatively less unmarked due to the fact that they are often chosen as epenthesis, and they are often the result of markedness reduction in unstressed syllables; on the other hand, they are more marked when they act as the nuclear, because they are the least sonorant vowels according to the sonority scale proposed in Gordon (2016), as follows:

Low V	Middle V	High V	Mid-central V	High-central V
æ. a	e. o	i,u	ɔ	ɨ

High sonority ⟵⟶ Low sonority

It is noted that schwa is often the markedness reduction as in this case from Zhangzhou to Xiamen to Quanzhou, which is a manifestation of segmental and syllabic markedness reduction, as indicated in Zhang (2011):

(4)

Cognates		Southern Min	
	Zhangzhou	Xiamen	Quanzhou
果 "fruit"	kue	ke	kə
火 "fire"	hue	he	hə

Zhang (2011) proposes that the transition from Zhangzhou to Xiamen to Quanzhou is the reduction from the deletion of preglide as in Xiamen to further centralization as in Quanzhou. Phonologically speaking, the feature specification of schwa is usually the minus feature, such as [-high], [-low], [-round]. [ə] can be described as a "neutral vowel" (Chomsky & Halle 1968) or as a "targetless vowel" (Browman & Goldstein 1992), since its realization makes no special demands of the articulators, due to which it is a good choice as in reduction, as in the following examples:

(5)

Cognates	MC	Quanzhou	Chaozhou	Fuzhou	Sanming	Jianou
飞 "fly"	* pjwei	pə	pue	puei	puɛ	yɛ
吹 "blow"	* tshjwe	$ts^hə$	ts^hue	ts^huei	$tɕ^hyɛ$	$ts^hyɛ$

As indicated in (5), for the cognates such as 飞 and 吹, [puei] and [ts^huei] of Fuzhou are more similar to those forms of MC, which are followed by the less marked forms such as [pue] as well as [ts^hue] of Chaozhou in Southern Min and [puɛ] as well as [$tɕ^hyɛ$] of Sanming in Central Min. [pə] and [$ts^hə$] of Quanzhou are remarkably the least marked in terms of segment and syllable structure.

Schwa is often specified with negative values such as [-high], [-front] and [-back]. Besides, schwa often bears such features as [-tense] and [+ATR]. In different languages, the active features of schwa are different, for example in English, schwa is specified with [-tense], while in the languages with [ATR] harmony, schwa is often specified with [+ATR] (Zhu 2013: 78). How is the schwa of Quanzhou specified in terms of contrastive features? This will be discussed in the following section.

4.1.1.2 High central vowel /ɨ/

The "peripheral" vowels are the front unrounded, back rounded and low vowels, all of which lie along the margins of the available phonetic space. It should be noted, however, that the high central vowels, although they occupy one of the margins of the phonetic space, do not fall within the peripheral category; this more restricted definition of peripherality is justified on phonological grounds, as the high central vowels tend not to pattern with the true peripheral vowels in natural languages, and they are also less common than peripheral vowels. Thus, high central /ɨ/ and /ʉ/, along with the remaining phonetically centralized vowels, constitute the set of "interior" vowels (Maddieson 1984: 139).

In Quanzhou, the high central vowel /ɨ/ can also occur as a final by itself as a simplex final. Consider the following examples:

(6) $tɨ^{33}$	"pig"	$t^hɨ^{55}$	"store"
$lɨ^{55}$	"female"	$sɨ^{55}$	"mouse"
$kɨ^{33}$	"cart"	$gɨ^{14}$	"fish"

The examples in (6) reveal that like the other two high vowels /i/ as well as /u/, /ɨ/ can stand alone as an independent final and form contrastive minimal pairs with /i/ and /u/.

Cross-linguistically speaking, /ɨ/ is not a common vowel, and this vowel is also not found in the other sub-dialects of Min. Then is it a common vowel in Southern Min? Wu (2009) provides a list of cognates of Southern Min, as follows:

(7)

Cognates	Southern Min				
	Penghu	Zhangzhou	Quanzhou	Shantou	Jieyang
	u	i	ɨ	ɨ	ə
舒 "cozy"		tsʰi	tsʰɨ	tsʰɨ	tsʰə
猪 "pig"	tu	ti	tɨ	tɨ	tə
箸 "chopstick"	tu	ti	tɨ	tɨ	tə
鼠 "mouse"	tsʰu	tsʰi	tsʰɨ	tsʰɨ	tsʰə
汝 "you"	lu	li	lɨ	lɨ	lə
锯 "saw"	ku	ki	kɨ	kɨ	kə
鱼 "fish"	hu	hi	hɨ	hɨ	hə

It is obvious that *ɨ* finds its counterpart in *u* in Pengpu, *i* in Zhangzhou, *ə* in Jieyang. Zhang (2011: 96 – 103) also makes a comparison of the cognates of Yu Final between Quanzhou, Xiamen and Zhangzhou in Southern Min, as follows:

(8)

Cognates	吕 "surname"	猪 "pig"	鼠 "mouse"	去 "go"	鱼 "fish"
Quanzhou	lɨ	tɨ	tsʰɨ	kʰɨ	hɨ
Xiamen	lu	ti	tsʰu	kʰi	hi
Zhangzhou	li	ti	tsʰi	kʰi	hi

All these cognates, which belong to Yu Final of other Chinese dialects in Middle Chinese, are found to be *ɨ —u/i—i* from Quanzhou to Xiamen to Zhangzhou. Zhang (2011) proposes that in these cognates that *u* in Xiamen comes from *ɨ* of Quanzhou, and *i* in Xiamen finds its source of *i* in Zhangzhou, and the common source of *ɨ* of Quanzhou and *i* of Zhangzhou lies in *y*. According to Zhang's (2011) assumption, *ɨ* in Quanzhou is derived from *y*. Is it suitable to stipulate such assumption that the source of *ɨ* comes from *y*? Before answering this question, it is necessary to find out the patterning of *ɨ* of Quanzhou in comparison with the cognates of the other sub-dialects of Min. Take a look at the following examples (Lin 1993: 3626; Feng 1998: 43 -45):

(9)

Cognates	Quanzhou / Southern Min	Fuzhou / Eastern Min
	* pɨ	* py
猪 "pig"	tɨ	ty
女 "women"	lɨ	ny
书 "book"	tsɨ	tsy
锯 "saw"	kɨ	ky
虚 "modest"	hɨ	hy

According to (9), from the comparison of these cognates of Fuzhou and Quanzhou, *ɨ* of Quanzhou seems to correspond with *y* of Fuzhou, since both *ɨ* in Quanzhou and *y* in Fuzhou can follow all the initials except the labial initials. Hence *ɨ* in Quanzhou has a similar patterning to *y* of Eastern Min. However, is it solid enough to stipulate that *ɨ* is a direct counterpart of *y* just due to such patterning. Since Min dialects are "notoriously" noted for their complexity in the historical strata, it may be better to look into the possible strata of Min dialects involved in these cases in consideration of the relation of *ɨ* with the other single vowels either in Southern Min or in Eastern Min. For the possible historical strata that may be involved in this case, Chen Zhongmin (2013: 221-265) provides an insightful proposal about this issue, as follows:

(10)

Historical Strata	Quanzhou	Xiamen
The first stratum	-ue(ɔ)	-ue(ɔ)
The second stratum	-ɯ	-i
The third stratum	-u	-u

According to Chen Zhongmin (2013: 265), within Southern Min, for the cognates of Yu Final, -ɯ in Quanzhou (which is transcribed as *ɨ* in this book) is indeed found to correspond to *-i* in Xiamen, both of which belong to the second stratum of this rhyme. As for the question of the correspondence of-*ɨ* with the other subdialects of Min such as Eastern Min, it will be a more complicated case with different sub-dialects of Min through a comparison, presented as follows (Chen Zhongmin 2013: 221):

(11)

Historical Strata	Southern Min	Eastern Min	Puxian	Northern Min	Central Min
The first stratum	ue	ø	ø	ɔ	o
The second stratum	ɯ				
The third stratum	u	y	y	y	y

According to Chen Zhongmin (2013: 221), the finals of Yu Final in Min dialects are divided into three strata, the second stratum of *ɯ* in Southern Min is noted for being active in both literate stratum and colloquial stratum, while *y* in Eastern Min belongs to the literate stratum. Therefore, it is not suitable to come to a quick answer with respect to the relation of *ɯ* with its counterpart in the other sub-dialects of Min.

As an uncommon vowel, /ɨ/ is not a stable segment in Quanzhou. A comparison of some cognates of Nan'an (a sub-county of Quanzhou) and Quanzhou may help understand the changes of this segment, as follows (Du 2014: 176):

(12)

Final	Cognates	*Hui Yin Miao Wu*	Nan'an	Quanzhou
	处 "location"	ɨ	ɨ/u	ɨ/u
	贮 "store"	ɨ	ɨ/u	ɨ
	书 "book"	ɨ	ɨ/u	ɨ
Yu(鱼)	庶 "plebeian"	ɨ	ɨ	ɨ
	储 "reserve"	ɨ	u	u
	据 "occupy"	ɨ	ɨ	ɨ
	御 "imperial"	ɨ	ɨ	ɨ
	与 "give"	ɨ	ɨ	ɨ

It is observable that for all these cognates, the finals of more than two hundred years ago in the rhyme book *Hui Yin Miao Wu*[①] was *ɨ* , in contrast with which, this final form is still *ɨ* in Quanzhou, yet it is remarkable that in Nan'an, there is an obvious alternation between *ɨ* and *u* for these cognates. Hong (2001) also puts forward that *ɨ* as a marked segment results in some alternants such as *u* in Xiamen and Zhangzhou, *i* in Huian, and *ə* in Chaozhou, due to its unstability.

As one member of the central vowels, does /ɨ/ have some similar patterning with the schwa? A comparison of two central vowels' combination with initials may give some clue to the patterning of these two central vowels, as follows:

(13)

Final	Initials		
	labial stops	coronal stops	dorsal stops
ɨ		√	√
ə	√	√	√

As is indicated in (13), both two central vowels can follow coronal stops and dorsal stops. While the schwa /ə/ can follow labial stops, the high central vowel /ɨ/ can not. Why is there a gap in terms of the combination of /ɨ/ with the labial initials? A further comparison with the back vowel /u/ can give a hint about the gap.

(14)

Final	Initials		
	labial	coronal	dorsal
ɨ		√	√
u	√	√	√

The observation from (13) as well as (14) indicates that both schwa /ɨ/ and the back vowel /u/ can follow labial initials, while /ɨ/ can not. In fact, in southern Min dialects, including the Quanzhou dialect, there is a universal

① *Hui Yin Mian Wu* is one dialect book compiled by Huangqian of Qing Dynasty, which records the phonetic data and lexical characteristics of Quanzhou about two hundred years ago (Dong 2006).

co-occurring combination restriction. This combination restriction does not allow the co-existence of * [αround][αround] in rhyme, for example * [um] and * [om] are not allowed; but it does not extend its restriction in the combination between initials and finals, so /pu/ is permitted.

Dresher (2009: 164 – 165) points out that the addition of central vowels will alter the markedness of the other vowels. In a vowel system with a front and back vowel, say /i, a, u/, either /i/ or /u/ may pattern as marked with respect to phonological activity, because only one contrast is required to distinguish front unrounded vowels from back rounded vowels (say, [labial] or [coronal], but not both). However, if a central vowel such as /ɨ/ or /ə/ is added, the prediction is that both the front and back vowels will pattern as marked with respect to the central vowel. This follows from the assumption that there is no feature [central], with the consequence that now both [labial] and [coronal] are required to distinguish the vowels from each other. It thus follows that the central vowel must be unmarked, a prediction that is empirically supported (Rose 1993; Walker 1993; Rice 2007).

Based on the above discussion, it is found that the high central vowel /ɨ/ and the middle central vowel /ə/ share three similar properties: firstly, both /ɨ/ and /ə/ are observed to have no combination with glide; secondly, both /ɨ/ and /ə/ in Quanzhou find their counterparts in the other sub-dialects of Southern Min in the peripheral vowels of the same height revealed in such patternings as /ɨ ~ u ~ i/ and /ə ~ e ~ o/; thirdly, both /ɨ/ and /ə/ display the similar unstable state. Hence it is plausible to classify these two central vowels /ɨ/ and /ə/ as a natural class.

4.1.2 Peripheral vowels

There are five peripheral vowels in Quanzhou, including three middle vowels as well as two high peripheral vowels in Quanzhou. Do they have similar patterning as peripheral vowels? How are they different from the other vowels of the simplex final inventory of Quanzhou?

4.1.2.1 Middle vowels

There are three peripheral middle vowels /e/, /o/ and /ɔ/ as finals in the Quanzhou dialect, as presented in (15).

(15) a. pe^{24} "climb"
b. po^{24} "grandma"
c. $pɔ^{24}$ "seize"

As seen, all three peripheral middle vowels in Quanzhou can form minimal contrastive pairs under the same tone. From the perspective of the system, it seems not so systematic to have two back middle vowels corresponding to one front middle vowel. Gordon (2016) gives the most common vowel inventories of different sizes compared with those of the same size predicted to occur by Liljencrants & Lindblom (1972), in which there are some cases with two front vowels corresponding to one back vowel, but there is no case with more back vowels than front vowels. Crothers (1978) presents a study of vowel inventories in the world's languages and formalizes general patterns in vowel systems, one of which indicates that the number of height distinctions in front vowels is equal to or greater than the number in back vowels (Zhang Jisheng 2006: 73). Why does the Quanzhou dialect have two back middle vowels? What is the relationship between these two back middle vowels? A careful observation of phonotactics of vowels in Quanzhou will reveal that these three middle peripheral vowels are not quite patterned in their phonological behavior, which will be discussed in details in the following section.

4.1.2.2 High front vowel /i/

The high front vowel /i/ is observed to have a rather wide distribution in Quanzhou, as follows:

(16)	pi^{24}	"spleen"	tsi^{24}	"water chestnut"
	$p^{h}i^{24}$	"skin"	$ts^{h}i^{24}$	"last"
	bi^{24}	"eyebrow"	si^{24}	"time"
	ti^{24}	"pool"	ki^{24}	"strange"
	$t^{h}i^{24}$	"cry"	gi^{24}	"doubt"
	li^{24}	"separate"	hi^{33}	"scarce"

As indicated, /i/ can occur after all the initials. Cross-linguistically, /i/ is relatively unmarked compared with the other vowels. In many languages, i is chosen as an epenthetic vowel. In Bao Zhiming's analysis on sub-syllabic process and the southern Min syllables, he puts forwards a language game La-pi of Taiwan as follows:

(17)	a. be	>	le	bi	"buy"
	b. kam	>	lam	kin	"sweet"
	c. tsin	>	lin	tsin	"very"
	d. aŋ	>	laŋ	in	"red"
	e. tsap	>	lap	tsit	"ten"

From the data above, one important observation is that in the case of the second vowel as the result of the word splitting, i is chosen as the default vowel in this process.

Besides, i is often the reduction result in many languages. As for i of Quanzhou, Wu (2014: 67) points out the change from [* -ie > -i] is an important innovation of Southern Min as an independent dialect from Proto-Min. Here it is proposed that the change from [* -ie > -i] is a markedness reduction process which transfers the more marked syllable structure CVV to CV which is the least marked syllable structure among all the syllable structures.

The fact that i in Quanzhou tends to be the result of markedness reduction can also be seen in the following example (Wu 2010):

(18) Southern Min

	Quanzhou	Yongchun	Zhangzhou	Dongshan	Shantou	Jieyang
彭	p^hĩ	p^hĩ	p^hɛ̃	p^hẽ	p^hẽ	p^hẽ
盲	bĩ	bĩ	bɛ̃	bẽ	mẽ	mẽ
生	sĩ	sĩ	sɛ̃	sẽ	sẽ	sẽ
更	kĩ	kĩ	kĩ	kẽ	kẽ	kẽ

As indicated, the other sub-Min dialects show up as the middle vowel e or ɛ, while Quanzhou turns out to be i. Wu Ruiwen proposes that the Quanzhou dialect has undergone a systematic vowel raising such as *ɛ̃ > ĩ.

4.1.2.3 High back rounded vowel /u/

As one peripheral vowel, /u/ is quite common typologically. In Quanzhou, there are two cases where /u/ occurs, the first of which is as nuclear of rhyme, the second of which is as glide of rhymes. Similar to the front high vowel /i/, /u/ in Quanzhou has a wide distribution, as follows:

(19)

a.	[pu^{24}]	"toast"	h.	[ts^hu^{24}]	"young"
b.	[p^hu^{24}]	"float"	i.	[su^{24}]	"potato"
c.	[bu^{24}]	"no"	j.	[ku^{24}]	"surname"
d.	[tu^{24}]	"kitchen"	k.	[k^hu^{33}]	"mould"
e.	[t^hu^{24}]	"dawdle"	l.	[ku^{33}]	"tortoise"
f.	[lu^{24}]	"child"	m.	[gu^{24}]	"cow"
g.	[tsu^{55}]	"main"	n.	[hu^{24}]	"capture"

The examples indicate that /u/ can follow all the different initials as a nucleus vowel. More than that, /u/ is in minimal pair with all the other high vowels under the same tone.

4.1.2.4 Low vowel

In the Quanzhou dialect, there is only one low vowel /a/. The vowel /a/ is quite stable in the Quanzhou dialect in that it can't only stand by itself as a final, but also be followed by all three stop codas, all three nasal codas, as well as the glottal stop coda. Furthermore, the low vowel can have [i] and [u] either as preglide or as offglide. The phonological behavior of /a/ has no parallel in other vowels in the inventory of Quanzhou. Why is the low vowel so stable in its combination with all the consonant codas as well as the glides? According to Gordon (2016), the low vowel is the most sonorant vowel in the sonority hierarchy, which makes it the most suitable as the nuclear of rhymes for which the higher sonority, the better. Hence, when the low vowel combines with the glide [i] as well as [u], the sonority difference between the low vowel and the glide [i] as well as [u] is larger than those between the middle vowel with the glides, which means more stable. And its flexibility in combining with consonant codas as well as glides is in accord with properties of unmarked segments proposed in Rice (2007: 80), according to which, unmarked segments appear in more grammars and are implied by marked ones.

4.1.3 Hierarchy of the contrastive features of simplex-final vowels in Quanzhou

Why do the simplex-final vowels of Quanzhou the have the distribution as discussed above? Why do some vowels have similar pattern in contrast with the other vowels? It is proposed that the unique phonological behavior of these simplex vowels is concerned with complexity in representations, which is driven by both contrast and markedness (Dresher 2009: 163).

Dresher & Zhang (2004) propose that contrastive feature values are phonologically active, triggering phonological rules, whereas redundant feature values are phonologically inert. In order to determine which feature values are contrastive in any given segment, an ordering of features must be established. This ordering, or contrastive hierarchy, determines the relative contrastive scope of each feature. The account presented here depends on a particular way of arriving at contrastive specifications. Since Saussure, it has been commonly asserted that contrast is central to linguistic theory; nevertheless, how one determines whether a particular feature is contrastive or redundant in a particular phoneme has remained an elusive matter. The author will adopt the view that contrastive specifications derive from ordering features into a contrastive hierarchy (Jakobson & Halle 1956; Dresher 1998, 2003a, 2003b; Dresher & Zhang 2004). The author will propose a particular feature hierarchy for Quanzhou, and show how it accounts for the synchronic and diachronic patterns of Quanzhou vowel systems.

It has long been assumed that phonological criteria for determining markedness relations can be found in the asymmetrical patterning of features (or sounds) in inventories and phonological processes (Trubetzkoy 1969; Archangeli 1984; Kiparsky 1985; Paradis & Prunet 1991a, 1991b). In constructing the feature hierarchy of simplex-final vowels of Quanzhou, the most markable simplex vowel is the low vowel, which is noted for its stability and flexibility in the related phonological processes. With regard to the specification of the low vowel, besides the common [low] feature, the low vowel is (typically) phonetically [+back] and [-round], but these features are not contrastive in Quanzhou. In other words, though the low vowel is relevant to these features, it is not necessarily in the contrastive scope of these features (Dresher 2009: 56). In Quanzhou, the low vowel is deemed as not being specified with the feature of [back], which makes it possible to combine with the glide with [-back] feature as well as [+back] feature. Therefore, in constructing the feature hierarchy, the only feature needed in separating the low vowel from the other vowels is [low], indicated as follows:

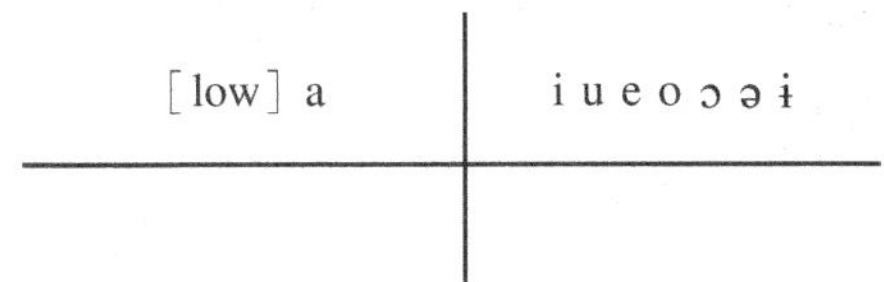

Diagram 4-2 Division of low vowels and non-low vowels

For the rest non-low vowels, it is found that the high central vowel /ɨ/ and the middle central vowel /ə/ share three similar properties: firstly, both /ɨ/ and /ə/ are observed to have no combination with glides; secondly, both /ɨ/ and /ə/ in Quanzhou find their counterparts in the other sub-dialects of Southern Min in the peripheral vowels of the same height revealed in such patternings as

/ɨ ~ u ~ i/ and /ə ~ e ~ o/; thirdly, both /ɨ/ and /ə/ display the similar unstable state. Hence it is plausible to classify these two central vowels /ɨ/ and /ə/ as a natural class. Then which feature is needed in separating these two vowels from the other vowels? Accordingly, it is proposed to use the feature [-peripheral] to separate these two central vowels from the other peripheral vowels, as follows:

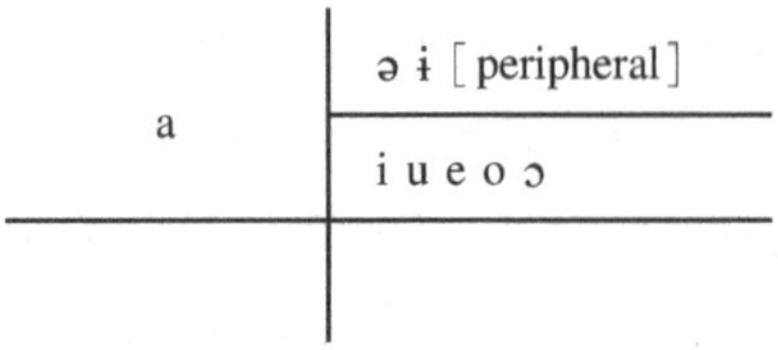

a

ə ɨ [peripheral]

i u e o ɔ

Diagram 4-3 Division of non-peripheral vowels and non-peripheral vowels

For the division of non-front vowels and front vowels, it appears likely to employ the feature [back] to divide them from front vowels, as follows:

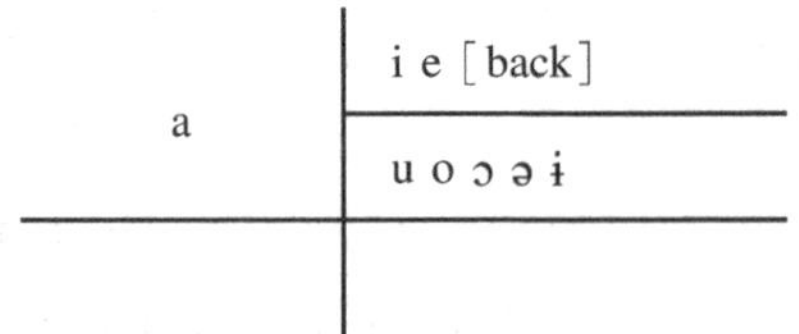

Diagram 4-4 Division of back vowels and non-back vowels

For peripheral vowels, there are two possibilities of dividing them, either with the feature [back] or with the feature [high]. With peripheral vowels divided into back vowels and non-back vowels, it will mean that /i/, /e/ will be separated from /u/, /o/, /ɔ/ which are under the same node [+back]. If peripheral vowels are divided with the feature [high], it will mean that two high vowels /i/ and /u/ will be separated from the other three vowels. Is it reasonable to include all the non-front vowels under the node of [+back] or separate the high vowels from the non-high vowels? According to Dresher (2009: 173), deciding on the scope of a feature is particularly important when there are asymmetries in a phoneme inventory. The specification of the same contrastive features will mean the similar phonological behavior for the related segments since phonological activity serves as the chief heuristic for determining what the feature hierarchy is for a given language (Dresher 2009: 161). In fact, the two non-back vowels /i/ and /e/ are not found to have similar patterning in Quanzhou, while both the high front vowels of Quanzhou play the similar role in being the segments as the markedness reduction results in vowel raising. Accordingly, for further dividing high vowels and middle vowels such as /i u e o ɔ/, it is suggested that in this book to use the feature [high] to separate these two high peripheral vowels from the other vowels, as follows:

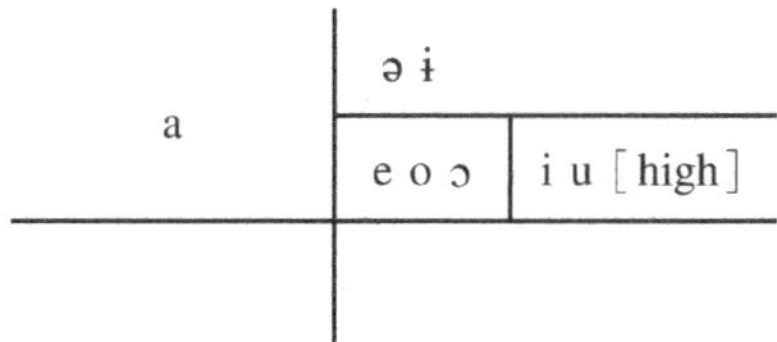

Diagram 4-5 Division of high vowels and non-high peripheral vowels

For the remaining three middle vowels, in contrast with /ɔ/, the other two peripheral middle vowels /e/ and /o/ in Quanzhou are noted to have wider distribution in their combination with preglides. How to differentiate /o/ as well as /e/ from /ɔ/? According to Zhang Jisheng (2006: 88 – 89), the differentiation of /o/, /e/ and /ɔ/ can resort to [ATR] or [tense], depending on the patterning of concrete cases. [+tense] vowels like /i, e, a, o, u/ are produced with a more peripheral and somewhat closer tongue position than their [-tense] counterparts /ɪ, ɛ, ɔ, ʊ/, while [ATR] involves a forward position of the tongue body, with concomitant enlargement of the pharynx (Gussenhoven & Kaike 2011: 84). The features [tense], and [ATR] while phonetically somewhat different, appear never to co-occur in the same language (Ladefodge & Maddieson 1996: 300). The choice of [tense] or [ATR] can refer to the behavior of the other vowels such as schwa in this language system. If /ə/ is similar to /ɛ/ and /ə/, then the common feature is [tense], but if /ə/ is similar to /o/ and /e/, the common feature is [ATR] (Zhu 2013). In Quanzhou, schwa is found to have similar patterning with /o/ as well as /e/, both of which are found to have no similar behavior with /ɔ/. Therefore, it is suggested to employ [ATR] to differentiate /o/ and /ɔ/, as follows:

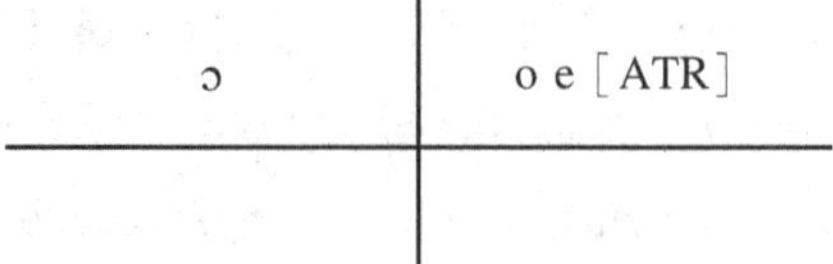

Diagram 4-6 Division of three central vowels

For the further separation of these two middle vowels /e/ and /o/, the feature [back] is enough, which can also be used to separate the high front vowel /i/ and the high back vowel /u/.

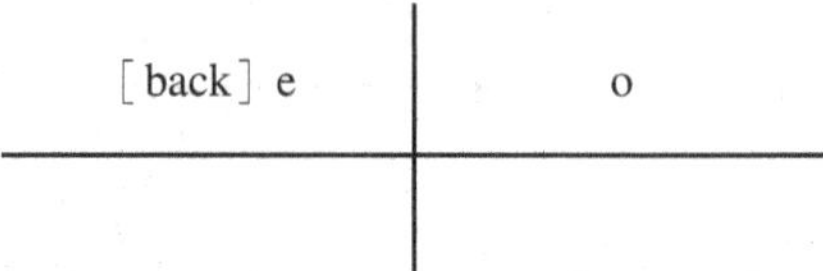

Diagram 4-7 Division of middle front vowel and middle back vowel

On the basis of the division of simplex final vowels in Quanzhou, the feature hierarchy of these simplex vowels can be constructed as follows:

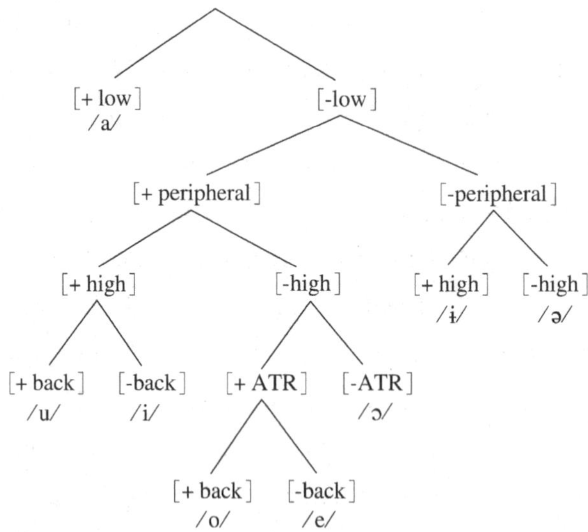

Diagram 4-8 Hierarchy of contrastive features of simplex vowels of Quanzhou

4.2 Complex finals of Quanzhou

The complex finals discussed in this subsection narrow down to the rhymes such as GV, VG and GVG, excluding finals ending with nasal or oral stops. There has been discussion in literature on whether GV in Southern Min is GV or VV as in Taiwan Southern Min and Xiamen dialect. This subsection will be devoted to this topic and claim that GV in Quanzhou is in fact also VV in this book.

4.2.1 GV or VV

In Quanzhou, there are eleven complex finals ending with an oral vowel or a nasalized vowel, or a nuclear vowel followed by a vocalic off-glide ([i] or [u]), of which six have a nuclear vowel preceded by [i] and five preceded by [u], as follows:

(20)	ia	ua	iã	uã
	io	ue	iũ	
	uai	iau	iãu	uãi

The syllabic status of the prenuclear [j] and [w] has been the topic of many Chinese linguistic studies. Are they vowels or glides? Glides are distinguished from corresponding high vowels by the feature [syllabic] in Chomsky & Halle (1968). Padgett (2008: 1939 – 1940) puts forward that within a language a glide might be realized as either semi-vocalic or consonantal, according to context and other factors. In many languages, high vowels and glides are in complementary distribution. For example, French is typical in that a high vocoid will surface as a vowel or glide depending on how it is syllabified. Also in Russian, the glide [j] is consonantal at the beginning of a stressed syllable and semi-vocalic elsewhere (Avanesov 1972: 89 – 94). Cheon (2002) argues that Korean glides behave like consonants both phonologically and phonetically when in either initial or coda positions. Zhang Jisheng (2006: 105) points out that in Mandarin, all on-glides are [-voc] but offglides can be [+voc]. Thus, it can be said that the prenulear [i] and [w] in Quanzhou are glides. Are they semi-vocalic or consonantal? Or are these two types attested in Quanzhou?

Levi (2008) proposes that there are two types of glides, "phonemic" glides and "derived" glides. The former is phonemically different from corresponding vowels and patterns with other sonorant consonants. However, the latter is a positional variant of corresponding vowels and shows vowel-like behavior. Therefore, the variable behavior has made glides problematic when we consider whether they are allophonic variants of corresponding vowels or distinct phonemes that contrast with vowels. Cross-linguistically, "phonemic" and "derived" glides co-occur in some languages like Karok, Sundanese and Pulaar (Levi 2008), whereas some languages such as Latin (Steriade 1984) only have "derived" glides. Mandarin is one of those languages that only have "derived" glides (Duanmu 2007). Are the glides in Quanzhou phonemic or derived?

From the synchronic perspective, the glides in Quanzhou can be found to have two main sources. The first is the glide shared with the other sub-Min dialects, as follows (Wu 2002):

(21)

Cognates	Fuzhou	Ningde	Quanzhou	Xiamen	Jianou	Putian
	ieu	iau	iau	iau	iau	iɐu
雕 "engrave"	tieu	tiau	tiau	tiau	tiau	tiɐu
调 "melody"	tieu		tiau	tiau	tiau	
了事 "finish"	lieu	liau	liau	liau	liau	liɐu
萧 "surname"	sieu	siau	siau	siau	siau	
尧 "surname"	ŋieu			giau	iau	
晓 "know"	hieu	hiau	hiau	hiau	xiau	hiɐu

As indicated, all the cognates in sub-Min dialects share the preglide [j], which is transcribed as [i] in the above data. Due to its common historic correspondence, such a preglide can be deemed as the phonemic glide of Min dialects. Alongside of this kind of glide, there is a special preglide in Quanzhou, as follows:

(22)

Cognates	Southern Min		
	Quanzhou	Zhangping	Chaoyang
挨 "in sequence"	ue	ei	oi
买 "buy"	bue	bei	boi
街 "street"	kue	kei	koi

(23)

Cognates	Southern Min			Eastern Min	Northern Min
	Quanzhou	Zhangping	Chaoyang	Fuzhou	Jianyang
八 "eight"	pueʔ	pei	poiʔ	paik	pai

It is interesting to observe that compared with VG structure in the other sub-dialects of Southern Min and Eastern Min as well as Northern Min, Quanzhou is noted to have GV structure for these cognates. In fact, such unique preglide of Quanzhou is not limited to some sporadic cases. According to the comparison of cognates of sixteen finals of Quanzhou on the basis of Zeng (2013) and Yuan (2010), Quanzhou is observed to have more examples with such preglide as summarized in the following tableau:

(24)

Cognates	Middle Chinese	Quanzhou	Fuzhou
辣 "spicy"	lɑt	uaʔ	aʔ
拔 "pull"	b^{w}iɐt	uat/ueʔ	eiʔ
莲 "lotus"	len	ũĩ	eiŋ
截 "tug-of-war"	dzet	ueʔ	eiʔ
段 "section"	d^{w}ɑn	ũã	auŋ
反 "reverse"	p^{hw}iɐn	ũĩ	eiŋ
县 "county"	ɦ^{w}en	ũĩ	aiŋ
血 "blood"	h^{w}et	uiʔ	aiʔ

Why does Quanzhou display so distinctive characteristics of having the rounded preglide? Is this a systematic feature of Quanzhou? This will be further addressed in the following section. In fact, according to the data provided in Zhang (1989), there are some enlightening clues to such preglide of Quanzhou as follows:

(25)

Cognates	Eastern Min	Northern Min	Southern Min		
	Fuzhou	Jianyang	Chaoyang	Zhangping	Xiamen
八 "eight"	paik	pai	poiʔ	pei	pueʔ
拔 "pull"	pɛik	vai	poi		puiʔ
獭 "otter"			thuaʔ	thua	thuaʔ
辣 "spicy"		lue	luaʔ	lua	luaʔ
撒 "scatter"		sue	suaʔ	sua	suaʔ
割 "cut"		kue	kuaʔ	kua	kuaʔ
拔 "pull"		poi	phuaʔ	pua	puaʔ
抹 "wipe"		moi	buaʔ	bua	buaʔ
阔 "wide"		khue	khuaʔ	khua	khuaʔ

As indicated, it is interesting to note that in contrast with the consistent preglide reflected in the cognates in (25), the cases of Chaoyang and Zhangping of Southern Min indicated the intermediate stage of co-existence of preglides and non-preglides.

For the rounded preglide, Hong (2001) makes an analysis of transformation of the schwa to the peripheral vowel glides, as follows:

(26)

Cognates	Southern Min						
	Xizhi	Quanzhou	Tongan	Xiamen	Zhangzhou	Zhangping	Chaozhou
底 "buttom"	təe	tue	tue	tue	te	tei	toi
细 "thin"	səe	sue	sue	sue	se	sei	soi
侪 "fellow"	tsəe	tsue	tsue	tsue	tse	tsei	tsoi
鸡 "chick"	kəe	kue	kue	kue	ke	kei	koi

As indicated in (26), Hong (2001) proposes that in Xizhi, where the elder people still retain the pronunciation [əe], some young people have begun to pronounce it as [ue]. Based on this observation, [ə] is turning to a more stable peripheral glide [u].

Furthermore, such unique glide in Quanzhou is not limited to the rounded preglide, but also extends to the unrounded preglide [i], as listed in Hong (2001):

(27)

Cognates	Yong-chun	An-xi	Quan-zhou	Tong-an	Xia-men	Chang-tai	Zhang-zhou	Zhang-ping	Chao-zhou	Hai-kou
后 "behind"	həu	hou	hio	hɔ	hɔ	heu	hɔ	hou	hou	hou
厚 "thick"	həu	hou	hio	hɔ	hɔ	heu	hɔ	hou	hou	ɦou
贸 "trade"	bəu	bou	bio	bɔ	bɔ	beu	bɔ	bou	mou	mou
愁 "worried"	ts^{h}iu	ts^{h}iu	ts^{h}io	ts^{h}iu	ts^{h}iu	ts^{h}iu	ts^{h}iu	ts^{h}iu	ts^{h}iu	ɕou

Why does Quanzhou have GV when the other Min dialects have VG for the same lexical terms? What is the motivation for the occurrence of such GV in Quanzhou? The [u] in [ue] of Quanzhou is the result of the transition of the vowel in the process of ＊ai > oi > ue, which is not like the [i] in [ei], an inserted offglide. Based on this presumption, this preglide in Quanzhou should be deemed as a derived glide from the corresponding vowel. Although the proto-form of this final is not what this book is going to discuss yet, it aims to discuss those questions concerning what phonological characteristics are embodied in such preglides of Quanzhou, whether they are vocalic preglides or consonantal preglides, whether they are part of the rhymes of syllables or part of initials, and what is implied in such GV structure of Quanzhou.

Cheon (2002: 626) proposes that whether preglide is part of diphthong or part of initial consonant cluster depends on its position in syllable. As for the question whether the preglide of Quanzhou belongs to initials or finals, there are divergent opinions. Duanmu (1990a, 1990b) suggests that such preglide belongs to initials on the basis of the labial occurrence restriction. Some other scholars such as Bao (1990b), Chung (1997) proposes putting such a preglide under the node of finals. Luo (2014: 192) proposes that such preglide belongs neither to the initials or finals on the inspiration of Zhang Jisheng's analysis of Mandarin and the Shaoxing dialect. As for determining the nature of such preglide of Quanzhou, the phonological processes are good ways.

The rhyming in Chinese poems always play a key role in the phonological analysis of Chinese phonology. Therefore, the poetic rhyming will be a good evidence in determining the location of the preglide of Quanzhou. According to the 200 plays of Liyuan opera of Quanzhou investigated by the author, it is found that 54 plays involve the rhyming of preglides. The rhyming of these plays is found to display one remarkable characteristics, namely only the characters with the same preglide can rhyme with each other, and there are no cases of rhyming between characters with different preglides, which indicates that preglides are important part of the rhymes of syllables.

These preglides of Quanzhou are different from the consonantal prelgides in their combination with initials, namely the vocalic prelgides can follow all kinds of initials. Such case of preglides can also find similar examples in some other Chinese dialects. For example, Zhengzhang Shangfang (2008: 78) holds that that there are two types of [i] in Wenzhou, namely a long [i] and a short [i] which are different in that the long [i] can follow whatever initials while the short [i] can only follow the initial /tɕ/. Zhu (2013: 87) also proves that the long [i] corresponds to the high vowel and is noted for its duration which is remarkably longer than the short [i] which only occurs in the case of such initial as /tɕ/ and is consonantal preglide.

Therefore, it is suggested in this book that the seemingly GV in Quanzhou is rising VV in essence. Such observation can also find related evidences in some other sub-dialects of Southern Min such as the case of Xiamen (Luo 1956) and Taiwan Southern Min in Hsu (2004).

As indicated, it is obvious that there are GV structures in Quanzhou, but the VG structures are absent from it, namely /oi/ and /eu/ are missing from Quanzhou dialect. Then why are such sequences absent from this dialect? Chung (1996: 56) proposes a V-neutralization rule to account for this; namelys there is vowel neutralization when non-low vowels co-occur with another vowel. He also employs the conflict between maximized and minimized contrasts (Flemming 2005) to explain such a phenomenon. But here is an awkward situation that /io/ and /ue/ compared with /oi/ and /eu/ are the same in terms of contrast. In this book it is put forward that some other approaches may be needed to account for such a gap. Before our approach is proposed, it is necessary to pay attention to one detail mentioned in Chung (1996: 56) that in some speakers of Taiwanese there is alternation between [eu] and [io], such as [keu] – [kio]. In fact, [eu] can be found in Eastern Min, as indicated in the following comparison of several sub-dialects of Min (Dai 2005: 64):

(28)

Final	Southern Min	Eastern Min	Middle Min	Northern Min	Western Min
	Quanzhou	Fuzhou	Xianyou	Jianou	Yongan
Hou 侯	io	eu	iau	e	ø
You 尤	io	eu	iau	e	ø

Hence it is proposed that the synchronic absence of /eu/ in Southern Min should be the result of the transition from /eu/ to /io/. Then what motivates the transition from /eu/ to /io/ instead of /eu/ to /oi/? The following feature analysis may shed light to answering this question.

(29) /eu/ – /oi/ [-back, -high, -low][+back, +high]→[+back, -high, -low][-back, +high]

/eu/ – /io/ [-back, -high, -low][+back, +high]→ [-back, +high][+back-high, -low]

From the feature changes of these pairs of rhymes, it is clear that in the first pair the features that are involved in the change are the backness as well as roundeness of the vowel, while in the second pair it is the height of vowels that are changed. Compared with backness of vowel, the height feature is relatively more unmarked, vowel systems may fail to exploit either frontness or roundness, but "no language is known which does not have some distinctions of height" (Maddieson 1997: 636). Typologically speaking, there are no "horizontal" vowel systems, but there are some vertical vowel systems of three vowels, such as /ɨ, ə, a/ which have no contrast of backness or roundness but have height contrast. Hence it is proposed that why there is /io/ instead of /oi/ in Quanzhou may be related to the markedness. The transition from /eu/ to /io/ involves more changes of markedness reduction.

4.2.2 Finals ending with nasals

In this subsection, I will discuss all the VN forms in Quanzhou. Altogether there are 16 such complex finals in Quanzhou, presented as follows:

(30)							
	labial	/am/	/iam/	/im/	/əm/		
	coronal	/an/	/ian/	/uan/	/in/	/un/	/ən/
	dorsal	/aŋ/	/iaŋ/	/uaŋ/	/iŋ/	/ɔŋ/	/iɔŋ/

To have a better view of the phonotactics of nasal codas in Quanzhou, the author provides the combination of these nasal codas with vowels as follows:

(31)	Vowels	m	n	ŋ
	a	√	√	√
	i	√	√	√
	u		√	
	e			
	o			
	ə	√		
	ɨ			

As indicated, all three nasal codas can follow the low vowel /a/ and the high front /i/, while only the coronal nasal coda [n] can follow the high back vowel /u/ and the labial nasal coda can come after schwa. Why is there such an absence of ＊uŋ or ＊um in Quanzhou? This will be further addressed in the following section.

4.2.2.1 Co-existence of three nasals

The co-existence of three nasal codas which have merged to be the velar nasal coda in Eastern Min can still be found in Quanzhou. Here is one example which can help illustrate this point:

(32)

Cognates	Eastern Min (Fuzhou)	Southern Min (Quanzhou)	Mandarin
斩 "chop"	tsaŋ	tsam	tʂan
真 "real"	tsiŋ	tsin	tʂən
名 "name"	miaŋ	biŋ	miŋ

As indicated, the co-existence of three nasals in Middle Chinese, which have merged to be the velar nasal as well as the coronal nasal in Mandarin and merged to be the velar nasal in Eastern Min, is still retained in Quanzhou. Along with the co-existence of three nasal codas, there are traces of the evolution of vowels preceding these nasal codas. It is noticeable that the vowel contrast before the labial coda is lost earlier than those before the coronal nasal coda and the velar nasal coda. This is in line with the implication that the contrasts of vowels before the labial coda implies the contrasts of vowels before the coronal nasal coda and the velar nasal coda, but the reverse does not hold.

From (31), the observation about VC structure in Quanzhou shows that there is no back high vowel followed by the velar nasal coda and that there are also no middle vowles /e/ and /o/ followed by nasal codas. Why is there no /uŋ/ in the inventory of Quanzhou? Is it a system gap? Chen (1973) points out all the Wu dialects have preserved at least some of the velar nasal endings, especially when these are preceded by high and middle back vowels /u/, or /o/. In other words, the Middle Chinese final [uŋ] has kept its velar nasal endings in Wu dialects (cf. Chao 1928). In fact, although synchronically there is no high back rounded vowel followed by the velar nasal in Quanzhou, it is observed that the rhyme consisting of the high back rounded vowel and the velar nasal coda in Middle Chinese finds its counterpart in the Quanzhou dialect with the vowel lowering to the middle back rounded vowel or even low vowel, which is indicated as follows:

(33)

Example	Quanzhou	Middle Chinese
弄 "lane"		
公 "male"	ɔŋ/aŋ	uŋ
红 "red"		

According to the observation in (33), the [uŋ] in Middle Chinese is lowered to the [ɔŋ] or [aŋ]. As to why the co-existence of /u/ and the velar nasal coda is forbidden in Quanzhou will be further discussed in the following section.

4.2.2.2 Merger of nasal codas

Despite the co-existence of three nasal codas synchronically, there have been traces of the merger of certain nasal codas in Southern Min. According to Dai (2005: 104) and Zhang (2009: 5), some labial nasals have turned to coronal nasals. Here are some examples which may help illustrate:

(34)

Example	Middle Chinese	Quanzhou
品 "grade"	p^hɯim	p^hin

This seems to be in alliance with the observation of the evolution of nasal codas of Chinese dialects proceeding from "the front to the back", namely from the labial to the velar nasal (Chen 1973). Yet, there is another interesting case of nasal coda merger, which appears not to be in accord with this observation as follows:

(35)

Cognates	Quanzhou	Xiamen	Jieyang
瓶 "bottle"	pan	paŋ	paŋ
零 "zero"	lan	lan	laŋ
踢 "kick"	t^hat	t^hat	t^hak

It is observed that the velar nasal has turned to coronal nasal in Quanzhou while it is still retained as the velar nasal in Xiamen as well as Jieyang. As for the merger from the velar nasal to the coronal nasal in Quanzhou instead of the velar nasal, it is proposed that this is the unmarkedness of coronals in Quanzhou as discussed that accounts for such merger result.

4.2.2.3 Finals with nasalized vowels

Nasalization of vowels is quite common in Chinese dialects, but few can be compared with that of Southern Min (Dai 2005). The nasalized vowels of Quanzhou are also noted for their wide distribution, even the syllables with the glottal stop can be nasalized. The nasalized vowels of Quanzhou are listed as follows:

(36)	ã	iã	uã	uãi	iãu	ãŋ	iãŋ	ãiŋ	ãuŋ	iãuŋ
	ĩ	uĩ	ĩʔ	uĩʔ						
	ɔ̃	ɔ̃ʔ								
	ẽ	ẽʔ								
	iũ	iũʔ								

From (36), there are some observations: firstly, the nasalized vowels are different in height, including not only low vowel and middle vowels, but also high vowels; secondly, high back vowel /u/ and back middle vowel /o/ have no independent nasalized counterparts; thirdly, nasalized low vowels have quite various syllable structures, including not only CGV structure, but also CGVGC structure.

There is cross-linguistic evidence that the surface syllable-final nasal vowels are underlying sequences of an oral vowel + a nasal consonant. For example, Zhang Jisheng (2006: 60) assumes that the underlying forms of the surface nasalized vowels of Shaoxing are VN combinations. As for the nasalization of Quanzhou, there are three sources: firstly, the merger of the nuclear vowel and the following nasal coda, which is the main source of nasalization of Quanzhou; secondly, the influence of the nasal initial, for example 娜 $nã^{24}$, 骂 $mã^{41}$, 傲

ŋɔ̃^{41}, the main vowels of which include some of /ã/, quite a lot of /ɔ̃/ and all of /ẽ/; thirdly, the source of nasalization is unclear as indicated in Zhang (2012), and the syllables of this type mostly have glottal fricatives as their initials. The discussion of the nasalization of Quanzhou in this book focuses on the first type of nasalization, which will preclude the nasalized vowels with the middle vowels as its nuclear that are the result of the reduction of nasal initials followed by the vowel or the nasalized vowels following the glottal fricative initial. Syncrhonically in Quanzhou, the nasalized vowels from the vowel + nasal sequence have two most common vowels as their nuclear, either low vowel or high vowel. This conforms to the observation made in Hayes et al. (2004: 4) and Crothers (1978: 136) that if the system of the nasalized vowels is smaller than that of the oral vowels, it is usually the nasalized middle vowels that are missing from the system. Why does the nasalized vowel system from the sequence of vowel + nasal coda only have the high nasalized vowel and the low nasalized vowel? Or why are the nasalized middle vowels absent from this system? Does nasalization begin from the low vowel or the high vowel?

Chen (1975) puts forward that nasalization tends to spread from low vowel to high vowel. Cross-linguistically speaking, there are some similar cases. For example, in Breton phonemic vowel nasality arose first with /a/ (Ruhlen 1973). Why does the low vowel show more tendency to be nasalized? It is proposed that the stronger tendency of the low vowel to be nasalized should be associated with the unmarkedness of the low vowel in terms of its highest sonority in the sonority hierarchy (Gordon 2016), which assures it best as the nuclear of syllable as well as the best locus of nasalization.

Alongside with the nasalized low vowel, there are some noticeable nasalized high vowels. Are these nasalized high vowels the direct result of the nasalization of the high vowel or the result of the raising of nasalized vowels? Ma (2002) makes a comparative analysis of some sub-dialects of Southern Min, which may give a hint to the answer of this question, as follows:

(37)	Example	Quanzhou	Zhangzhou
	张 "surname"	iũ	iɔ̃
	长 "long"		

A comparison of three sub-dialects of Southern Min is indicated as follows:

(38)	Example	Quanzhou	Xiamen	Chaoyang
	生 "live"	sĩ	sĩ	sẽ
	更 "midnight"	kĩ	kĩ	kẽ
	争 "content"	tsĩ	tsĩ	tsẽ

As indicated, it is obvious that the nasalized vowel in Chaoyang is still the nasalized middle vowel, while that of Quanzhou has been raised to a high vowel. Here is another example which can further embolden the raising of the nasalized vowel in Quanzhou:

(39)	Cognates	Southern Min				Eastern Min
		Quanzhou	Chaozhou	Zhangping	Chaoyang	Fuhzou
	闲 "idle"	ũĩ	õĩ	ẽĩ	ãĩ	ᴇiŋ
	苋 "amaranth"	hũĩ	hõĩ		kãĩ	kᴇiŋ
	拣 "pick"	kũĩ	kõĩ		kãĩ	kᴇiŋ

As indicated, the nasalized vowel is the low nasalized vowel in Chaoyang while it is the middle nasalized vowel in Zhangping and Chaozhou, and then the high nasalized vowel in Quanzhou. It is suggested that the high nasalized vowel in Quanzhou should be the result of vowel raising. The reference to the forms of these finals in Middle Chinese and Ancient Chinese can also offer a clue, as follows (Pan 2000; Zhengzhang 2003):

(40)

Cognates	Ancient Chinese	Middle Chinese
闲 "idle"	greːn	ɦɯæn
苋 "amaranth"	greːns	ɦɯæn
拣 "pick"	greːns	len

According to (40), the nuclear vowels of these cognates are middle vowel e or the middle low vowel æ. Therefore, it is reasonable to think the nasalized high vowel of Quanzhou is the result of vowel raising. In fact, such raising of the nasalized vowel may occur in one sub-dialect of Southern Min. For example, Chung (1996: 50) points out in Taiwan Southern Min, /io/ and /iu/ are in contrast, but the nasalized [ĩ õ] and [ĩ ũ] are not in contrast, but in complementary distribution. In this book, it is proposed that the raising of the nasalized vowel is a preparation for the further reduction to the syllabic consonant. What is more interesting is that the nasalized vowel, raising of the nasalized vowel as well as the syllabic nasal sometimes can co-exist in the same case, as indicated in the following example (Zeng 2013: 130):

(41)

	Geng Rhyme			
Example	兵 "solider" 平 "flat" 命 "destiny" 迎 "welcome" 影 "shadow"	命 "destiny" 迎 "welcome" 影 "shadow" 丙 "third"	平 "flat" 病 "illness"	影 "shadow"
Quanzhou	iəŋ	ĩ ã	ĩ	ŋ

In (41), all these words are the same rhyme of Middle Chinese, which indicates that they might have the same form originally. But synchronically in the Quanzhou dialect, they have evolved into different forms, ranging from V + N sequence to the nasalized vowel to the syllabic nasal. Such co-existence of different states can even be found in the same word, as follows:

(42)	Geng Rhyme	Quanzhou		
	影 "shadow"	iəŋ	ĩ ã	ŋ

Hence, the evolution of vowel nasalization in the Quanzhou dialect may be seen as a clear case of markedness reduction of syllable structure from GVN to GV to C. This is quite different from the Wu dialect in which the nasalized vowels are reduced directly to the oral vowel.

In the inventory of the nasalized vowels in Quanzhou, it is obvious that there is no nasalized high back vowel /ũ/. Is it the systematic gap or the result of the reduction of nasalized vowel? Chen (1973) provides support from Chinese dialects for the notion that NV's are denasalized in the reverse order from that in which they were nasalized. The Breton dialects also provide supporting evidence for this hypothesis. In the Tregorrois dialect, /ũ/ has been denasalized first, but the other nasalized vowels /ĩ ỹ ẽ õ ã/ remain. In both Osage and Siriono /ũ/ is missing from the series of high nasalized vowels (Ruhlen 1973). Does this observation also hold for the nasalization of uN? Is the first denasalization of /u/ in Quanzhou responsible for the present absence of /ũ/ in Quanzhou? To answer this question, it is necessary to observe another absence of /u/ followed by the dorsal nasal. Synchronically, there is no high back round vowel followed by the velar nasal in Quanzhou. The rhyme consisting of the high back round vowel with the velar nasal coda in Middle Chinese finds its counterpart in the Quanzhou dialect with the vowel lowering to the middle back round vowel or even the low vowel, which is indicated as follows:

(43)	Cognates	Middle Chinese	Quanzhou	Mandarin
	锋 "sharp"	uŋ	ɔŋ/aŋ	əŋ
	风 "wind"			
	蜂 "bee"			

According to the observation in (43), the uŋ in Middle Chinese is lowered to the ɔŋ or aŋ. Why is the high back round vowel lowered instead of undergoing nasalization directly? Zhang (2012) points out that the chance of nasalization of the low vowel is the same if the tongue body moves forward; if the tongue body moves backward, there is difference with regards to distance. In /vŋ/ structure, /a/ is more likely to be nasalized than /ɔ/ and /o/, which are easier than /u/ in terms of nasalization. /uŋ/, which is more difficult than the low vowel as well as the middle vowels to be nasalized, needs to be lowered before undergoing nasalization. Hence it is suggested that the reason why there is no /ũ/ in Quanzhou lies in that the /u/ is lowered to be prepared to go through nasalization.

4.2.3 Finals ending with stops

In this subsection, I will give a brief introduction to all the V + stop forms in Quanzhou. There are altogether 30 such complex finals in the VC structure in Quanzhou, as follows:

(44)

			uʔ	
		iʔ	uiʔ	
	aʔ,ɔʔ,oʔ,əʔ,eʔ, ɨʔ,auʔ	iaʔ,ioʔ,iuʔ,iauʔ	uaʔ	
			ueʔ	
With stop codas	ŋʔ, mʔ			
		ip		
	ap	iap		
		it	ut	
	at	iat	uat	
	ak	iak		
	ɔk	iɔk		

To have a better understanding of the combination of vowels and stop codas, the possibility of vowels followed by stop codas is listed as follows:

(45)

Vowels	p	t	k	ʔ
a	√	√	√	√
i	√	√		√
u		√		√
e				√
o				√
ə				√
ɨ				√
ɔ			√	

As indicated, the most active stop coda is the glottal stop which can appear after all the vowels, which is followed by the coronal stop /t/ which can occur after /a/, /i/ as well as /u/. There are some observations about (45): along with three stop codas in Quanzhou, there is also a glottal stop coda. Chung (1996: 22) analyzes the glottal stop as an E-tone feature instead of a full segment. In this book, it is proposed that Chung's analysis of the glottal stop as an E-tone feature instead of a full segment is not so solid. Chung (1996: 25) proposes an argument against the glottal stop following the falling diphthongs in Taiwan Southern Min as a full segment for a generalization that no falling diphthongs can be followed by a consonant, which is quite general among Chinese languages. But a comparison within Min dialects may indicate this generalization is not so complete, such as in the Fuzhou dialect, there are quite some falling diphthongs followed by a glottal stop such as /eiʔ/ /ouʔ/ /øyʔ/. Chung's another argument against the glottal stop as a full segment is that no nasalized vowels occur in syllables closed with a consonant, but the glottal stop is the only phoneme allowed, so the glottal stop is not an independent phonemic segment. But a further observation of the nasalized vowels followed by the glottal stop reveals that most of the nasalized vowels followed by glottal stops are oral pronunciation without corresponding writing characters, while a few nasalized vowels followed by glottal stops find their counterparts in Middle Chinese with stop codas, such as the following three words:

(46) Cognates from Quanzhou MC

捏	lĩʔ	"pinch"	net
合	hãʔ	"togehter"	ɦəp
膜	mɔ̃ʔ	"membrane"	mɑk

Hence, in this book, it is proposed that the glottal stop in these words is a full segment. The nasalization of these words are a latter phenomenon, which has nothing to do with glottal stops.

Then what is the source of the glottal stop in Quanzhou? Zhang Jisheng (2006: 150) points out that the glottal stop in Shaoxing is the relic of the three stop codas, which results from debuccalization, in which process the segmental place component is lost, but the manner component often remains and is interpreted as a (new) segment. Many studies (Chomsky & Halle 1968; Clements 1985; Steriade 1987) claim that /ʔ/ and /h/ have no (oral) place component. Actually, the glottal stop in Quanzhou is also the reduction result of three stop codas. Why are different stop codas reduced to the glottal stop? This could be inferred from the articulatory and perceptual perspective. Compared with their nasal counterparts, final stops (especially when unreleased) provide much less distinct perceptual cues for the discrimination of the place of articulation. This perceptual factor accounts for, in part, the greater propensity of final stops to reduction (a glottal stop) and eventual loss (Chen 1973: 50). And in contrast to the highly complex patterns of vowel nasalization and of merger-splits of nasal endings, the phonological conditioning of the merger and neutralization of stop endings is relatively straightforward and unconditional altogether (cf. Chen 1973). Then how about the processes of the debuccalization in three stop codas? Do three stop codas debuccalize at the same time or in succession? Chen (1973) believes that the directionality of merging of the stop endings is virtually a replica of that of the nasal endings. In both cases the direction is invariably from the front to the back along the dimension of the place of articulation, which implies that the labial stop as the most marked coda is the first one to disappear. This can get evidence from the faster disappearance of the sequence of vowel with labial stop codas in Quanzhou.

Then before concluding the discussion of this section, how to address the question posed by Chung (1996: 25) about why the syllable structure Vʔ sometimes patterns with V, which is used by him as an argument against treating the glottal stop as a phonemic segment? In fact, the similar patterning of V as well as Vʔ in Quanzhou can find some similar corresponding phenomenon in Fuzhou dialect of Eastern Min, in which the non-final syllable ending with a glottal stop has similar effect as the syllable ending with a vowel in triggering the change of the initial of the following syllable. Based on the phonological behavior of the glottal stop, it is proposed in this book to employ the method in Chan (1985: 65) which treats the glottal stop in Eastern Min as a floating segment to treat the glottal stop in Quanzhou as a floating segment instead of as an E-tone feature as mentioned in Chung (1996: 22). In this way, it can not only account for the glottal stop as the dubaccalization result of the stop coda counterparts in Middle Chinese, but also explain why it is ignored in determining whether a syllable is open or closed, whether other post-vocalic consonants are not similarly treated. The glottal stop's similar behavior as syllables ending with vowels can be deemed as a reflection of the markedness reduction process from CVC to CV.

4.3 Syllabic nasals

De Lacy (2007: 180) points out that any of the thresholds in syllabicity may define the set of syllabic segments in a language. For example, the set of syllabic segments includes vowels in Bulgarian, vowels and liquids in Slovak, vowels, liquids and nasals in English, and all segments in Imdlawn Tashlhiyt Berber (Zec 1988, 1995). What kinds of syllabic segments can be found in Quanzhou? What characteristics can be found in these syllabic segments of Quanzhou?

The syllabic consonants can be found in a lot of languages. In some languages, the syllabic consonants are related to morphology. In some other languages, syllabic consonants are only a phonological phenomenon, for example, in English, /n/ in "button" and /ɫ/ in "bottle" form a syllabic consonant when they occur at the end of the coda (Trask 1996). The syllabic consonants of Quanzhou dialect is a phonological phenomenon. This subsection is going to discuss what kinds of syllabic consonants can be found in Quanzhou and what are the distinctive characteristics of the syllabic consonants of Quanzhou dialect.

De Lacy (2007: 183) thinks that syllabic segments have some implicational relations. If one language allows nasals to be syllabic segments, it should also allow liquids to be syllabic segments. Zhang Jisheng (2006) shows that syllabic segments in Shaoxing include not only nasals but also liquid. But there are also some languages that allow nasals to be syllabic segments, but not liquid, such as Swahili (Ashton 1944). In the Quanzhou dialect, the syllabic consonants only include bilabial nasals and velar nasals.

Then what is the distribution environment for these syllabic nasals? Here are some examples about the nasal syllabics in Quanzhou, as follows:

(47) m̩^{24} match-maker "媒" ŋ̩^{24} yellow "黄"
hm̩ŋ^{24} silent "沉默" hŋ̩^{24} park "公园"
tŋ̩^{24} stammer "结巴"

The syllabic velar nasal① in the Quanzhou dialect is so active that it can combine with almost all kinds of initials. Furthermore, the syllabic nasals can not only have consonant initials, but also can have consonant coda in the Quanzhou dialect. Syllabic consonants in traditional New Mexico Spanish (TNMS) share with vowels in the ability to function not only as syllable heads

① According to Lin (1993), in the combination between /ŋ/ and the initials, there is a transitional schwa between the initials and /ŋ/.

but also as stress-bearing units. As is shown in these example words, the syllabic nasals in the Quanzhou dialect serve not only as syllable heads but also as tone-bearing units.

Syllabic consonants are subject to two universal alignment constraints that govern their distribution by forcing them to be co-articulated with another consonant, based on the observation that syllabic consonants always occur adjacent to another consonant (Mohanan 1979). He further points out that although languages may vary as to whether the syllabic consonant is coarticulated with a preceding or a following consonant, there are no languages where syllabic consonants appear between two vowels or between a vowel and a pause precisely because in such environments there is no adjacent consonant available for co-articulation. Contrary to the observation of Piñeros (2005), the distribution environment of the syllabic nasals of Quanzhou can be presented as follows:

$ (consonant) + ____(consonant) $

This distribution environment of the syllabic nasals of Quanzhou dialect means that they can not only occur independently between syllable boundaries underlyingly, but also have consonant initials before them as well as consonant codas following them. This is different from the syllabic consonants in the Shaoxing dialect of Wu in which the syllabic sonorants occur on their own between syllable boundaries underlyingly.

As shown in these example words, the syllabic nasals in the Quanzhou dialect consist of labial nasals and velar nasals. Are there any difference between the labial syllabic nasal and the velar syllabic nasal in terms of their origin?

Michaud (2012) argues that in various Loloish languages some or all of the nasals occur as syllabic. In most such cases, the diachronic source for the syllabic nasals is syllables with a nasal initial and a high vowel, which evolved to be nasal syllabics in some dialect while to be a nasal plus a high vowel in some other dialects. Shen (2006: 83) points out that in the syllable structure of

Chinese, nasal consonants can be at the initial or final position of the syllables. Thus, the syllabic nasals in various dialects can be analyzed accordingly into two different kinds of changes. On the one hand, some syllabic nasals are developed from initials, on the other hand some from endings. For those syllabic consonants from endings in Quanzhou, they are found to have correspondence not only with the velar nasal coda of Middle Chinese, but also with the coronal nasal coda of Middle Chinese as follows:

(48)	Cognates	Quanzhou	Mandarin	Cognates	Quanzhou	Mandarin
	钻 "drill"	tsŋ^{41}	zuan	朋 "friend"	pŋ^{24}	peŋ
	算 "count"	sŋ^{41}	suan	长 "long"	tŋ^{24}	tɕ^{h}aŋ
	劝 "persuade"	kŋ^{41}	tɕ^{h}uan	床 "bed"	ts^{h}ŋ^{24}	tɕ^{h}uaŋ

The syllabic labial nasal segment and the syllabic velar nasal segment in Quanzhou are also different in their origins, as indicated in the following:

(49)	Cognates	Quanzhou	Mandarin	Cognates	Quanzhou	Mandarin
	媒 "match-maker"	m̩^{24}	mei^{35}	帮 "help"	pŋ̍^{33}	baŋ^{55}
	姆 "aunt"	m̩^{55}	mu^{213}	等 "wait"	tŋ̍^{55}	deŋ^{213}
	呣 "no"	m̩^{41}	mu^{35}	损 "hurt"	sŋ̍^{55}	sun^{213}

In (49), it is found that the syllabic labial nasal in Quanzhou mainly finds correspondence with the nasal initials of the counterparts of Middle Chinese, while the syllabic velar nasal is mainly noted to correspond with the nasal coda of the counterparts of Middle Chinese.

How did this active velar nasal segment in Quanzhou come into being? Why did the nasal codas transform to the velar syllabic nasal instead of the syllabic nasal of the other place such as the coronal?

On the basis of the survey of 85 languages, Bell (1978) finds that the most common source of syllabic segments is the transfer of the syllabicity to the neighbouring consonant with the disappearing of vowel. In the Quanzhou dialect, the vowel from which the syllabicity is transfered is usually the high vowel or schwa. Ye (2011) points out that part of the velar syllabic nasals have [ɤŋ] as their rhyme before the reduction of the vowel. Zhu (2012) proves that [ɯəŋ] in the Quanzhou dialect evolved to be [ŋ] in four hundred years with the deletion of glides as well as vowels. The independent evidence for the syllabic velar nasal coming from the reduction of the high vowel can be told from a comparison between Xiamen and Haifeng, another Min dialect, as shown below (Zhang 2011):

(50)

Cognates	糖 "sugar"	霜 "frost"	糠 "chaff"	变 "change"	染 "dye"	钱 "money"	扇 "fan"	见 "see"	圆 "round"
Xiamen	tŋ	sŋ	khŋ	pĩ	nĩ	tsĩ	sĩ	kĩ	ĩ
Haifeng	tŋ	sŋ	khŋ	pŋ	nŋ	tsŋ	sŋ	kŋ	ŋ

Zhang (2011) gives more example words, which is a good indication of the syllabic nasal as the whole rhyme in Xiamen which is similar to Quanzhou in these cases, but a counterpart [uĩ] rhyme in the Zhangzhou dialect, as follows:

(51)

Cognates	MC	Zhangzhou	Quanzhou
饭 "rice"	b^{w}iɐn	puĩ	ŋ
门 "door"	muon	muĩ	
断 "broken"	d^{w}ɑn	tuĩ	
卵 "egg"	l^{w}ɑn	nuĩ	
酸 "sour"	s^{w}ɑn	suĩ	
光 "light"	k^{w}ɑŋ	kuĩ	
远 "far"	$ɦ^{w}$iɐn	huĩ	

It is clear that for these cognates, the nasalized high vowel finds the counterparts in syllabic nasal [ŋ]. As to why the underlying nasal codas of different places of articulation surface as the syllabic velar nasal segment instead of the coronal nasal, it may have something to do with the sonority markedness of consonants (De Lacy 2006). As initials, the lower sonority, the more natural; as the nuclear, the higher sonority, the better. According to the element theory (Harris 1994; Zhang Jisheng 2006: 152), the three places of articulation of consonants are represented as [U] which represents the labial, [I] which stands for the coronal and [A] which is related to the dorsal. According to Torre (2003: 51 – 59) it is proposed that many cross-linguistic evidences prove that [U] is the consonantal element and [A] is the vowel element. In the sonority hierarchy, the feature element [A] is of the highest sonority, which implies the [A] in consonant is also relatively more sonorant than [U] and [I]. For nasals, the hierarchy of sonority is labial < coronal < dorsal. Hence velar nasal is the best choice in terms of serving as nuclear. This accounts for the observation of Quanzhou dialect.

4.4 Phonological changes of the finals of Quanzhou

In the related literature, Quanzhou is not described to have displayed notable systematic sound changes. However, on the basis of the researches made by Ma (2002), Hong (2001), it is found that Quanzhou still manifests some sound changes that can not be neglected.

4.4.1 Vowel raising

Some comparison of the cognates in some sub-dialects of Southern Min is as follows:

(52)

Cognates	Southern Min		
	Quanzhou	Zhangping	Chaoyang
当 "when"	toŋ	taŋ	taŋ
郎 "man"	loŋ	laŋ	laŋ
康 "health"	koŋ	laŋ	laŋ
航 "sail"	hoŋ	haŋ	paŋ
行 "walk"	hiŋ	hin	heŋ
杏 "apricot"	hiŋ	hin	kʰeŋ

It is clear that compared with those cognates of Zhangping and Chaoyang, the vowels preceding the velar nasal coda are raised in Quanzhou, which is different from the lowering of vowels preceding the velar nasal in Wenzhou as discussed in Zhu (2013: 88). What triggers such raising of vowels preceding the velar nasal coda?

Sagey (1986: 274) puts forward the feature [DORSAL], which includes /k/, /ŋ/, and /g/, which are specified with [+high] and [+back]. Padgett (2011) points out velar consonants, which are [dorsal], can cause raising of vowels, one example of which is Maxakali (Clements 1991) in which the [high] feature of the dorsal causes the vowel preceding it to rise. Similar to this, the dorsal nasal coda in Quanzhou also spreads its [high] feature leftward to raise the vowel preceding it.

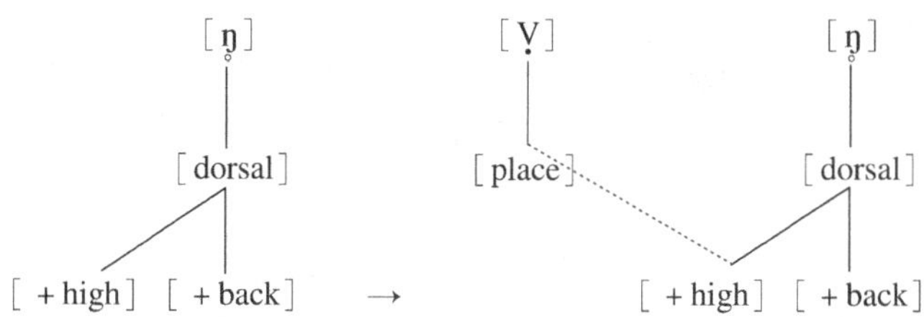

Diagram 4-9 Regressive assimilation of [+high] feature

As shown, the vowel raising as just discussed about Quanzhou is in the context of being followed by a nasal coda. Is such vowel raising of Quanzhou only restricted in the case of being followed by nasal codas? Can such vowel raising be observed in other cases of Quanzhou? Ma (2002) provides cognates in some sub-dialects of Southern Min, which may give a hint to the answer to this question, as follows:

(53)	Example	Quanzhou	Zhangzhou
	张"surname"	iũ	iɔ̃
	长"long"		

A comparison of three sub-dialects of Southern Min, which is a clear illustration, is indicated as follows:

(54)	Example	Quanzhou	Xiamen	Chaoyang
	生"live"	sĩ	sĩ	sẽ
	更"midnight"	kĩ	kĩ	kẽ
	争"content"	tsĩ	tsĩ	tsẽ

As shown, it is obvious that the nasalized vowel in Chaoyang is still the nasalized middle vowel, while that of Quanzhou has risen to the high vowel. Here is another example which can further embolden the raising of the nasalized vowels in Quanzhou:

(55)	Cognates	Southern Min				Eastern Min
		Quanzhou	Chaozhou	Zhangping	Chaoyang	Fuhzou
	闲"idle"	ũĩ	õĩ	ẽĩ	ãĩ	ᴇiŋ
	苋"amaranth"	hũĩ	hõĩ		hãĩ	hiŋ
	拣"pick"	kũĩ	kõĩ		kãĩ	kᴇiŋ

As indicated, the nuclear vowel of these cognates is the low nasalized vowel in Chaoyang while it is the middle nasalized vowel in Zhangping and Chaozhou, and then the high nasalized vowel in Quanzhou. It is suggested that the high nasalized vowel in Quanzhou is the result of vowel raising. The reference to the forms of these rhymes in Middle Chinese and Ancient Chinese may offer a clue, as follows (Pan 2000; ZhengZhang 2003):

(56)	Cognates	Ancient Chinese	Middle Chinese
	闲 "idle"	greːn	ɦɯæn
	苋 "amaranth"	greːns	ɦɯæn
	拣 "pick"	greːns	len

As shown, the nuclear vowels of these cognates are the middle vowel e or the middle low vowel æ. Therefore, it is reasonable to think the nasalized high vowels of Quanzhou are the result of vowel raising. Such vowel raising of Quanzhou can also be observed in the data provided in Hong (2001):

(57)	Cognates	Baozhong	Quanzhou	Tongan	Xiamen	Zhangzhou	Zhangping	Chaozhou	Haikou
	千 "thousand"	ʦɨ̃i	ʦhũi	ʦhãi	ʦhiŋ	ʦheŋ	ʦhẽi	ʦhãi	sai
	肩 "shoulder"	kɨ̃i	kũi	kãi	kiŋ	keŋ	kẽi	kãi	kai
	间 "room"	ɨ̃i	ũi	ãi	iŋ	eŋ	ẽi	ãi	ai

It is remarkable that all the sub-dialects of Eastern Min and Northern Min as well as some sub-dialects of Southern Min bear the middle vowels as the nuclear vowels of these cognates, except Quanzhou in which the nuclear vowel is the high vowel u. It is believed that the high back vowel u in these cases is the rcsult of vowel raising.

In fact, such raising of nasalized vowels may occur in one sub-dialect of Southern Min. For example, Chung (1986: 50) points out in Taiwan Southern Min, /io/ and /iu/ are in contrast, but the nasalized [ĩõ] and [ĩũ] are not in contrast, but in complementary distribution. In this book, it is proposed that the raising of the nasalized vowels is a preparation for the further reduction to the syllabic consonant. What is more interesting is that the nasalized vowels, raising of nasalized vowels as well as the syllabic nasal sometimes can co-exist in the same case, as indicated in the following example (Zeng 2013: 130):

(58)

	Geng Rhyme			
Example	兵 "soldier" 平 "flat" 命 "destiny" 迎 "welcome" 影 "shadow"	命 "destiny" 迎 "welcome" 影 "shadow" 丙 "third"	平 "flat" 病 "illness"	影 "shadow"
Quanzhou	iəŋ	ĩã	ĩ	ŋ

As shown, all these words are from the same rhyme, which indicates that they had the same form originally. Although these rhymes may come as the result of influences of different strata, the co-existence of these rhyme forms is a good indication of different degree of markedness reduction.

In fact, such vowel raising observed in Quanzhou can also be attested in the data provided in Wu (2010):

(59)

	Southern Min					
Cognates	Quanzhou	Yongchun	Zhangzhou	Dongshan	Shantou	Jieyang
彭 "surname"	p^hĩ	p^hĩ	p^hɛ̃	p^hẽ	p^hẽ	p^hẽ
盲 "blind"	bĩ	bĩ	bɛ̃	bẽ	mẽ	mẽ
生 "Sir"	sĩ	sĩ	sɛ̃	sẽ	sẽ	sẽ
更 "more"	kĩ	kĩ	kĩ	kẽ	kẽ	kẽ

As indicated, it is observable that for these cognates, the rhyme of Southern Min includes both middle vowels and high vowels. What is more interesting is that Zhangzhou is found to have the co-existence of high vowels and middle vowels. To have a better understanding of changes of these cognates, it is better to take the same cognates of Eastern Min into consideration:

(60)

Cognates	Eastern Min					
	Zherong	Shouning	Ningde	Minqing	Yongtai	Fuqing
彭 “surname”	p^{h}aŋ	p^{h}aŋ	p^{h}aŋ	p^{h}aŋ	p^{h}aŋ	p^{h}aŋ
盲 “blind”	maŋ	maŋ	maŋ	maŋ	maŋ	maŋ
生 “Sir”	saŋ	saŋ	saŋ	saŋ	saŋ	saŋ
更 “more”	kaŋ	kaŋ	kaŋ	kaŋ		keŋ

As indicated, it is clear that while the rhymes of Eastern Min and Northern Min are diphthongs, in contrast the rhymes in Quanzhou are the front high vowel i. Why is there such big contrast between Quanzhou and the other Min dialects for all these cognates? Wu (2014: 67) points out the change from ∗-ie > -i is an important innovation of Southern Min as an independent dialect from Proto-Min. Here it is proposed that the change from ∗-ie > -i is a markedness reduction process which transfers the more marked syllable structure CVV to CV which is the least marked syllable structure among all the syllable structures. Furthermore, such markedness reduction process is not influenced by coda of syllables. The following example from Zhang (2011) is a good example to the vowel raising of Southern Min:

(61)

Cognates	Southern Min		
	Xiamen	Chaozhou	Quanzhou
莲 “lotus”	naĩ	noĩ	nuĩ
前 “front”	tsaĩ	tsoĩ	tsuĩ

Accordingly, it may be reasonable to propose that vowel raising that has happened in Quanzhou is a systematic phenomenon instead of sporadic case.

4.4.2 Segment merger

Merger is a phonological change in which a previously existing contrast between two or more phonemes is lost. There are two types of merger: a merger applying only to restricted contexts, thus introducing a neutralization, is a conditioned merger, and the other one which applies to all contexts, thus reducing the number of phonemes in the language, is an unconditioned merger (Trask 1996; Zhang Jisheng 2006: 80). Which merger do the cases of Quanzhou belong to?

As indicated in the preceding discussion, it is noted that there are three middle vowels in Quanzhou, two back middle vowels and one front middle vowel, as follows:

(62)			
	poʔ^{55}博	peʔ^{55}伯	ɔʔ^{24}呕
	toʔ^{55}桌	teʔ^{55}硩(压)	
	tsoʔ^{55}作(做工)	tseʔ^{55}仄	
	koʔ^{55}廓	keʔ^{55}格	
	pio^{33}镖	pue^{33}杯	
	tio^{33}兜	tue^{55}底	
	tsio^{33}招	tsue^{24}罪	
	sio^{33}烧	sue^{33}梳	
	kio^{33}钩	kue^{55}鸡	

It is clear that two middle peripheral vowels /o/ and /e/ can have the glottal stop /ʔ/ as a coda to form rhymes such as /oʔ/ and /eʔ/ which can follow different initials, while /ɔ/ can only occur in one case as indicated. Furthermore, /e/ and /o/ can follow a preglide to form diphthongs such as /ue/ and /io/ with different consonants as initials, which does not occur in the case of /ɔ/. What leads to such difference? How to account for the co-existence of two back middle vowels in the inventory of Quanzhou?

Middle vowels are often proposed to be more marked with respect to high vowels and low vowels. Phonologically, middle vowels are not common in epenthesis and are not result from neutralization; in addition, middle vowels are not frequent in inventories, and generally, the presence of middle vowels in an inventory implies the presence of high vowels (Rice 2007: 82). Typologically speaking, the middle vowels are under more restriction than the high and low vowels. Weijer (1994) points out in the unstressed syllable all the other vowel contrasts still remain, while the middle vowels will disappear. Katamba (1989: 109) proposes in some Bantu languages only the marginal vowels can occur in some noun-prefix, while the middle vowels can not. Wang (2012) puts forward that in Anduo Tibetan, the middle vowels will first disappear in the vowel + nasal sequence. Zhu (2013: 82) points out the middle vowels in Wenzhou can not be a final by itself and should be followed by high vowels. Why are the middle vowels restrained in more aspects? Do the middle vowels in Quanzhou also display any special behavior?

Cross-linguistically speaking, the markedness of middle vowels may influence their phonological behavior. The middle vowels in Quanzhou are noted for some restriction in their combination with glides, namely the middle vowels can not be followed by an off-glide that disagrees with them in feature [back], such as *[eu], *[oi]. Alongside of this restriction, the middle vowels are also restrained in their combination with preglides. These restriction rules can be stipulated as follows:

1) *[+back][+back]
2) *[-back][-back]
3) *[labial][labial]

According to these rules, the following segment sequences are permitted in Quanzhou:

1) *uo *uoo (*uom *uon *uoŋ
2) *ou *oou
3) *ie
4) *ei

It is observed that the middle vowels are not allowed to co-exist with preglides that agree with them in terms of the features such as [round] or [back]. Due to these constraints, the following rhymes such as *-uɔ, *-uoŋ, *-uok disappear, which leads to some quite noticeable merger in the Quanzhou dialect.

As discussed above, there are two types of merger: a merger applying only to restricted contexts, thus introducing a neutralization, is a conditioned merger, and the other one which applies to all contexts, thus reducing the number of phonemes in the language, is an unconditioned merger (Trask 1996; Zhang Jisheng 2006: 80). The merger in Quanzhou is a conditioned merger, which only happens when the middle vowels are the nuclear of rhymes. Wu (2009: 220) offers a list of cognates of Southern Min and Eastern Min, which is a clear indication of the merger in Quanzhou, as follows:

(63)

Cognates	Southern Min					
	Shantou	Jieyang	Chaozhou	Chenghai	Quanzhou	Zhangzhou
	ou	ou	ou	ou	ɔ	ɔ
布 "cloth"	pou	pou	pou	pou	pɔ	pɔ
肚 "belly"	tou	tou	tou	tou	tɔ	tɔ
吐 "spit"	tʰou	tʰou	tʰou	tʰou	tʰɔ	tʰɔ
粗 "coarse"	tsʰou	tsʰou	tsʰou	tsʰou	tsʰɔ	tsʰɔ
糊 "muddy"	kou	kou	kou	kou	kɔ	kɔ
五 "five"	ŋou	ŋou	ŋou	ŋou	ŋɔ	ŋɔ

Wu (2009) proposes to reconstruct the ancient form of these cognates to be *-ɔw, which is preserved as diphthong from Shantou to Chenghai of Southern Min while it is merged to be monothong [ɔ] in central areas of Southern Min such as Quanzhou and Zhangzhou.

(64)

Cognates	AC	MC
布 "cloth"	paːs	puo
肚 "belly"	l'aːʔ	duo
吐 "spit"	lʰaːs	tʰuo
粗 "coarse"	tʰjog	tɕʰiok
糊 "muddy"	gaː	ɦuo
五 "five"	ŋaːʔ	ŋuo

Regarding ɔ in Quanzhou, Chen Zhongmin (2013) also points out that it turns up as alternant in two cases of Yu Final. Firstly, in the case of mixture of Yu Final (鱼) and Yu Final (虞), the final following affricate/fricative initials is [ɔ] while that following the other initials is [u], as follows:

* u > ɔ/Affricate/Fricative initials_

> u/the other initials_

Secondly, in the case of distinction of Yu Final (鱼韵) and Yu Finale (虞韵), [ɔ] which only occurs following the dorsal initial is the alternant of [ue] which turns up after the other initials as discussed in Yang (1991), as follows:

* ue > ɔ/Dorsal initials_

> ue/the other initials_

It is noticeable that the occurrence of /ɔ/ in Quanzhou displays the trace of markedness reduction from diphthongs to monothong. Does such merger also hold for the other two middle vowels /e/ and /o/? The following examples may give a hint to this answer (Wu 2002: 138):

(65)

	Eastern Min		Southern Min		Northern Min		Central Min	Western Min
Cognates	Fu-zhou	Ning-de	Xia-men	Jie-yang	Jian-ou	Jian-yang	Putian	Yongan
	ie	i	e	e	i	i	i	ie
剃 "shave"	t^hie	t^hi	t^he	t^he	t^hi	hie	t^hi	t^hi
弟 "brother"	tie	ti	te	ti	ti	tie	ti	ti
济 "many"	tsie		tse	tsi	tsie			tsi
鸡 "chick"	kie	ki	ke	ke				
启 "enlighten"	k^hie	ki	k^he	k^hi	k^hi	k^hie		k^hi
系 "system"	hie	hi	he	hi	hi			

In the cognates provided by Wu Ruiwen, he offers the cognates of Xiamen, which are replaced by the cognates of Quanzhou here. For the ancient form of these cognates, Wu Ruiwen suggests the form reconstructed which is * iei to be a reasonable form. Viewed from this ancient form, [e] of Quanzhou in some cases is a merged result of the corresponding ancient form.

These examples are important in two senses: the first is that it reveals the markedness reduction of syllable structures from CGVG to CVG, and the second is that the middle vowel /o/ in Quanzhou, even including some other sub-dialects of Southern Min such as Zhangzhou, is the merger result of the corresponding diphthongs in Eastern Min and Northern Min.

Why are the middle vowels more restrained compared with the three corner vowels /a, i, u/? Why are the the middle vowels prone to be the target of reduction? Crosswhite following Steriade presents arguments showing why specifically the middle vowels are targeted by so many reduction systems, and why the resulting systems of unstressed vocalism are so often /i, u, a/. The arguments are familiar from the phonetic literature on crosslinguistic regularities in the shape of vowel inventories: she cites specifically optimal dispersion in the vowel space (Liljencrants & Lindblom 1972), the quantal stability of the corner vowels, meaning the tendency to keep stable acoustic realizations even with a degree of articulatory variation (Stevens 1986), and the tendency for certain pairs of formants to approach and enhance one another in each of the corner vowels (Stevens 1986), increase their perceptual salience, while the middle vowels are less robust than the corner vowels perceptually, and hence prone to effacement (Barnes 2002: 74). Hence, from the perceptual perspective, the middle vowels are less prominent than the high and low vowels. This may account for the dissimilation of the nuclear middle vowels and glides in Quanzhou, which can help to enhance the perception of these rhymes.

The more interesting implication embodied in segment merger of Quanzhou is the result of bringing in markedness reduction of syllable structure of Quanzhou. In fact, such markedness reduction of syllable structure reflected in Quanzhou in contrast with Fuzhou is observed to cover a quite range of final groups, as follows:

Table 4-2 Markedness contrast of syllable structure of QZ&FZ
(L indicates the literate stratum, and C means the colloquial stratum.)

Finals	Quanzhou	Fuzhou	Markedness Contrast of Syllable Structure of QZ & FZ	
Ge Final 戈韵	ɔ	ɔ	V	V/GV
		uɔ		
	ua	uai	GV	GVG
		ai		VG
	ə	uei	V	GVG
		æy		VG
		øy		VG
Zhi Final 支韵	a	ia	V	GV
	i	ie	V	GV
	ɯ	y/øy	V	V/VG
	ə	uei	V	GVG
Xian She & Shen She 咸摄 &深摄				
Xian Final 咸韵	ã	aŋ	V	VN
Xian Final 衔韵	ã	aŋ	V	VN
Tian Final 添韵	ĩ ũĩ/iam	ieŋ eiŋ	V GV/GVN	GVN VGN
Qin Final 侵韵	ã	aŋ	V	VN

As indicated, it is remarkable that the markedness reduction of syllable structures in Quanzhou is a systematic phenomenon, which covers a wide range of final groups. In contrast, the syllable structures of Fuzhou for these cognates turn out to be more marked.

4.4.3 Dissimilation

Middle vowels are often proposed to be more marked with respect to high vowels and low vowels. Phonologically, middle vowels are not common in epenthesis and do not result from neutralization; in addition, middle vowels are not frequent in inventories, and generally, the presence of middle vowels in an inventory implies the presence of high vowels (Rice 2007: 82). The middle vowels in Quanzhou are noted for some restriction in their combination with glides, namely the middle vowels are restrained in their combination with preglides. These restriction rules can be stipulated as follows (Chung 1996):

1) * [+back][+back]

2) * [-back][-back]

3) * [labial][labial]

According to these rules, the following segments sequences are not permitted in Quanzhou:

1) * uo * uoo (* uom * uon * uoŋ

2) * ou * oou

3) * ie

4) * ei

It is observed that the middle vowels are not allowed to co-exist with preglides that agree with them in terms of the features such as [round] or [back]. Due to these constraints, the following rhymes such as * -uɔ, * -uoŋ, * -uok disappear. What can be observed sychronically are only two rhymes with middle vowels as nuclear such as [ue] and [io], which are suggested to be the result of dissimilation.

Dissimilation of Quanzhou can also be glimpsed through the combination of nuclear vowels and codas, which is clearly indicated in the case of /u/. Unlike /i/ which is not restricted in its combination with nasal codas and obstruent codas, the distribution of /u/ is restrained in its combination with codas when it is the nuclear of rhymes, as shown in the following example:

(66)

coda	m	n	ŋ	p	t	k	ʔ
/u/	×	√	×	×	√	×	√
/i/	√	√	√	√	√	√	√

As indicated, the vowel /u/ can not be followed by the labial coda as well as the dorsal coda. Bao (2000) employs the syllable structure to account for why the vowel /u/ can not be followed by the coda with [+ round] feature. But there is little discussion about why /u/ is forbidden in combination with velar nasal codas as well dorsal stop codas? Is this a systematic gap? As discussed, it is mentioned that there is a co-occurrence restriction targeted at the middle vowel, namely *[α back][α back]. In fact, this restriction can be extended to the high vowel. This restriction rule can be revised to be such as the violation of *[α Feature][α Feature] in segment clusters and such violation should not be more than one. The nuclear /u/ and the dorsal coda /ŋ/ and /k/ share [+back] as well as [+high], so /uŋ/ and /uk/ are ruled out because they violate twice the constraint *[α Feature][α Feature], namely *[+back][+back] as well as *[+high][+high]. Such co-occurrence restriction can be explained from the perspective of the maximal contrast. It is supposed that the maximalization of contrast (which is driven by dissimilation) is highly ranked in Quanzhou, which requires that the sharing of features of the co-occuring segments can not be more than one. As a contrast, /ɔk/ is allowed in Quanzhou due to the fact that although they share the feature /back/, they are different in height. Another example is /bu/ which is permitted in Quanzhou because two segments of it though sharing the feature [round] differs in [backness].

4.5 Summary

This chapter provides a detailed analysis of the characteristics in phonology of the Quanzhou finals. The patterning of the finals of Quanzhou can be summarized to have the following characteristics:

a. As for the simplex oral vowels, Quanzhou vowel system contains five most unmarked peripheral simplex vowels as well as two non-low central vowels. Two non-peripheral vowels in Quanzhou find their counterparts in the other sub-dialects of Southern Min in the peripheral vowels of the same height. The specification of [peripheral] of Quanzhou can still be viewed as the division of the vowels from the main parameter of vowel such as [backness].

b. In Quanzhou, the contrastive features of the main parameters of vowels such as height and backness are dominant in the successive division of the inventory. The dominance of the feature [high] over the feature [back] in

Quanzhou highlights the biased importance of the height distinction in Quanzhou, which is reflected in the final reduction that is pervasive in Quanzhou which tends to result in high vowels including both the front high vowel and the back high vowel as discussed.

c. In terms of syllable structure, Quanzhou tends to show a less marked syllable structure, which is systematically reflected in the literate system and the colloquial system, alongside with the reduced segments such as schwa and syllabic nasal.

d. Regarding the phonological processes, Quanzhou is found to have manifested such processes as dissimilation, merge, regressive assimilation, which is related to markedness in some way.

Chapter 5

Phonological Characteristics of the Fuzhou Finals

This section will be devoted to the analysis of the finals of Fuzhou, including simplex finals and complex finals. Unlike the finals of Quanzhou, the finals of Fuzhou are simple in terms of coda systems but are more complicated due to the synchronic final alternation process. Moreover, the finals of Fuzhou are also different from those of Quanzhou in terms of syllable structures.

5.1 Final inventory of Fuzhou

The finals of Fuzhou can be divided into three types, namely the finals ending with vowels, the finals ending with nasals, and the finals ending with stops. The exact inventory of finals in Fuzhou is an issue with some controversies which differ in the transcription of final alternation of Fuzhou. In Feng's (1998: 8) transcription, every final of Fuzhou has its own alternation form, as follows (Feng 1998: 8):

Table 5-1 Finals of Fuzhou (Feng 1998: 8)

a/ɑ	ɛ/ɑ	o/ɔ	œ/ɔ	ai/ɑi	au/ɑu	ɛu/ɑu	
i/ɛi	ia/iɑ	ie/iɛ				iau	ieu/iɛu
u/ou	ua/uɑ		uo/uɔ		uai/uɑi		uoi/uɔi
y/ɔy			yo/yɔ	øy/ɔy			
	aŋ/ɑŋ						ŋ(n, m)

(continuous)

iɛ/ɛiŋ	iaŋ/iɑŋ	ieŋ/iɛŋ			ɛiŋ/aiŋ		
uŋ/ouŋ	uaŋ/uɑŋ		uoŋ/uɔŋ			ouŋ/ɔuŋ	
yŋ/øyŋ			yoŋ/yɔŋ	øyŋ/ɔyŋ			
	aʔ/ɑʔ	ɛʔ	oʔ/ɔʔ	œʔ			
iʔ/ɛiʔ	iaʔ/iɑʔ	ieʔ/iɛʔ			ɛiʔ/aiʔ		
uʔ/ouʔ	uaʔ/uɑʔ		uoʔ/uɔʔ		ouʔ/ɔuʔ		
yʔ/øyʔ			yoʔ/yɔʔ		øyʔ/ɔyʔ		

Different from the complex final inventory provided in Feng's (1998: 8), Chen (1998: 12) narrows the final alternation down to certain final form according to his description and the intuition of native speakers, as follows (Chen 1998: 12):

Table 5-2 Finals of Fuzhou (Chen 1998: 12)

Types	I	II	III
Finals ending with vowels	a ɛ o/ɔ œ ia ie ua uo yo	au ai iau uai euui iu	i/ei u/ou y/øy øy/oy
Finals ending with stops	aʔ ɛʔ oʔ/ɔʔ œʔ iaʔ ieʔ uaʔ uoʔ yoʔ		iʔ/eiʔ eiʔ/aiʔ uʔ/ouʔ ouʔ/auʔ yʔ/øyʔ øyʔ/œyʔ
Finals ending with nasals	aʔ iaʔ ieʔ uaʔ uoʔ yoʔ		iʔ/eiʔ eiʔ/aiʔ uʔ/ouʔ ouʔ/auʔ yʔ/øyʔ øyʔ/oyʔ

According to Chen (1998), the finals of Fuzhou are divided into three groups: the first are the finals ending with [a, o, ɛ, e, œ] accompanied with their corresponding final forms ending with nasal codas as well as stop codas; the second are the finals ending with [i] and [u] with no corresponding finals ending with nasal codas and stop codas; the third are the finals which are noted for their alternation with their transformed forms under certain tones.

Since the final system of Fuzhou is remarkably noted for its complexity due to its final alternation, Yuan (2010: 257 – 258) presents her final system of Fuzhou as follows:

Table 5-3 Finals of Fuzhou (Yuan 2010: 257 – 258)

	i-(ei)	u-(ou)	y-øy-(œy)
ɛ	ie		
a	ia	ua	
œ			
ɔ		uɔ	yɔ
ai		uai	
ɛu-au	ieu		
		uei	
	iŋ-eiŋ-(aiŋ)	uŋ-ouŋ-(auŋ)	yŋ-øyŋ-(œyŋ)
aŋ	iaŋ	uaŋ	
	ieŋ		
		uɔŋ	yɔŋ
	iʔ-eiʔ-(aiʔ)	uʔ-ouʔ-(auʔ)	yʔ-øyʔ-(œyʔ)
aʔ	iaʔ	uaʔ	
ɔʔ		uɔʔ	yɔʔ
	ieʔ		

As indicated in Table 5-2 and 5-3, both final systems of Chen Zeping and Yuan Bixia are noted to highlight the brevity and consistence of final alternation of Fuzhou in which some final forms both serve as the transformed final of some original forms and as the original final forms with their own transformed final form. The systems of Chen Zeping and Yuan Bixia are different from the final systems of Feng (1998) and Lin (2002), both of which highlight every final form has their transformed final form. According to Chen (1998) and Yuan (2010), despite the complexity of final alternation of Fuzhou, it is not reasonable to stipulate every final form has one transformed final form since such final alternation sometimes is so intricate that the native speakers can not differentiate them. Accordingly, Chen (1998) and Yuan (2010) propose to highlight those final forms whose transformed final forms are commonly accepted in the inventory of finals of Fuzhou, as indicated in Table 5-2 and 5-3. Before further analysis, it is necessary to compare the final inventory of Chen Zeping and Yuan Bixia. It is found that the final inventories of Zeping Chen and Bixia Yuan agree in most cases, except in the following cases:

Table 5-4 Comparison of finals of Fuzhou in Chen Zeping (1998) and Yuan Bixia (2010)

Chen Zeping (1998)	Yuan Bixia (2010)
o/ɔ	ɔ
uo	uɔ
yo	yɔ
uoŋ	uɔŋ
yoŋ	yɔŋ
ɛʔ	
œʔ	
oʔ/ɔʔ	ɔʔ
uoʔ	uɔʔ
yoʔ	yɔʔ

It is observable in Table 5-4 that the main difference between Chen (1998) and Yuan (2010) lies in the status of [o] and [ɔ], namely [o] is stipulated as the phonemic vowel in Fuzhou which is accompanied by its transformed rhyme [ɔ] in Chen (1998), while [ɔ] is deemed as the phonemic vowel in Yuan (2010). According to Chen (1998: 90), the rhyme system of *Qi Lin Ba Yin* of more than three hundred years ago is stipulated and it should have such middle vowels as [o], [e], and [œ], among which [e] has observed to lower to be [ɛ] paralle to [œ] as described in Chen (1998) and Yuan (2010). Hence the description of [o] with its transformed form [ɔ] in Chen (1998) and [ɔ] in Yuan (2010) both indicate the lowering of vowels of Fuzhou. In this book, the rhyme system of Chen (1998) as well as Yuan (2010) is cited as the basis for further discussion.

This section will be devoted to the finals ending with vowels, which can be further divided into simplex finals and complex finals. The simplex finals refer to the finals with one vowel as the rhyme of syllable, while the complex finals are such finals as GV, VG, or GVG. Among the finals ending with vowels, some rhymes are remarkable to have their transformed forms such as i/ei, u/ou, y/øy, øy/oy as well as o/ɔ.

5.2 Simplex finals

The simplex finals refer to the finals with one vowel in a syllable. The simplex finals of Fuzhou are found to consist of the following vowels (Yuan 2010: 257 – 258):

(1)

Types	Front		Central		Back	
high	i	y				u
middle	ɛ	œ				ɔ
low			a			
	non-round	round	non-round	round	non-round	round

It is obvious that in the Fuzhou dialect there are three high vowels, three middle vowels, and one low vowel; among the non-low vowels, four vowels are rounded vowels, two times more than non-rounded vowels. The arrangement of the simplex vowels of Fuzhou in (53) gives a rather symmetrical picture with respect to features of height and roundness. Such pattern of Fuzhou is in alliance with the observation made in Maddieson (1984: 136) who held that in most of deviations from the predicted patterns there is nonetheless evidence that vowels tend toward a balanced and wide dispersion in the available phonetic space. It also follows the general pattern observed by Maddieson (1984: 124) in which some interesting asymmetries are mentioned when the interactions of the three basic parameters are examined, namely there are more high front vowels than high back vowels, and in the middle range, more front rounded vowels than back unrounded vowels.

Diachronically speaking, the vowels in the simplex finals of Fuzhou seem to be rather stable. Chen (1998: 84 – 88) found that there was little change in terms of the vowel system of Fuzhou in his comparison of the simplex finals of Fuzhou about three hundred years ago with that of the present day, except some minor adjustment of features of some diphthongs.

5.2.1 Low vowel

The low vowel /a/ is the only vowel that can occur under all tones in the final system of Fuzhou. It is remarkable that this is the only vowel in the Fuzhou dialect that can bear all tones, since all the vowels in Southern Min such as the Quanzhou dialect can occur under all tones. More than that, the low vowel is the only vowel in this inventory that can combine freely with glides /i/ and /u/, which is different from some other Chinese dialects such as Shaoxing dialect of Wu in which both the low vowel and the middle vowel can combine with glides /i/ and /u/ (Zhang Jisheng 2006: 40). The unique status of the low vowel compared with the other vowels in the system is not unimaginable since the low vowel is a most common vowel, and is the most typical marginal vowel cross-linguistically. I will explain why the low vowel is the only vowel that can exist under all tones in the following section. Hooper (1976: 238) argues that /a/ in Spanish has never undergone reduction or deletion, while all other vowels have been deleted in post-tonic position (Bauer 2008). The low vowel /a/ in Fuzhou did not undergo the vowel splitting like those underwent by the high vowels.

5.2.2 Middle vowels

Totally, there are three middle vowels, including the front middle vowels such as /ɛ, œ/ and one back middle vowel such as /ɔ/. Do these middle vowels share the same phonological behavior?

5.2.2.1 /ɛ/ and /œ/

The vowels that can be independent finals under certain tones include two front middle low vowels /ɛ/ and /œ/ which are not typical marginal vowels.

According to Maddieson (1984), /ɛ/ and /œ/ are marked vowels. These two vowels can not be found in Southern Min. In Wenzhou dialect of Wu, /ɛ/ can not be an independent final except when it co-exists with the high vowel /i/ and /u/ or /y/. While in the Fuzhou dialect, these two middle vowels are active.

As one of the two middle low vowels, /ɛ/ can serve as independent finals like the low vowel, as follows (Chen 1998: 21).

(2) pa^{33}把 "control" ta^{53}茶 "tea" tsa^{55}渣 "residue"
pɛ^{33}摆 "array" tɛ^{53}题 "subject" tsɛ^{55}斋 "room"
pœ^{33}叵 "impossible" tœ^{53}除 "rid" tsœ^{55}糟 "bad"

As indicated, /ɛ/ can stand alone as a final and can occur following the same initials under the same tones as /a/ and /œ/ do. This vowel, as mentioned above, can not be found in Southern Min. In fact, this vowel is found to have an interesting patterning if viewed from the perspective of Min dialects, as follows (Wu 2002):

(3)

Cognates	Eastern Min		Southern Min		Northern Min		Central Min	
	Fuzhou	Ningde	Xiamen	Jiayang	Yong'an	Putian	Jianou	Jianyang
	ɛ/a	ɛ	ue	oi	e	e	ai	ai/ɔi
底 "below"	tɛ	tɛ	tue		te	te		tɔi
犁 "plough"	lɛ	lɛ	lue	loi	le	le	lai	lɔi
齐 "trim"	tsɛ	tsɛ	tsue		tse	tse	tsai	lai
洗 "wash"	sɛ	sɛ	sue	soi	se	ɬe	sai	sai
鸡 "chicken"			kue	koi	ke	ke	kai	k^hai

It is interesting to see that ɛ in Fuzhou finds its counterpart in diphthongs such as ue or oi in Southern Min and in monophthong such as e in Central Min dialects such as Yong'an or Putian and in ai in Northern Min. For ɛ in Fuzhou, Chen (1998: 61) provides some examples containing this vowel, as follows:

(4)

Cognates	Middle Chinese	Fuzhou	Mandarin
牌 “board”	ai/wai	ɛ	ai
买 “buy”			
差 “allocate”			
解 “unite”			ie
街 “street”			
低 “low”	iei/iwei		i
泥 “mud”			
蹄 “hoof”			
底 “buttom”			
体 “body”			

In (4) it is found that ɛ in Fuzhou finds its counterpart in two Middle Chinese rhymes: ai and ei. Is /ɛ/ in Fuzhou a result of monothongization. These cognates in Southern Min can be seen as the result of backing of vowels in such a following sequence as ai > oi > ue. Along this line, is it possible that the same cognates in Eastern Min may be the result of further reduction such as ai > oi > ue > ɛ? Without more evidence to support such a presupposition, it is too hasty to reach such a conclusion, which may need further studies in future research. In fact, based on the comparison of cognates of Qi Final such as “稗买街鞋”① ue in Xiamen finds its counterpart in ɛ in Fuzhou (Yuan 2010: 86). Then why is ɛ chosen as the final form instead of ue in Fuzhou? It is suggested that it may be that the forms such as oi and ue do not agree with such a constraint that is active in Fuzhou as [α Feature][α Feature] which requires that the more agreement of two parts of a diphthong, the better.

As for the vowel /œ/, this middle front rounded vowel can occur as a final, either by itself or in a combination such as /œʔ/. As an independent final, it can only occur under such tones as Yinping, Yangping and Shangsheng. The tones it can not occur with is Qusheng. Consider the following examples:

① 稗“weeds”, 买“buy”, 街“street”, 鞋“shoe”

(5) a. pœ^{33}叵 "English"　　e. tsœ^{55}糟 "English"
b. mœ^{53}模 "model"　　f. sœ^{55}梳 "comb"
c. tœ^{53}除 "rid"　　g. kœʔ^{24}嗝 "gulp"
d. nœ^{53}驴 "donkey"　　h. k^{h}œʔ^{5}咳 "cough"

The vowel œ is common in Eastern Min, but it is rare in Southern Min. What are the counterparts of œ in the other sub-dialects of Min? Chen Zhongmin (2013: 221) provides the strata correspondence of these cognates:

(6)

Central Min	Yu Final	Southern Min	Eastern Min	Puxian	Northern Min
The first stratum	* ue	* ø	* ø	* ø	* o
The second statum	* ɯ				
The third stratum	* u	* y	* y	* y	* y

For the cognates of Yu Final mentioned in Chen Zhongmin (2013: 214) which is transcribed as ø, Feng (1998: 19) and Chen (1998: 61) and Yuan (2010) transcribe as œ. Therefore, œ in Fuzhou finds its counterparts in Southern Min, Puxian, Northern Min and Central Min as follows:

(7)

Yu Rhyme	Southern Min	Eastern Min	Puxian	Northern Min	Central Min
The first stratum	* ue	* œ	* œ	* ɔ	* o

These two middle low vowels /ɛ/ and /œ/ are noted for their flexibility in combining with initials: /ɛ/ can follow whatever initials, while /œ/ can follow the initials except the dorsal initial, as follows:

(8)

Initials	Rhyme			
	ε		œ	
p, p^h, m	排 [pε]	"row"	叵 [pœ]	"impossible"
t, t^h, n	低 [tε]	"low"	除 [tœ]	"except"
ts, ts^h, s	斋 [tsε]	"room"	糟 [tsœ]	"bad"
k, k^h, ŋ, x, o	街 [kε]	"street"	呵 [xœ]	"exclamation"

These two middle low vowels /ε/ and /œ/ are different from the two middle high vowels such as /e/ and /ø/ which are noted that they can not serve as independent rhymes, but need co-occur with the high vowels /i/ and /y/ in such forms as ie and øy. This is different from the Wenzhou dialect of Wu in which two vowels that can not exist without glides are the two middle low vowels /ε/ and /ɔ/. The restriction of /ø/ in Fuzhou is also different from that in the Fuqing dialect a sub-dialect of East Min adjacent to Fuzhou, in which /ø/ needs not co-exist with a glide, but exists in more independent forms such as ø, øŋ, øʔ. The restriction of /e/ and /ø/ set them different from the corresponding middle low vowels such as /ε/ and /œ/, which can serve as independent rhymes.

5.2.2.2 /ɔ/

The middle rounded back /ɔ/ is similar to the other two middle low vowels such as /ε/ and /œ/ in that all these three middle vowels can only occur under certain tones instead of all the tones. According to Yuan (2010: 121), ɔ is the main literate form of Hao Final of Fuzhou, as follows:

(9) Hao Final of Fuzhou Dialect 豪韵 Xiao She 效摄

ɔ	毛 mɔ^{53}	"hair"	刀 tɔ^{55}	"knife"
	^{父}老 lɔ$^{33\,L}$	"fellow countryman"	早 tsɔ^{33L}	"early"
	操 ts^{h}ɔ^{55L}	"gym"	臊 ɔ^{h}ɔ^{55}	"smelly"
	骚 sɔ^{55}	"tarty"	草^{木皆兵}ts^{h}ɔ^{33L}	"grass"
	高 kɔ^{55}	"tall"	浩 xɔ^{213}	"vast"
au	老^{母} lau$^{242\,C}$	"old"	扫^{地} sau^{C}	"sweep"
	操 ts^{h}au$^{55\,C}$	"gym"	^{麦}草 ts^{h}au$^{33\,C}$	"grass"
	灶 tsau^{213}	"kitchen stove"		
a	早^{操} tsa$^{33\,C}$	"early"		
ua	^{六}扫^{除} sua$^{213\,L}$	"get rid of"		

Besides, ɔ of Fuzhou finds its counterpart in the other sub-dialects of Eastern Min, as follows:

(10)

Fuzhou	Minqing	Fuqing	Gutian	Ningde	Fuan	Zhouning	Fuding	Zherong
ɔ	ɔ	o	o	ɔ	ɔ	ɔ	o	ɔ

It is noticeable that for the literate form of Hao Final in Eastern Min ɔ and o alternatively occur in Eastern Min, and ɔ has turned to be the dominant form in Eastern Min.

5.2.3 High vowels

When serving as an independent final, the high front round vowel /y/ finds its unrounded counterpart in other Min dialects, as follows (Du 2014: 211):

(11)

Cognates	East Min			Southern Min		
	Fuqing	Gutian	Zherong	Quanzhou	Zhangzhou	Chenghai
	y/øy	y	y	ɯ	i	ə
煮 "boil"	tsy^{33}	tsy^{42}	tsy^{51}	tsɯ^{55}	tsi^{53}	tsə^{52}
猪 "pig"	ty^{55}	ty^{55}	ty^{42}	tɯ^{33}	ti^{44}	tə^{33}
锄 "hoe"	t^{h}y^{53}	t^{h}y^{33}	t^{h}y^{21}	tɯ^{24}	ti^{13}	tə^{55}
鼠 "rat"	ts^{h}y^{33}	ts^{h}y^{42}	ts^{h}y^{51}	ts^{h}ɯ^{55}	ts^{h}i^{53}	ts^{h}ə^{52}
鱼 "fish"	ŋy^{53}	ŋy^{33}	ŋy^{21}	hɯ^{24}	hi^{13}	hə^{55}
许 "that"	hy^{33}	hy^{42}	xy^{51}	hɯ^{55}	hi^{53}	hə^{52}

It is clear that the final is the front rounded high vowel in Eastern Min in uniform, while it is the unrounded vowel of different forms in Southern Min.

What characterizes the distribution of y in Fuzhou? Chen (1998) makes a list of three sources of y/øy in Fuzhou, as follows:

(12)

Cognates	Middle Chinese	Fuzhou	Mandarin
女 "female"	/ ĭo/ / ĭu/	y/øy	y
鱼 "fish"			
遇 "meet"			
猪 "pig"			u
书 "book"			
刺 "stab"	/ĭə/		i
试 "try"			

It is observable that all these cognates have evolved into three high vowels in Mandarin, but find their counterparts in a front rounded vowel with its transformed final under certain tones in Fuzhou. Pulleyblank (1984) presents some evidence from Chinese rhyme books that in Chinese phonology there is a tradition of treating front-rounded vowel [y] as a combination of fronting and (back-) rounding. Zhang Jisheng (2006: 80) also puts forward that [y] in Shaoxing is not an underlying vowel, but a merged vowel in surface representation. Ladefoged's (1982: 211) characterizes front-rounding as secondary articulation in some languages (e. g. Twi and other Akan languages) (Chan 1985:74). In the Fuzhou dialect, the front rounded vowel y patterns consistently in the minimal contrastive pairs with the other two high vowels both as independent finals, as follows:

(13)	y	女 ny^{33}	"female"	吕 ly^{33}	"surname"
		徐 sy^{53}	"surname"	猪 ty^{55}	"pig"
		书 tsy^{55}	"book"	黍 sy^{33}	"millet"
		如 y^{53}	"as if"	举 ky^{33}	"raise"
		鱼 $ŋy^{53}$	"fish"	许 xy^{33}	"surname"
	u	驴 $lu^{53\,L}$	"donkey"	初 ts^hu^{55L}	"first"
		阻 tsu^{33}	"stop"	梳 su^{55L}	"comb"
	i^C	来 li^{53}	"come"	苔 t^hi^{53}	"moss"
		腮 ts^hi^{55}	"cheek"	鳃 ts^hi^{55}	"gill"

Accordingly, it seems that /y/ is an independent segment in Fuzhou, which is in contrast with the other high vowels. While in accordance with Chen Zhongmin (2013), Yu Final of Middle Chinese in Min dialects is so complicated in their correspondence as well as in their strata, it is too hasty in coming to a conclusion that all cases of y of Fuzhou are independent segments.

In terms of [i] of Fuzhou, it is more clearly related to its markedness. Languages may vary in whether low or non-low vowels are less marked. If low vowels are less marked, the epenthetic vowel will be [a]; setting aside the low vowel, the least marked vowels are [ɨ] and [ə]. Where they are not, languages will choose the least vowel possible (Lombardi 2002). In the Fuzhou dialect, there being no central vowels, which vowel will be the epenthetic vowel, the low vowel or the nonlow vowel? There is a phonological process which reduplicates the verb forms in three successive syllables in the Fuzhou dialect. There is some observation about this process: in the first syllable the initial of the verb is retained and the final of this syllable is replaced by [i] in a uniform way, the second syllable and the third syllable copy initials and finals of the original syllable. Take a look at the following examples (Chen 1998: 116):

(14)				
	听 "listening"	t^{h}iaŋ^{55}→t^{h}i^{21} t^{h}iaŋ^{55} t^{h}iaŋ^{55}	画 "draw"	ua^{242}→ i^{21} ua^{53} ua^{242}
	行 "walk"	kiaŋ^{53}→ ki^{21} kia^{33}kiaŋ^{53}	讲 "talk"	kuoŋ^{33}→ ki^{21} kouŋ^{24} kouŋ^{33}
	扫 "sweep"	sau^{213}→ si^{21} sau^{24} sau^{33}	看 "look"	k^{h}aŋ^{213}→ k^{h}i^{21} k^{h}aŋ^{53} k^{h}aŋ^{213}
	写 "write"	sia^{33}→ si^{21} sia^{24} sia^{33}	拣 "pick"	keiŋ^{33}→ ki^{21} keiŋ^{24} keiŋ^{33}
	啜 "sip"	ts^{h}uoŋ→ts^{h}i^{21}ts^{h}uo^{53}ts^{h}uoŋ^{24}	食 "eat"	sieŋ^{5}→ si^{21} sie^{33} sieŋ^{5}

It is clear that in this phonological process, it is the unrounded front high vowel [i] that is inserted as epenthesis. [i] as epenthesis can also be observed in some other cases in Fuzhou, for example, Feng (1998: 362) points out that the syllabic nasal [ŋ] as a negative indicator can have three alternants such as [ŋ, m̩, n̩] according to the place of articulation of the following initial consonant. But it turns to be [iŋ] on emphasis, with [i] as epenthetic vowel. Why is the high front unrounded vowel [i] chosen as the epenthetic vowel in Fuzhou?

In the Fuzhou dialect, there is another high rounded back vowel, namely [u] which is also involved in the final alternation. What is more remarkable about [u] is its role in being a preglide, which will be further discussed in the following section.

5.3 Hierarchy of the contrastive features of simplex vowels in Fuzhou

As discussed, there are totally seven simplex final vowels which form minimal contrastive pairs. How are these simplex vowels patterned with each other in their phonological processes? What features are needed in differentiating these vowels?

5.3.1 Feature [low]

In the Fuzhou dialect, the low vowel is the most stable vowel diachronically and the only vowel in this vowel system that can occur under all tones. The low vowel /a/ can freely combine with the front high vowel as well as the back high vowel and is more stable in its combination with consonant codas than the middle vowels. Hooper (1976: 238) argues that /a/ in Spanish has never undergone reduction or deletion, while all other vowels have been deleted in post-tonic position (Bauer 2008). The low vowel /a/ in Fuzhou does not undergo the vowel splitting like those underwent by the high vowels and can occur under all the tones. Hence in the feature hierarchy of vowels in Fuzhou, it is suggested that the feature [low] should rank the highest.

The low vowel can both combine with the front high unrounded glide [i] as well as the back high rounded glide [u]. The flexibility of the low vowel may be concerned with the feature specification of the low vowel. There is cross-linguistic evidence that specification of [back] for [a] differs from language to language (Ladefoged & Maddieson 1996). For example, [a] is a front vowel in the Cardinal Vowel System (Jones 1975); [a] is [+back] in SPE (Chomsky & Halle 1968: 332); [a] in Shaoxing is unspecified for [back] (Zhang Jisheng 2006: 90). According to the phonological performance of the low vowel /a/ in Fuzhou, it is suggested that the low vowel in Fuzhou is unspecified for the feature [backness], which accounts for its freedom in combination with glides.

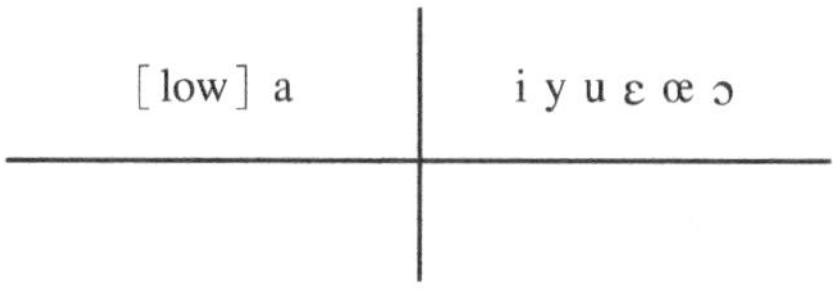

[low] a	i y u ɛ œ ɔ

Diagram 5-1 The first step of successive division algorithm based on the feature [low]

5.3.2 [round] vs [back]

In terms of the classification of non-low vowels, there are two possibilities of division: based on the feature of [back], the non-low vowels can be divided into two groups:/u, ɔ/ and /i, ɛ; y, œ/; according to the feature of [round], the non-low vowels can classified as /u, ɔ; y, œ/ as well as /i, ɛ/. Which ordering of features is more suitable to the Fuzhou dialect? Which features are contrastive? According to SDA, the contrastive specification of features is related to the ordering of features. Since the non-low vowels include high vowels as well as the middle vowels, it is suggested to take the high vowels into consideration first, all of which can be glides as well as nuclear vowels. Therefore, if /i/, /u/, and /y/ are fully specified, they are as follows:

(15)

	i	y	u
[back]	–	–	+
[round]	–	+	+

If the feature ordering is [back]≥[round], the contrastive feature specification is as follows:

(16) a. [back] u > i, y

b. [rounded] y > i

Then the contrastive feature specification of /i/, /u/ and /y/ is as follows:

(17)

	i	y	u
[back]	–	–	+
[round]	–	+	

If the ordering of features is [round] ≥ [back], then the contrastive feature specification is as follows:

(18) a. [round] i≥y,u

b. [back] y≥i

Then the contrastive feature specification of /i/, /u/ and /y/ is as follows:

(19)

	i	y	u
[round]	−	+	+
[back]		−	+

Then which case can better account for the phenomenon of Fuzhou? An example of assimilation in the diachronic process may shed light on the priority of [round] or [back] in the Fuzhou dialect. In *Qi Lin Ba Yin* two hundred years ago, Xiang Rhyme and Qiao Rhyme began with the glide [i], which was assimilated to be [y] under the influence of the nuclear vowel. This can get evidence from *The Dictionary of Fuzhou* published in 1870, in which Xiang Rhyme was transcribed to be [iong] and [iok], and Qiao Rhyme was transcribed to [io] and [ioh]. At that time the glides of these two rhymes can be transcribed to be [i] or [y]. In the current inventory of Fuzhou, this rhyme has totally turned to [yo]. This is in accord with the Contrastivist Hypothesis which states that phonologically active features are contrastive (Dresher 2009: 175). In the same line, the triggers of the rounding assimilation in Fuzhou also should be contrastive features. This means that the feature [round] in Fuzhou is a contrastive feature, which is phonologically active. Accordingly, it is assumed to divide the non-low vowels first into rounded vowels and unrounded vowels, namely [roundedness] ≥ [backness]. This feature hierarchy constrains such phonological activity as potentially triggering rounding of adjacent vowel in a diphthong.

Zhang Jisheng (2006: 87) holds that the roundness parameter plays the least active role among the three parameters in constructing a vowel inventory, because the great majority of the world's languages have a predictable relationship between the phonetic backness and rounding dimensions (Ladefoged & Maddieson 1996). Front vowels are usually unrounded and back vowels are usually rounded, so that the unroundedness of front vowels and roundness of back vowels can be regarded as predictable. The Fuzhou vowel inventory is interesting in that the roundness parameter has played a key role in the diachronic process of vowels. Accordingly, it is suggested that the non-low vowels be divided with the feature [round].

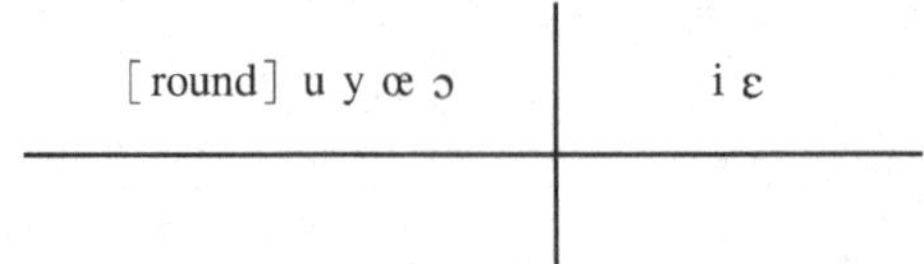

Diagram 5-2 The second step of successive division algorithm based on the feature [round]

The contrastive marked values of [round] for all the rounded vowels in Fuzhou account for the fact that these rounded vowels can trigger rounding assimilation process, as they have a relevant contrastive feature, which is different from the case of Classical Manchu in which /u/ and /ʊ/ have no contrastive specification for [labial] (= [round]), despite the fact that they are phonetically rounded vowels (Dresher 2009: 177).

5.3.3 Feature [high]

The third division is based on the fact that the three high vowels in the Fuzhou dialect are the first segments that underwent the vowel splitting and ushered in the phenomenon of high vowels co-existing with the corresponding diphthongs in a complementary distribution under all tones. Hence for the third step of division, the feature [high] is needed in separating /u, y/ as well as /i/ from the middle back vowels /ɔ/, /ɛ/ as well as /œ/.

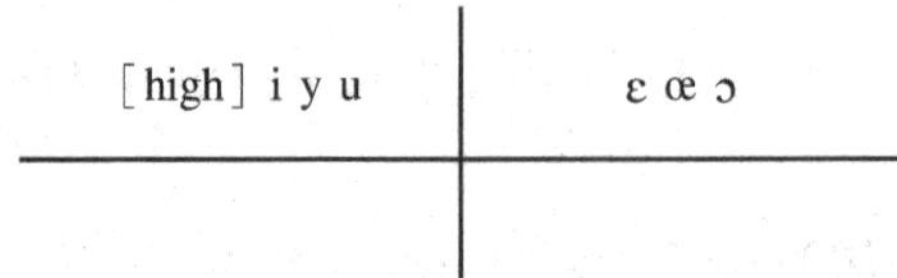

Diagram 5-3 The third step of successive division algorithm based on the feature [high]

5.3.4 Feature [back]

As for the last step of dividing, the feature [back] is needed, which can separate /y/ and /u/.

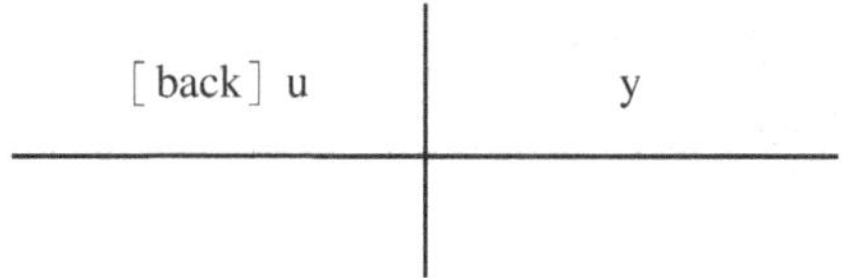

Diagram 5-4 The fourth step of successive division algorithm based on the feature [back]

The final vowel hierarchy of Fuzhou can be constructed as follows:

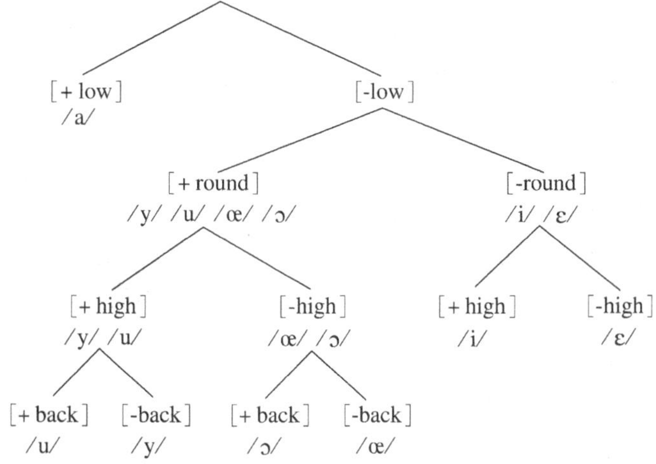

Diagram 5-5 Final vowel hierarchy of Fuzhou

It is noted that the vowel inventory of Fuzhou is remarkable for its variety of front vowels. He (2004: 12) proposes an assumption that languages may be divided into backness prominent languages in which backness feature is more marked and there are more sub-division of back segments in these languages or frontness prominent languages in which front segments are more various than back segments and more prominent in changes. Accordingly, Fuzhou can be deemed as frontness prominent dialect. As is known to all, Fuzhou is also rich in rounded vowels which play an active role in Fuzhou. Accordingly, it may be reasonable to call Fuzhou dialect a roundness prominent dialect.

5.4 Complex finals

Totally, there are 16 complex finals, including [ia], [ie], [ua], [uo], [yo], [au], [ai], [eu], [ui], [iu], [ei], [ou], [øy], [oy], [iau], [uai].

From the perspective of the diachronic changes, the rhymes mentioned above can be divided into the following types:

(1) Stable rhymes: ai, au

(2) Rhymes from splitting: i—ei y—øy u—ou

(3) Rhymes from the insertion of glides: a—ia

(4) Rhymes as the result of assimilation: yo

Of all the diphthongs, /ai/ and /au/ are the most stable ones. Why are these rhymes most unaffected of all the rhymes? It is noted that the vowel height difference between two segments in /ai/ and /au/ is the greatest, which may account for their stability in diachronic change, since the greater the sonority, the better to be nuclear. The same phenomenon of the stability of these two rhymes can also be observed in the Wenzhou dialect (Zhu 2013).

The diphthongs of [ei], [øy] and [ou] on the surface in Fuzhou are most interesting for their complementary distribution with the corresponding high vowels. Are the diphthongs [ei], [ou], [øy] observed on the surface the same finals underlyingly? According to Chen (1998: 12), the diphthongs [ei], [ou] and [øy] play a double role: on the one hand, they serve as transformed final of the corresponding high vowels; on the other hand, they are original finals with their own transformed finals.

Apart from the complementary distribution of [ei], [ou] and [øy] as transformed finals with [i], [u], [y] as the original forms, there is an interesting question about [ei], [ou], [øy] which were labelled as 灯,钉,东 as the original finals whether they experience the development from monothong to diphthong or the reverse development? Chen (1998: 83) provides a parallel comparison of the cognate 灯 in sub-dialects of Eastern Min as (20):

(20)	Cognates	AC	MC	Fuzhou	Fuqing	Longtian	Tangdong
	灯 "light"	tɯːŋ	təŋ	eiŋ	e^{i}ŋ	eŋ	eIŋ

Chen Zeping proposes that according to the synchronic observation about the cognate 灯 in sub-dialects of Eastern Min, the patterning of this cognate such as

灯(light) in Fuzhou as [eiŋ], [eŋ] in Longtian, [eɪŋ] in Tangdong and [eᴵŋ] in Fuqing implies that the final of this cognate 灯 (light) as an original final also underwent changes from monothong to diphthong when the high vowels as original finals began to come into the complementary distribution with diphthongs as the corresponding transformed finals. Chen (1998: 89) puts forward that the diphthongization of the rhymes of 灯,钉,东 also happens in VC counterparts of these finals, which forms the VVC structure as a result of the insertion of glides rather than the splitting of high vowels. Chen Zeping's proposal is very interesting and enlightening. But there is some problem about this proposal: why is the process supposed from the monothong to diphthong such as [eᴵŋ] - [eᴵŋ] - [eɪŋ] - [eiŋ] instead of the reverse from diphthong to monothong as it is generally observed that it is usually the diphthongs evolving to be monothongs in the diachronic process as in the case of Wu dialects? As in (20), according to the reconstruction of this cognate in Ancient Chinese which was a long vowel and Middle Chinese which was a short vowel, it is hard to suppose whether the contemporary form of 灯 (light) in Fuzhou [eiŋ] is the result of monothong or diphthong since Min is considered to be split from Proto-Chinese ahead of the other Chinese dialects which are thought to split from Middle Chinese. Accordingly, this question needs further probing when more data are available.

5.4.1 GV structure and GVV structure

The syllabic status of the prenuclear glides has been the topic of many Chinese linguistic studies. Zhang Jisheng (2006: 62) claims that the prenuclear glides in Shaoxing are not in the initials and are also not in the nuclear constituent due to the fact that they are not in the rhyming unit as in Mandarin as well as the fact that they are not TBU since they are non-moraic (Howie 1976). Then how about the syllabic status of the prenuclear glide in Fuzhou dialect? How to account for the glides on the surface in Fuzhou?

5.4.1.1 Glide /y/

In the Fuzhou dialect, there are totally seventeen GV(X) structures, and the glides involved in them include [i], [u] and [y]. The rhymes include:

(21)	iɛ	iɛʔ	iɛŋ	ia	iaʔ	iaŋ	iau
	uo	uoʔ	uoŋ	ua	uaʔ	uaŋ	uai
	yo	yoʔ	yoŋ				

Of the three glides, [i] and [u] are common glides in ancient Chinese phonology while [y] is not (Tang 2013: 34). Then is the glide [y] an underlying form in Fuzhou? Chen (1998: 87) points out that the finals with [y] as the preglide most likely came from Dang She and Shan She in Middle Chinese, the glide of which was [i]. This can find the evidence from the *Fuzhou Dictionary* published in 1870, in which this glide was spelled as [i]. Then this glide was assimilated by the rounded feature of the nuclear vowel /o/ and turned to [y]. Here is an example that indicates the rounding process of this glide under the assimilation of the nuclear vowel, as follows (Wu 2010:318):

(22)	Cognates	Zherong	Shouning	Fuqing	Quanzhou	Zhangzhou	Shantou
	借 "borrow"	tsyøʔ	tsyø	tsyoʔ	tsioʔ	tsioʔ	tsioʔ
	略 "omit"	lyøk		lyoʔ	lioʔ	lioʔ	lioʔ
	著 "write"	tyøʔ	tyøʔ	tyo/tyoʔ	tioʔ	tioʔ	tioʔ
	脚 "leg"	kyøk	kyøʔ	kyo	kioʔ	kioʔ	kioʔ

It is clear from these cognates that the glide of these cognates in Fuzhou has been assimilated by the nuclear vowel in terms of the feature of roundness when the glide of the corresponding rhyme in the other sub-dialects of Eastern Min still retains [i].

Alongside of these diachronic changes from [i] to be [y], there is some synchronic evidence which can further support that the surface [y] may have another source. In the east suburb of Fuzhou ranging from Min'an County (闽安县) in the south to Lianjiang County (连江县) in the north, the finals which are pronounced as [-uoŋ], [uoʔ] in the rural part of Fuzhou are pronounced as

[-yoŋ], [yoʔ] when following the coronal initials, for example (Chen 1998: 73):

(23)

Regions	砖 "brick"	川 "river"	箱 "box"	张 "surname"	粮 "grain"
East Suburb	tsyoŋ55	tshyoŋ55	syoŋ55	tyoŋ55	nyoŋ53
Rural	tsuoŋ55	tshuoŋ55	suoŋ55	tuoŋ55	nuoŋ53

It is found that [yoŋ] in East Suburb finds its counterpart as [uoŋ] in Rural area. Chen (1998: 74) puts forward the opinion that the pronunciation of rural area conforms to that of *Qi Lin Ba Yin*① about three hundred years ago. The similar alternation between [u] and [y] can also be found in Wu (2010: 314)

(24)

Cognates	Zherong	Shouning	Ningde	Minqing	Yongtai	Fuzhou
借 "borrow"	tsyøʔ		tsyøʔ	tsyoʔ	tsuoʔ	tsuoʔ
席 "mat"	tshyøʔ	tshyøʔ	tshyøʔ	tsyoʔ	tshuoʔ	tshuoʔ
石 "stone"	syøʔ	syøʔ	syøʔ	syoʔ	suoʔ	suoʔ

Why does the preglide [u] turn to be [y] when following the coronal initials in the case of [-uoŋ], [uoʔ]? Here I propose this is a means to meet the correlation between initials and finals.

5.4.1.2 Inserted glide

Chen Zeping (2010: 65) proposes that the rhymes of 嘉 and 山 in *Qi Lin Ba Yin* of 1870 were pronounced as [a, aʔ, aŋ, ak]. In the urban area of Fuzhou, the final [au] directly follows the affricate initials, while the same final and the same initial are broken up by an inserted glide in the suburb area of Fuzhou such as Lingtou, Hongliao north to Fuzhou, which is indicated by the following examples:

---

① *Qi Lin Ba Yin*: The earliest rhyme book known on the Fuzhou dialect was compiled by a military official, Qi Jiguang (戚继光), who is often referred to as Qi Canjun or Qi Canjiang according to his military title. One of the few sources that provide background information on this dictionary is Luo (1956), who referred this dictionary as *Ba Yin Zi Yi Bian Lan* (《八音字义便览》) "eight – sounds + word – meaning – convenient – reading" (Chan 1985).

(25)

Cognates	Mandarin	Fuzhou	
		Urban Areas	Suburb Areas
糟 "bad"	sao^{55}	tsau^{55}	tsiau^{55}
巢 "nest"	ɕao^{35}	tsau^{53}	tsiau^{53}
臭 "stinky"	ɕou^{51}	tsau^{213}	tsiau^{213}

According to Chen (1998: 74) the pronunciation in the urban areas is the same as that in the *Rhyme Book of Fuzhou* about one hundred years ago, and the pronunciation in the suburb areas is a new innovation. Since this glide only appears after the affricate initial, this is deemed as an inserted glide. What is the reason for the insertion of [i] when following the affricate initial in this final? This will be further discussed in the following section.

With the insertion of the preglide in Fuzhou, there is also an insertion of off-glide. For example, the Ge (歌韵) Final in Fuzhou includes such words as 大 tuai^{242}(big), 我 ŋuai^{33}(I/me), as follows:

(26)

Cognates	Eastern Min	Northern Min	Southern Min	Mandarin
	Fuzhou	Jianyang	Quanzhou	
大 "big"	tuai^{242}	tue^{43}	tua^{41}	ta^{51}
我 "I/me"	ŋuai^{33}	ŋue^{31}	gua^{55}	wo^{213}

It is observable that Fuzhou contains GVG when Northern Min as well as Southern Min retain GV and Mandarin has V. This final in Fuzhou came into being from * ɑ-o-uo-uai. Accordingly, Fuzhou is noted for its insertion of off-glide [i] which is not found in other sub-dialects of Min.

5.4.1.3 Preserved glide

The Fuzhou dialect is noted for its preservation of glides in Middle Chinese, for example the glides in [ia], [ua], [uo] and [ie] all correspond to those in Middle Chinese (Chen 1998: 61 - 62). The minute change of these rhymes is the adjustment of nuclear vowel in the rhymes. This change can be deemed as phonetic change. It is also observable that the preglide [u] in -uei and -uən that has disappeared in Mandarin still exists in Fuzhou, as follows:

(27)

Cognates	Middle Chinese	Fuzhou	Mandarin
杯 "cup"	uɒi	pui	pei
背 "back"		pui	pei
梅 "plum"		mui	mei
飞 "fly"	iĭwəi	hui	fei
肥 "fat"		hui	fei
尾 "tail"		ui	wei

There is a tendency in Chinese dialects: the disappearing of preglide u in -uei and -uən is related to initials: the glide u is the easiest to disappear when following the labial initial p, and the glide remains most stable when following the dorsal initial (Zhang Guangyu 2006). Why does this glide remain following the labial initial in Fuzhou? In this book, it is proposed that the preservation of glide following the labial initial is due to the markedness preservation to highlight the labial initial, which is similar to the insertion of high front glide [i] following the sibilant consonant as mentioned.

5.4.1.4 Vocalic glide or consonantal glide

Zhang Jisheng (2006: 64) proposes that only the falling VG is a real diphthong, and the rising GV is not a diphthong in Mandarin or many other Chinese dialects. What is the phonological status of the preglide of Fuzhou? Is GV structure [ie] in Fuzhou also not a diphthong?

In a dialect investigation conducted by Peking University in 1989, it is found that the preglides in Fuzhou, as well as in Xiamen dialect, Chaozhou dialect, and Jianou dialect of Min do not show the short duration as observed in the other Chinese dialects, and concludes that the preglides in these Min dialects are not consonantal. Are all the preglides in Fuzhou vocalic? For the preglide [i] in Fuzhou, there are also two kinds of glides, namely vocalic and consonantal glides co-exist. As discussed above, the perglide [i] is only inserted between the affricate initial and the rhyme [au] in the suburb area of Fuzhou such as Lingtou, Hongliao north to Fuzhou. The preglide [i] in this case is a consonantal glide, since it only follows the affricate initial. While the preglide [i] in [ie] is vocalic essentially, since this final can follow any kind of initial in Fuzhou, as indicated as follows:

(28)

Initial Finals	ie	ieŋ	ieʔ
p, pʰ, m	√ (except /m/)	√	√
t, tʰ, n	√	√	√
ts, tsʰ, s	√	√	√
k, kʰ, ŋ, h, 0	√	√	√

5.4.2 Finals ending with nasals

The evolution of VN structure in Chinese dialects is complicated not only in the changes of main vowel and nasal codas, but also in the relationship between nasal codas and nuclear vowels as well as the markedness of syllable structures.

Fuzhou did go through considerable phonological changes, especially in its finals. For example, the rich variety of consonant codas in Middle Chinese has disappeared, such as [n], [m], [p], [t], and [k]. The only two consonant codas that can be observed in Fuzhou now are [ʔ] and [ŋ].

Synchronically, the finals with nasal codas in Fuzhou include the forms, as follows (Chen 1998):

(29)

I		II	
aŋ		iŋ(eiŋ)	eiŋ(aiŋ)
iaŋ	ieŋ	uŋ(ouŋ)	ouŋ(auŋ)
uaŋ	uoŋ	yŋ(øyŋ)	øyŋ(oyŋ)
yoŋ			

It is noted that the finals ending with nasal codas are divided into two groups, namely those that go through final alternation and those that do not. In contrast with the rich variety of nasal codas in Southern Min, the nasal coda of Fuzhou is much simpler, that is the co-existence of three nasal codas from Middle Chinese has been replaced by the dominance of the velar nasal in Fuzhou. What is also interesting is that there is only one vowel that can independently be followed by the nasal coda, namely the low vowel. The three cases of high vowels followed by the nasal codas are not the independent finals but in complementary distribution with the related transformed diphthongs under different tones. Furthermore, the vowels followed by the nasal codas tend to be diphthongs.

5.4.2.1 Merger of nasal codas in Eastern Min

Coronal is said to be the most unmarked in many languages (Kiparsky 1985; McCarthy & Taub 1992). De Lacy (2006) also proposes a universal markedness hierarchy that sees coronal as being less marked than labial or dorsal. Place neutralizations are argued to have only two possible outputs, namely coronal and glottal. De Lacy (2006: 355) makes a clear prediction concerning the type of place neutralizations that are claimed to be not possible as synchronic rules: "No language ever ... neutralizes PoA to dorsal ..." The apparent cases of neutralization to dorsal that have been discussed in the literature (e.g. Rice 1996) can be explained in other ways such as historical perspective (De Lacy 2006). The case of Fuzhou which is deemed as "an even more gapped system" by De Lacy (2006) is one example in which three nasal codas have coalesced into the velar nasal. In fact, Rice (2007: 89) proposes that there are languages that neutralize the three-way place contrast among nasals to the velar nasal. There are also some similar examples in Chinese dialects. For example, the three nasal codas of the Wu dialect had merged to be velar nasal coda as far as the 15th century (Dai 2005). This conforms to the observation in Ye (2011), who compares 140 Chinese dialects and finds out that the most frequent nasal in Chinese dialects is the velar nasal which is about 97.1% among all the surveyed dialects, which is followed by the coronal nasal that is about 70.7%. Why is the velar nasal most preferable as the coda of a syllable in

Chinese dialects? From the perspective of place of articulation, the dorsal is more marked compared with the coronal. While Rice (1999) proposes that there are many dimensions of markedness, which do not necessarily converge on a single target cross-linguistically. For example, in the case of glottal stop, it is low marked on the * Place scale. But in other respects glottal stop can be a marked consonant, since it is not very perceptible. So glottal stop is unmarked in production terms but marked in perceptual terms. Therefore, glottal stop is unmarked on one dimension and marked on another (Lombardi 2002). Recently it has also been pointed out that any of the major places of articulation (labial, coronal, dorsal) can pattern as unmarked in some language, if one employs standard markedness diagnostics (Hume & Tserdanelis 2002; Hume 2003; Vaux 2003: 397). The markedness of the dorsal is concerned with the syllable position. In contrast with initials which prefer segments with lower sonority over those with higher sonority (De Lacy 2000; Smith 2002), codas prefer higher sonority elements over lower sonority ones. Zhang Jisheng (2007) points out the velar nasal coda is relatively unmarked than the coronal nasal as well as the labial nasal in his analysis of the markedness of codas of Chinese dialects. According to Torre (2003: 51 - 59), many cross-linguistic evidences prove that the labial consonant is more consonantal while the velar consonant is more vocalic and the velar consonant is relatively more sonorant than the labial consonant. Zhang (2012) also puts forward that the further back a nasal consonant is articulated, the less "consonantal" it is. Hence in the position of the coda of a rhyme which has a preference for the more sonorant element, the velar nasal which is more sonorant than coronal nasal coda and labial nasal coda is preferable. This may account for why the velar nasal is the most frequent nasal coda in Chinese dialects as well as the preferred merger target of nasal codas in Eastern Min.

Besides the coalescence of the nasal codas, the vowels preceding the nasal coda in Eastern Min display the tendency of diphthongization. As shown, the low vowel is the only vowel that can be an independent final with the nasal coda, which is in contrast with other Min dialects such as Putian in which all the vowels can precede the velar nasal as independent finals, such as [œŋ], [ɛŋ], [oŋ]. In addition to the low vowel as the nuclear, the other finals that can be followed by the velar nasal coda in Fuzhou are most diphthongs, as follows (Chen 1998: 63):

(30)

Cognates	Middle Chinese	Fuzhou
朋 "friend"	ĭəŋ	eiŋ/aiŋ
登 "climb"		
腾 "prance"		
萌 "cute"	ɐŋ	
烹 "cook"		
冷 "cold"		
办 "do"	æn	
斑 "spot"		
板 "plank"		
剪 "scissor"	ĭɛn/ien	
填 "fill"		
边 "edge"		
沉 "sink"	ĭən	
森 "woods"		
赚 "earn"	ɐm	
减 "subtract"		

The comparison of cognates of sub-dialects in Eastern Min can help reveal that VGN structure in Fuzhou finds parallel structure in VN structure of the other sub-dialects in Eastern Min, as indicated in Du (2014: 42):

(31)

Cognates	East Min				
	Fuzhou	Gutian	Zherong	Fuan	Ningde
闲 "idle"	ɛiŋ	eiŋ	ɛŋ	ɛiŋ	ɛŋ
糖 "sugar"	t^houŋ	t^houŋ	t^hɔŋ	t^hɔuŋ	t^hɔŋ
工 "work"	køyŋ	køyŋ	kœŋ	kœŋ	kœŋ

These cognates are noted in that the falling diphthongs are allowed in VN as nuclear, which is in contrast with the syllable structure of Chinese which is CMVE, namely onset + glide + nuclear + coda and the nuclear is usually the single vowel.

Why are only the low vowel and certain diphthongs allowed before the nasal coda? In this book, it is proposed that this is related to the requirement of the sonority of the nuclear vowel in Fuzhou that is more sonorous, more suitable to be nuclear. This will be attested in the following section.

5.4.3 Vʔ

As is well known, the syllables in Middle Chinese allowed a number of coda consonants, including [p], [t] and [k] (Wang 1963, 1985; Zhan 1991; Liu 2001; Zhang Jisheng 2006). During the diachronic process, the preservation of these coda consonants varies from dialect to dialect. Quanzhou nowadays still preserves four coda consonants; Mandarin misses all other consonants, except [n] and [ŋ]. In terms of the stop coda, in the Fuzhou dialect, there is only the existence of [ʔ] synchronically. In the dictionary of Fuzhou dialect in 1870, two oral stop codas such as [k] and [ʔ] could still be found. Chen (1998) provides the co-existence of two consonant codas more than one hundred years ago, as follows:

(32)

I	aʔ	ɛʔ	ɔʔ	øʔ/aøʔ	iʔ/eiʔ	
	iaʔ	ieʔ	ioʔ		uʔ/ouʔ	
	uaʔ		uoʔ		yʔ/øyʔ	
II	ak				ik/eik	eik/aik
	iak	iek	iok		uk/ouk	

There is some observation about the codas of Fuzhou over two hundred years. It is clear that the dorsal consonant coda following the middle vowels turned to the glottal stop earlier than that following the low vowel. What led to such difference?

The merger of the stop codas in Fuzhou is not a one-step process. By the time of *Qi Lin Ba Yin* rhyme dictionary of the sixteenth century, the coronal stop coda ∗-t and the dorsal stop coda ∗-k merged first, leaving the labial stop coda ∗-p behind. All three final stops merged by the time of *Zhuyu Tongsheng* rhyme dictionary a century later. Through further diachronic attrition, the syllable-final stops were finally reduced to the glottal stop seen in the contemporary Fuzhou dialect. However, what is interesting is that different segmental phonology of the finals with glottal stop still exhibit that the glottal stop has two sources, namely from classical Fuzhou ∗-ʔ and ∗-k (Chan 1985, 1990, 1996; Bao 2000). What is the status of the glottal stop in Fuzhou? Is it still a full segment? Is it moraic? It is believed that the weight of coda consonants is parameterized on a language-specific basis: some languages assign weight to coda consonants, in others, coda consonants are weightless. (e.g. Hyman 1985; Zec 1988; Hayes 1989) The weight status of the syllable-final stop also differs from Chinese dialect to dialect. In Cantonese, the syllable-final stop is weightless when it follows a long vowel, for example, [ta:p] "pile" (see Yip 1996, 2002; Zhang Jisheng 2006:79). For the status of the glottal stop in Fuzhou, Chan (1990) argues that the glottal stop derived from ∗-k occupies the nuclear position in Fuzhou. Chan (1996: 279) assumes that [ʔ] in [pɑʔ^5] is a disappearing glottal stop that occupies the same position as an off-glide in the nucleus, forming an open syllable so that it has the same length as an open syllable ending in a vowel. To support Chan's view, there are some facts that show the glottal stop occupies the nuclear position in Fuzhou, as follows (Chen 1998):

(33)

Example	Meaning	Word Splitting	Example	Meaning	Word Splitting
a. 吊	hang	tau—ta lau	e. 卷	reel	kuoŋ—kuo luoŋ
b. 塌	collapse	tʰaʔ—tʰa laʔ	f. 缠	twine	tieŋ—tie lieŋ
c. 腆	rich	tʰaiŋ—tʰa laiŋ	g. 夹	clip	keiʔ—ke leiʔ
d. 环	ring	kʰuaŋ—kʰua luaŋ	h. 拂	whisk	xouʔ—xo louʔ

These are some examples of word-splitting in the Fuzhou dialect, in which some monothongs can be split into two syllables to make them more vivid. The rules for such splitting are as follows: the portion from initials to the nuclear vowel in the original word is preserved for the first syllable in word splitting, and the second syllable retains the final part of the original syllable with [l] as the initial of the second syllable (since tones are irrelevant here, they are dismissed in these cases). It is clear that the parts deleted in the first syllable include the offglide as in example (a), the glottal stop as in example (b), the nasal coda as in (c), as well as the offglide with following glottal stop or nasal stop. Chan (1985) proposes that the Fuzhou dialect is an iambic language. Accordingly, the deletion of the off-glide, the nasal coda, the glottal stop coda following the nuclear vowel in the first syllable in word splitting may be seen as a means to reduce the weight of the first syllable to meet the prosodic requirement of Fuzhou. The example (b) 塌 is worthy in indicating that the glottal stop occupies the same position as offglide, which means the moraic status of such glottal stop is similar to that of offglide or of the nasal coda. However, if the glottal stop in Fuzhou is included as a full segment in all cases, it can not account for the following phenomenon:

(34)

Example	Word Splitting	Example	Word Splitting
石板 "slate"	suoʔ peiŋ→suo βeiŋ	白糖 "sugar"	paʔ t^houŋ→pa louŋ
烛斗 "candle"	tsuoʔ tau→tsuo lau	曲尺 "gauge"	k^huoʔ ts^huoʔ→kuo zuoʔ
石狮 "a city"	suoʔ sai→suo lai	伯公 "uncle"	paʔ kuŋ→pa uŋ

This is the categorical transformation phenomenon that can still be observed in the synchronic Fuzhou dialect, in which the initial consonant of the second syllable will transform according to the final segment of the first syllable, and the category of the final segment of the first syllable determines the change of the first consonant of the second syllable. When the first syllable ends in a glottal stop, it is common that the categorical transformation does not happen in the second syllable, which means the glottal stop as a full segment impedes the process of categorical transformation. However, as the examples in (34) indicate, despite the fact that the first syllables in these examples bear glottal stop codas, the categorical transformation still happens to the second syllables. Therefore, it is not suitable to define all the glottal stops as full segments.

Based on the same data, Bao (2000) proposes that the offglide and the final consonant form a constituent coda and puts forward that the offglide in the coda makes it impossible to place the glottal stop in the nuclear position in rhymes such as εiʔ and ouʔ. Bao further proposes to interpret Chan's view as considering the glottal stop in Fuzhou as not a full segment, but a glottal feature, namely [constricted glottis] (Halle & Stevens 1971) on the nuclear vowel, whether simple or diphthongal, which has been suggested for Southern Min (cf. Li 1989; Yip 1994). However, if the glottal stop in Fuzhou is treated as glottal feature instead of a full segment, it can not account for the following cases:

(35)

Phrases	Categorical Transformation	Phrases	Categorical Transformation
合倍 "double"	haʔ pui→ haʔ pui	泼水 "splash"	phuaʔ tsui→ phuaʔ tsui
拾起 "pick up"	khaʔ-khi→ khaʔ-khi	罚徛 "punish"	huaʔ khie→huaʔ khie

If the glottal stop is a feature on the nuclear vowel, then all the first syllables in these cases end with vowels. Then why do the second syllables in these examples not undergo the categorical transformation? Therefore, it is not reasonable to consider all the glottal stops just a feature on nuclear vowels.

It is clear that there are two kinds of glottal stops in Fuzhou: a loose glottal stop and a close glottal stop. The syllables with a loose final [ʔ] behave as though they end in a vowel or a glide, while syllables with a close [ʔ] coda behave as having a true consonant coda. It is suggested that two states of the glottal stops ask for two specification for them: for the close glottal stop, it is a full segment, while for the loose glottal stop, it has further been reduced to be feature hanging on nuclear vowels. Two states of glottal stop reveal the different reduction process of glottal stops. Accordingly, the glottal stops in Fuzhou can not be labeled under one category such as a feature or a full segment. The specific status of these glottal stops are dependent on their phonological behavior. This conforms to the view that most cross-linguistic variation in weight criteria is attributed to the parameterized application of Weight-by-Position to codas on a language-specific basis (Hayes 1989).

5.5 Phonological changes of the finals of Fuzhou

Fuzhou is remarkable for its complexity in sound changes in terms of tones, initials and finals, as discussed in Chen (1998), Feng (1998), Yuan (2010), etc. This sub-section will focus on the discussion of the sound changes of finals undergoing in Fuzhou.

5.5.1 Final alternation of Fuzhou

This section deals with the phonological motivation for the final alternation in Fuzhou. For the original finals and transformed finals in final alternation, there is some debate about which is the underlying form. In the analysis such as Yuan et al. (1989), Chao (1934), and Chan (1985, 1996), the original finals are taken as underlying, from which the transformed finals are derived; in some other analysis the transformed finals are taken as basic, and the original finals are derived accordingly (see Yip 1980; Wright 1983). In our analysis, we are supportive of the view held in Yuan et al. (1989), Chao (1934), and Chan (1985,1996) that the original finals are taken as underlying, from which the transformed finals are derived. Chen (1998: 79 – 84) makes a list of nineteen sub-dialects of Eastern Min, fourteen of which exhibit the final alternation phenomenon while four of which do not. Based on the comparison of these sub-dialects of Eastern Min, Chen Zeping concludes that the original finals are the basic form, from which the transformed finals come into being. Accordingly, the proposal that chooses the original final as underlying form is more in accordance with the diachronic development of this pervasive phenomenon in Eastern Min.

For the final alternation, the first glance of final alternation in Fuzhou may lead to the conclusion that the final alternation in Fuzhou is just a phenomenon of high vowel splitting, as indicated in the following table:

(36)	i/ei	u/ou	y/øy	iʔ/eiʔ	uʔ/ouʔ	yʔ/øyʔ	iŋ/eiŋ	uŋ/ouŋ	yŋ/øyŋ
			øy/œy	eiʔ/aiʔ	ouʔ/auʔ	øyʔ/œyʔ	eiŋ/aiŋ	ouŋ/auŋ	øyŋ/œyŋ

It is clear that all three high vowels are accompanied with diphthongs which are often the result of high vowel splitting. The high vowel splitting is a quite common diachronic phenomenon. Chomsky & Halle (1968) put forward that the diphthongization of high vowels often triggers the raising of the middle vowels and the low vowel. Schane (1984) proposes the Particle Analysis which holds that the raising of the middle vowels pushes the vowel shift, which is called pushing chain. Is the high vowel splitting in Fuzhou the result of the pulling chain? Here we propose that high vowel splitting in Fuzhou is not the result of the pulling chain since the high vowel splitting in Fuzhou did not lead to the raising of the middle vowels. Chen (1998) puts forward the view that the high vowel splitting that resulted in the distribution of two sets of finals under different tones is a new phenomenon which did not come into being until 300 years ago. The high vowel splitting was not accompanied by the raising of the middle vowels such as [e] and [o]. Instead, this phenomenon was accompanied by the lowering of the middle vowels, for example, the lowering of the middle high vowel [e] to the middle low vowel [ɛ]. A comparison of the final system about three hundred years ago and the synchronic final system (Chen 1998: 88-90) reveals that the synchronic final [ɛ] dates back to [e] three hundred years ago.

Then is the final alternation triggered by initial or coda? Peng (2008) proposes the physiological reason for the splitting of [u] following the coronal stop initial and affricate initial in the Xiang dialect, which, however, can not account for the splitting of the other high vowels. Xu (1996) suggests that it was the deletion of coronal nasal coda that led to the vowel shift. The high vowel splitting in Fuzhou has nothing to do with initial as well as coda.

In fact, with more final alternation in different sub-dialects of Eastern Min considered, it is found that final alternation as a pervasive phenomenon in Eastern Min is more various than just high vowel splitting, as follows:

Fuqing dialect: original final vs transformed final (Feng 1993: 35)

(37) i/e u/o y/ø e/ɛ o/ɔ ø/œ eu/ɛu
iʔ/eʔ uʔ/oʔ yʔ/øʔ eʔ/ɔʔ oʔ/ɔʔ øʔ/ŋʔ oi/ɔi
iŋ/eŋ uŋ/oŋ yŋ/øŋ eŋ/ɛŋ oŋ/ɔŋ øŋ/œŋ

Fu'an dialect: original final vs transformed final (Lan 1999)

(38) i/ei u/ou i/øi ui/oi øi/ɔi eu/ɛu iu/eiu
iŋ/eiŋ uŋ/ouŋ iŋ/øŋ ouŋ/ɔuŋ øŋ/œŋ eiŋ/aiŋ
ik/eik uk/ouk ik/øk ouk/ɔuk øk/œk eik/ɛik

Ningde dialect: original final vs transformed final

(39) i/ei u/ou y/øy iu/eu ui/oi iŋ/eŋ uŋ/oŋ yŋ/øŋ iŋ/eŋ uŋ/oŋ yŋ/øŋ

With the final alternation in Fuzhou, Fuqing, Fu'an and Ningde taken into consideration, it is clear that final alternation includes not only high vowel splitting, but also vowel lowering. Then what is the essence of final alternation in Fuzhou as well as in other sub-dialects of Eastern Min? In the previous research about this phenomenon, there is much argument for the view point that this final alternation is triggered by tones, such as Chen (1998). With more data on final alternation in Eastern Min taken into consideration, it is found that the tones accompanying final alternation may be simple tones (such as Fuqing) or complex tones (such as Fuzhou), high tones (Ningde) or low tones (Fuqing). Therefore, the perspective from tones either directly or indirectly can not account for this phenomenon. Is there any other possible approach to account for the vowel splitting of Fuzhou?

Zhu (2013: 109) proposes the requirement for the sonority of nuclear vowels in Wenzhou, which is enlightening for the case of the high vowel splitting of Fuzhou. The preference of vowels of higher sonority can also be observed in the diachronic development of vowel system of Fuzhou as discussed in Chen (1998) which proposes that the middle high vowel such as [e] has lowered to be [ɛ]. While the relation between the vowel alternation and sonority requirement of nuclear vowels can not account for why the vowel alternation only happen in the final position of a prosodic phrase, and when it comes to the non-final position, the transformed final turns back to the original rhyme as indicated in Chen (1998).

In this book, it is proposed that such final alternation in Fuzhou is related to the prosodic prominence of this language. The prosodic prominence of a language is usually manifested in forms such as pitch, duration or intensity, or the combined effect of these parameters. The prosodic prominent position may occur in the initial position, final position or the root of words (Trubetzkoy 1969; Beckman 1997; Crosswhite 2001; Smith 2002; Barnes 2002; Rachel 2011). As a common position of prosodic prominence, the final position of a prosodic unit is known for its lengthening of duration in many languages. The lengthening of duration is quite potential as a phonetic effect in different languages, but the realization of it is language-specific. Zhang (2001) puts forward that the contour tones tend to occur in the final syllable of words, since the duration of the final position better satisfies the requirement of duration of contour tones. The duration of vowels is related to the qualities of vowels, and the research of experimental phonetics (Nearey 1978) indicates that the duration of high vowel is shorter than that of low vowel, and the lower the vowel is, the longer the duration is. Some languages have special requirement for the qualities of the vowels that occur in the final position due to the characteristics of the duration of the final syllable. Some vowels turn to the vowels of greater sonority to meet the duration requirement of the final syllable. For example, in Bare, the high vowel in the final position will split to be [ie]. In these languages, the vowels turn to lower vowels to increase the sonority to satisfy the duration requirement of the final syllable, which is described as positional augmentation in Smith (2002) and such augmentation usually occurs in some prosodically strong positions (Barnes 2002: 242 – 244). In Fuzhou as well as the other sub-dialects that have complementary distribution between the original rhyme and the transformed rhyme, the new addition of vowels, namely the transformed rhymes, can only be realized in the final syllable, and the complete contrasts of new and old vowels can be accommodated in the final position, and the pre-terminal position can only host the contrasts of the underlying vowels. Hence it is proposed that the categorical vowel alternation in the final syllable in Fuzhou as well as the other sub-dialects of Eastern Min may be related to the prosodic prominence of this language. To support such hypothesis, it is necessary to investigate whether the duration of the final syllable in Fuzhou as well as the other sub-dialects show the significant lengthening. Wright (1983) indicates that phonetically, rhymes are shorter in non-final positions in Fuzhou. To further find out whether the lengthening of the final syllable in a prosodic phrase is a pervasive phenomenon in East Min, which is not influenced by the final position, we conducted a phonetic experiment to investigate the duration of the final syllable in a phonological phrase, excluding the influence of the final position. The experiment results are as follows:

(40)

Area	Result
Fuzhou	$F(1,158) = 17.145$, $p < 0.000$
Fuqing	$F(1,158) = 103.093$, $p < 0.000$
Fu'an	$F(1,158) = 42.067$, $p < 0.000$
Ningde	$F(1,158) = 208.831$, $p < 0.000$
Quanzhou (Southern Min)	$F(1,158) = 0.346$, $p < 0.000$

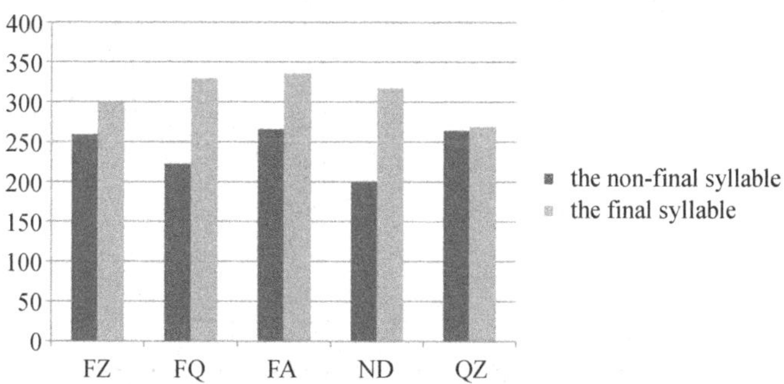

Diagram 5-6 Comparison of the duration between the non-final syllable and the final syllable

The comparison of duration of the final syllable and the non-final syllable in the domain of prosodic words indicates that the duration of the final syllable in four areas chosen from Eastern Min is significantly longer than that of the non-final syllable, which is not seen in Southern Min. Due to such significant correlation, it is argued that the alternation to be finals of greater sonority in the final syllable is closely related to the lengthening of duration of the final syllable. Here it is put forward that the final alternation triggered by the lengthening of duration is in the process, which has not been finally categorized phonologically. This may be the reason why this phenomenon has happened under certain tones instead of all tones. The reason why this phenomenon happened under certain tones instead of the other tones needs further investigation. Yet what is clear is that such rhyme alternation is not motivated directly by tones.

With the alternation between the original final and the transformed final in the synchronic Fuzhou vowel system, what is the possible result of such vowel complementary? One possible result of such vowel complementary is the rearrangement of vowel system. It is proposed that in the diachronic process, with the advent of splitting of /i/ to be the complementary distribution of [i] and [ei], it is quite likely that the finals with higher sonority will be more welcome in the final position whose longer duration greets more sonorant rhymes, just as the case in Fu'an (Dai 2008):

(41)

Area		Yinping	Yangping	Shangsheng	Yinqu	Yangqu
Fu'an	ei	碑"tomb" 知"know" 痴"silly"	脾"spleen" 皮"skin" 提"carry"		利"sharp" 智"witted" 记"memorize"	柿"persimmon" 地"floor" 技"skill"
	i			米"rice" 里"inside" 死"die"		
Fuzhou	ɛi				利智记	柿地技
	i	碑知痴	脾皮提	米里死		

As indicated, the final alternation in Fuzhou only happened under two tones such as Yinqu and Yangqu, while the final alternation for the same cognates happened under four tones in Fu'an. Therefore, it is predicted that the final alternation in Fuzhou may keep on evolving like that in Fu'an, ushering the more sonorant finals under all tones, or it may come into a halt just at this stage.

In fact, the increase of sonority of vowels under certain tones can also be seen from the following example: In *Qi Lin Ba Yin*, there are three finals, which have lowered under Yinqu, while Yangqu has become finals of greater sonority, as follows (Chen 1998: 77):

(42)

Xi(西)-Jia(嘉)		Gou(沟)-Jiao(郊)		Chu(初)-Ge(歌)	
街 $kɛ^{55}$ "street"	加 ka^{55} "add"	雕 teu^{55} "engrave"	兜 tau^{55} "pocket"	梳 $sœ^{55}$ "comb"	梭 so^{55} "shuttle"
蟹 xa^{242} "crab"	夏 xa^{242} "summer"	候 xau^{242} "wait"	校 xau^{242} "school"	初 $ts^hɔ^{213}$ "first"	糙 $ts^hɔ^{213}$ "rough"

As indicated, 街 $kɛ^{55}$ and 蟹 xa^{242} both belong to Final Xi (西), while the vowel of 蟹 xa^{242} which used to be [ɛ] has lowered to be [a], merging into Final Jia (嘉). The same situation can be found in the case of 雕 teu^{55} and 候 xau^{242} of Final Gou (沟).

5.5.2 Assimilation

Synchronically, there is one remarkable characteristic about diphthongs of Fuzhou, namely the assimilation of features in two parts of diphthongs, which are indicated as follows:

(43)	I	II	III	IV	V
	[ia]	[iu]	[ie]	[uo]	[eu]
	[ua]	[ui]	[ei]	[yo]	
	[au]			[oy]	
	[ai]			[øy]	
				[ou]	

It is observable that diphthongs from Column II to Column IV display the assimilation patterning in features of two parts of diphthongs. Three diphthongs such as [ei], [øy], [ou], [uo] are assimilated not only in terms of the feature [back] but also in terms of the feature [round]; [yo] and [oy] agree in the feature [round]; [iu] as well as [ui] agree in the feature of [high]. For the diphthong containing the low vowel, it will be discussed at the end of this section. Except the diphthongs from Column I to Column IV, there is one final [eu] in Column V which seems not to agree in neither of [back] nor [round], yet Chen (1998: 72 – 73) puts forward that there is an alternation between [eu] and [iu] in some areas of Fuzhou, which therefore does not influence the prominent feature assimilation of diphthongs in Fuzhou. Is such feature alignment in diphthongs a coincidence? How to account for such a assimilation patterning?

Duanmu (2000) proposes a harmony principle for combination of complex rhymes which holds that the [round] feature and the [back] feature of VX (X can either be glide or stop) must agree, namely the structures such as *[α back][-α back], *[α round][-α round] are not allowed by the harmony principle, with the physiological evidence which suggests that the speed of articulator is not fast enough to realize two segments with opposite features. The rising diphthongs and falling diphthongs in Fuzhou such as [ei], [øy], [ou] all conform to this harmony principle, agreeing not only in the feature of [backness] but also in [roundness]. Duanmu (2000) also proposes that the final harmony principle is based on contrastive specification (Steriade 1987). As discussed above, [round] as well as [back] are contrastive features in Fuzhou, which are responsible for triggering the rounding assimilation as well as the backing assimilation in Fuzhou.

For the agreement of feature of diphthongs, the comparison of cognates of Liu Final and Shao Final in the Fuzhou dialect as well as some sub-dialects may serve as a good illustrative example. These two finals were different in *Qi Lin Ba Yin* about three hundred years ago, but now the cognates of these two finals have merged to be the same in Fuzhou while they still keep contrast in other Eastern Min, indicated as follows (Chen 1998: 86):

(44)

Area	绸—潮		周—招		求—侨	
	"silk"	"tide"	"surname"	"recruit"	"beg"	"live abroad"
Fuzhou	tiu	tiu	tsiu	tsiu	kiu	kiu
Gutian	tiu	tiəu	tsiu	tsiəu	kiu	kiəu
Yangping	tiu	tieu	tsiu	tsieu	kiu	kieu

(45)

Area	辉—灰		肥—赔		翠—脆	
	"brilliant"	"ash"	"fat"	"compensate"	"green"	"crisp"
Fuzhou	xui	xui	pui	pui	tshui	tshui
Gutian	xui	xuəi	pui	puəi	tshui	tshuəi
Yangping	xui	xuoi	pui	puoi	tshui	tshuoi

The evolution of cognates of these two finals in different sub-dialects of Eastern Min displays that GVG in other sub-dialects of Eastern Min has transformed to be [ui] in Fuzhou. Here is another example of cognates as listed in Wu (2010: 318):

(46)

Cognates	Eastern Min			Southern Min		
	Zherong	Shouning	Fuqing	Quanzhou	Zhangzhou	Shantou
借 "borrow"	tsyøʔ	tsøyʔ	tsyoʔ	tsioʔ	tsioʔ	tsioʔ
略 "delete"	lyøk		lyoʔ	lioʔ	lioʔ	lioʔ
著 "write"	tyøʔ	tyøʔ	tyoʔ	tioʔ	tioʔ	tioʔ
脚 "leg"	(kyøk)	kyøʔ	kyo	kioʔ	kioʔ	kioʔ

As indicated, for these cognates, while Southern Min has such a rhyme form as [io], the sub-dialects of Eastern Min have the final forms with more feature agreement such as [yo], [yø]. In fact, the synchronic comparison of cognates of sub-dialects of Min may provide a better evidence for the assimilation of features of these finals, as follows:

(47)

Cognates	Middle Chinese	Quanzhou	Fuzhou
别 "farewell"	bɯiɛt	iat	ieʔ
言 "say"	ŋiɐn	ian	yɔŋ
歇 "rest"	hiɐt	ioʔ	yɔʔ
边 "edge"	pen	ian	ieŋ
节 "section"	tset	iat	ieʔ
全 "whole"	dz^{w}iɛn	uan	uɔʔ
沿 "along"	j^{w}iɛn	ian	yɔŋ
绝 "absolute"	dz^{w}iet	uat	uɔʔ
悦 "happy"	j^{w}iet	iat	yɔʔ
玄 "mysterious"	$ɦ^{w}$en	ian	ieŋ
血 "blood"	h^{w}et	iat	ieʔ
诀 "knack"	h^{w}et	uat	yɔʔ

As indicated, GVC structure in Fuzhou is noted for more agreement in features of GV, in contrast with those of Southern Min and Mandarin.

In fact, the feature agreement is not a sporadic characteristic of Fuzhou, which can be observed to occur in more final groups on the basis of the comparison of final groups of Fuzhou (Yuan 2010) and Quanzhou (Zeng 2013) as follows:

Table 5-5 Summary of assimilation of finals of Fuzhou

Rhyme	Quanzhou	Fuzhou
Qia Final II 洽韵	iap iap	eiʔ/ieʔ ieʔ
Yan Final III 盐韵	iam ian	ieʔ
Ye Final III 叶韵	iap iap/iʔ iat/iap iaʔ	ieʔ
Yan Final III 严韵	iam	ieŋ
Ye Final III 业韵	iap	ieʔ
Tie Final IV 帖韵	iap	ieʔ
Xian Final 仙韵	ian	ieŋ
	(ian)	yɔŋ
Xue Final 薛韵	iat	ieʔ
Yuan Final 元韵	ian	yɔŋ

Such a tendency of assimilation between preglides and nuclear vowels may also be responsible for the delinking of preglide in such reduction process as ai > oi > ue > e, which further lowered to be the monothong [ɛ] as discussed. This also accounts for why [œ] is the result of merger. It is assumed that there is a strong constraint that disprefers the co-existance of [+ feature] [-feature].

The low vowel can both combine with the front high unrounded glide [i] as well as the back high rounded glide [u]. The flexibility of the low vowel may be concerned with the feature specification of the low vowel. There is cross-linguistic evidence that specification of [back] for [a] differs from language to language (Ladefoged & Maddieson 1996). For example, [a] is a front vowel in the Cardinal Vowel System (Jones 1975); [a] is [+ back] in SPE (Chomsky & Halle 1968: 332); [a] in Shaoxing is unspecified for [back] (Zhang Jisheng 2006: 90). According to the phonological performance of the low vowel /a/ in Fuzhou, it is suggested that the low vowel in Fuzhou should be unspecified for the feature [backness], which accounts for its freedom in combination with glides.

5.6 Summary

This chapter provides a detailed analysis of the characteristics in phonology of Fuzhou finals. The patterning of Fuzhou finals can be summarized to have the following characteristics:

a. With regard to the simplex vowel system, Fuzhou is noted for its rich and systematic distribution of front vowels which are contrasted in [round] and [high]. The phonology system of Fuzhou displays the systematic preference for the more sonorant finals, which is also attested in the final alternation process triggered by the lengthening of the final syllable which brings about more sonorant finals.

b. Regarding the hierarchy of the contrastive features of the simplex vowels of Fuzhou, it is found that the hierarchy of the contrastive features of vowels is [low] > [round] > [high] > [back], which indicates the active role played by roundedness feature in the rounding assimilation in Fuzhou.

c. Regarding syllable structures, Fuzhou is noted to have marked syllable structure containing preglide as well as offglide such as GVG. The markedness of Fuzhou syllable structures is part of the preference for more weightier elements in Fuzhou phonological system. Besides, the diphthongs of Fuzhou are noted to have a remarkable assimilation especially in terms of [round] as well as [backness] feature. Such a markedness tendency of Fuzhou is also attested to be a systematic phenomenon rather than sporadic cases.

d. With respect to the phonological processes, Fuzhou is remarkably noted even among the Chinese dialects for its final alternation, which can still be observed synchronically. Besides, Fuzhou is also noted for manifesting an assimilation tendency especially in terms of [round] as well as [backness], which is found to be a systematic phenomenon rather than sporadic cases.

Chapter 6

Similarities and Differences of the Finals Between Quanzhou and Fuzhou

As discussed in Chapter 1, Quanzhou and Fuzhou are so different as to be divided into different dialect groups. How different are Quanzhou and Fuzhou in terms of finals? Are the finals of Quanzhou and Fuzhou remarkably different to contribute to the divergence of Quanzhou and Fuzhou? This chapter will be devoted to the analysis of the similarities and differences of Quanzhou and Fuzhou in terms of simple finals and complex finals from the perspective of the markedness of segments and syllable structures, after which the phonological processes of the two dialects will also be compared to have a more comprehensive view of the similarities and differences of the two dialects.

6.1 Comparison of markedness of simplex vowel inventories

In terms of the simplex vowel inventory, there are eight vowels in Quanzhou and seven vowels in Fuzhou, as indicated as follows:

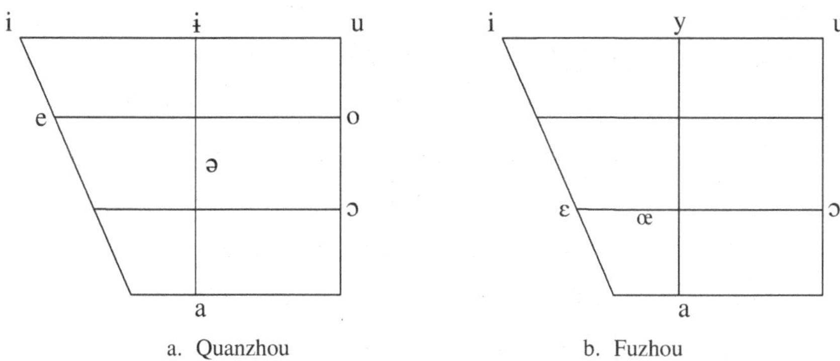

Diagram 6-1 Inventories of the simplex vowels of Quanzhou (a) and Fuzhou (b)

Cross-linguistically, a five-vowel inventory is more common, about 21.5% in UPSID, followed by a six-vowel inventory, about 13.6% (Maddieson 1984: 126). Yet the vowel inventories of Quanzhou and Fuzhou do not stray much from common vowel inventories as they are in accord with the observation about the vowel inventory size made in Maddieson (1984: 128) who mentions that in the samples of the languages surveyed almost two-thirds of the languages have between 5 and 7 vowels underlyingly, although up to 10 is still relatively common.

In the following section, the simplex-final vowels of Quanzhou and Fuzhou will be discussed from the perspectives of pattern of vowel inventory, sonority, roundedness, backness and height.

One common feature of phoneme inventories that is discussed in the context of vowel system is symmetry. A five-vowel inventory overwhelmingly has two front vowels and two back vowels balanced for height, while a seven-vowel system is strongly biased towards adding two second middle vowels in both the front and back planes (Grodon 2016: 65). It is noteworthy that the seven-vowel inventory of Quanzhou increases contrast by adding two schwas instead of the vowels of different heights. Schwa is typically simply added as an additional non-peripheral vowel without interacting with the spacing of the peripheral vowels (Grodon 2016: 62). The distribution of the simplex vowels in Quanzhou is accordingly noted for their symmetry from front to central to back. Clements (2003) provides an explicit formalization of the principles that lead to the formation of symmetrical inventories. According to the theory of feature economy in Clements (2003), which takes as a starting point long-standing observations about the structure of sound systems, languages prefer inventories that make maximal use of the minimum number of phonological features to expand their phoneme inventories (Grodon 2016: 65). The symmetric vowel inventory of Quanzhou which makes a maximal use of two basic parameters of backness and height of vowels just meets this observation. And the balanced and wide dispersion in the available phonetic space attested in the simplex vowel inventory of Quanzhou is also in line with the principle of vowel dispersion mentioned in Liljencrants & Lindblom (1972), Lindblom (1975), who propose that vowels tend to be evenly distributed in the available phonetic space and also widely distributed, within the limitations of the particular system (Maddieson 1984: 136).

In contrast with the simplex vowel inventory of Quanzhou, the simplex vowel inventory of Fuzhou are remarkable in its imbalance distribution of its vowel inventory. It is observed that the simplex vowel inventory of Fuzhou has a strong bias towards the front vowels including the unrounded front vowels and rounded front vowels in symmetric distribution, due to which the simplex vowel inventory of Fuzhou seems to be a remarkable front-vowel dominant language. For such imbalanced distribution of simplex vowels, the simplex vowel inventory of Fuzhou not only employs the basic vowel parameters such as backness and height but also the vowel heights, the evolution of which is reflected diachronically ranging from mid-high→mid-low as discussed in Chen (1998). Why does Fuzhou simplex vowel inventory have such disparity in terms of height? What is implied in the vowel height differences between Quanzhou and Fuzhou? Alongside with the parameters of height and backness, roundedness is another parameter employed by the vowel inventory of Fuzhou. The parameter of roundedness, though as a secondary vowel feature, plays a significant role in the simplex vowel inventory and the related phonological processes of Fuzhou.

With respect to sonority, the simplex vowels related to Quanzhou and

Fuzhou can be arranged according to the markedness in DTE as follows: ə, ɨ > i, u, y > e, o, ø > ɛ, ɔ, œ > a. This ranking indicates that the higher the sonority, the less marked in the position of DTE. In line with this sonority scale, the sonority hierarchy of the vowels in Quanzhou range from ə, ɨ > i, u, > e, o, > ɔ, > a and the vowels in Fuzhou cover the three stages of this sonority scale, namely i, u, y > ɔ, ɛ, œ > a, excluding the least sonorant vowels such as /ə/ and /ɨ/. It is clear that the simplex vowels in Fuzhou have greater sonority requirement than those of Quanzhou in excluding the lowest sonorant vowels such as /ə, ɨ/ in Quanzhou. Alongside with the higher demand of sonority of the simplex vowel inventory of Fuzhou, the higher demand of sonority in Fuzhou is also reflected in the systematic alternation between the original rhyme and the transformed rhyme under certain tones:

Table 6-1 Final alternation of Fuzhou

i/ei	u/ou	y/øy	iʔ/eiʔ	uʔ/ouʔ	yʔ/øyʔ	iŋ/ eiŋ	uŋ/ouŋ	yŋ/øyŋ
		øy/œy	eiʔ/aiʔ	ouʔ/auʔ	øyʔ/œyʔ	eiŋ/aiŋ	ouŋ/auŋ	øyŋ/œyŋ

It is seen that three high vowels in Fuzhou all alternate with their corresponding diphthongs irrespective of the syllable types.

De Lacy (2006) proposes that the rounded vowels are more marked than the unrounded vowels in light of feature geometry. From the perspective of roundedness, it is found that the Fuzhou dialect is rich in rounded vowels, which are not found in Quanzhou. The rounded vowels in Fuzhou not only include the less marked back rounded vowels such as /u, ɔ/, but also contain more marked front rounded vowels such as /y, œ/. Why does Fuzhou contain so many rounded vowels? In fact, a survey of vowel inventories of Min dialects can indicate that rounded vowels can only be found in Northern Min in a broad sense, which includes Eastern Min, Northern Min and Central Min, while the rounded vowels can not be found in Southern Min. What is responsible for such difference in terms of the existence of rounded vowels in Northern Min and Southern Min? It is possible to approach this question from the perspective of language contact. It is well-known that Eastern Min as well as some areas of

Northern Min are adjacent to the Southern Wu dialects such as the Wenzhou dialect. It is found that the Wenzhou dialect is noted for its rich variety of rounded vowels (Zhu 2013: 211). It is suggested that the rich variety of rounded simplex vowels in Fuzhou may be related to the influence of the Wenzhou dialect. In fact, there are some phonetic evidence for such speculation. This question can refer to Shi (2010).

In terms of backness, it is found that the simplex vowels in Quanzhou are quite symmetric, ranging from front vowels to central vowels to back vowels. In contrast, the Fuzhou dialect is noted for its rich variety of front vowels which range from high to middle to low range and are symmetric in terms of roundedness, as follows:

Table 6-2 Simplex vowel patterning of Quanzhou and Fuzhou

	Front		Central		Back	
	Quanzhou	Fuzhou	Quanzhou	Fuzhou	Quanzhou	Fuzhou
High	i	i, y	ɨ		u	u
Mid-high	e		ə		o	
Mid-low		ɛ, œ			ɔ	ɔ
Low			a	a		

Why does the Fuzhou dialect contain so many front vowels? There are controversial opinions as to whether front vowels are more marked or the back vowels are in Fuzhou. De Lacy (2006) proposes that back vowels are more marked than front vowels while Lombardi (2003) suggests that front vowels are more marked than back vowels. Rice (2007: 92) puts forward that the markedness of front vowels and back vowels are related to the contrasts of the phonological system of languages: if there are central vowels in this language, the unmarked vowel may be the central vowel; if there are only contrasts between front vowels and back vowels, either may be marked. As observed in the simplex vowel inventory of Fuzhou, there are no central vowels in Fuzhou, due to which it is unlikely to infer the markedness of front vowels and back vowels with reference to the central vowels. Rice (2007) defines the opposition between marked and unmarked in that marked elements appear in fewer grammars while unmarked elements appear in more grammars; marked elements cover smaller phonetic space while unmarked elements occupy larger phonetic space. That is, the marked member of a category may express fewer further morphological distinctions. Thus, in English pronouns, the unmarked singular distinguishes masculine, feminine, and neuter: he, she, and it. In the marked plural, no gender distinctions are expressed; instead, the only pronoun available is *they* (Bybee 2010: 134). In the same vein, the unmarked member of a phonological category may express more phonological distinctions. As observed, for front vowels in Fuzhou, there are more distinctions than back vowels, which accordingly indicates that front vowels are more unmarked in Fuzhou.

With respect to vowel height, it is clear that the Quanzhou dialect tends to have mid-high vowels while the Fuzhou dialect tends to have mid-low vowels /ɛ/ and /œ/. In fact, the simplex vowel inventory of Fuzhou about three hundred years ago revealed that the Fuzhou dialect had mid-high vowels /e/ and /ø/ instead of mid-low vowels /ɛ/ and /œ/ observed today (Chen 1998: 90). The preference of mid-low vowels /ɛ/ and /œ/ in Fuzhou are suggested to be related to sonority requirement of the Fuzhou dialect. Furthermore, the high vowels bear different importance in two dialects, namely two high vowels /i/ and /u/ in Quanzhou are often chosen as the results of the markedness reduction, while in Fuzhou three high vowels are forced to undergo the final alternations due to their low sonority, which result in their lack of the status as independent rhymes.

Based on the above discussion from the perspectives of roundedness, backness, height, sonority as well as the vowel inventory pattern, Quanzhou and Fuzhou have displayed more differences than similarities despite their common origin. To be more exact, the Fuzhou dialect is found to have more marked vowels than Quanzhou which tend to choose fewer marked vowels in terms of single vowel parameter. However, viewed contextually, the more marked vowels in Fuzhou turn to be less marked in the position of DTE while the unmarked vowels in Quanzhou show up as marked segments when they are in the position of DTE due to their different satisfaction of sonority requirement of DTE. Based on such a difference, it is proposed that the vowels of Quanzhou and Fuzhou are different in markedness, which needs to be considered both from the context-free perspective and from the contextual aspect. For these two dialects, which markedness mechanisms have more sway, markedness reduction or markedness preservation? What kind of tendency can be observed in terms of markedness mechanism about these two dialects? These questions will be further addressed in the following section.

6.2 Comparison of the hierarchies of contrastive features of vowels

The hierarchy of contrastive hypothesis holds that phonology computes only contrastive features, and only the contrastive features in a language are the triggers of related phonological processes. Contrastive features are assigned by language-particular feature hierarchies (Dresher 2009).

In accordance with the patterning of vowels in the related phonological processes, the hierarchy of contrastive features of vowels in Quanzhou is constructed as follows:

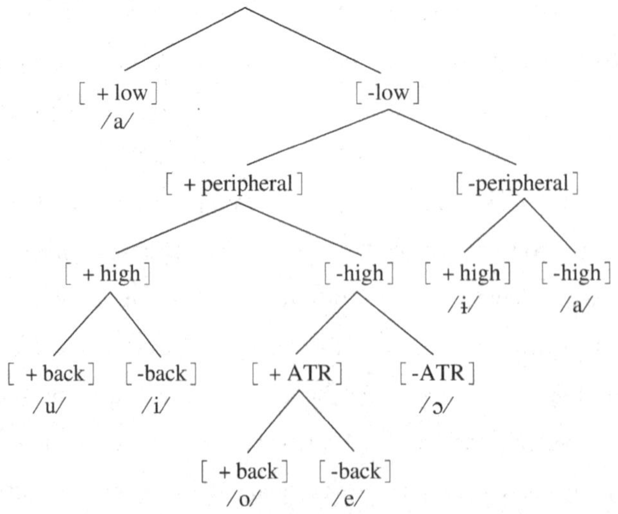

Diagram 6-2 Hierarchy of contrastive features of vowels in Quanzhou

Based on the related phonological processes of vowels in Fuzhou, the hierarchy of contrastive features of vowels in Fuzhou is established as follows:

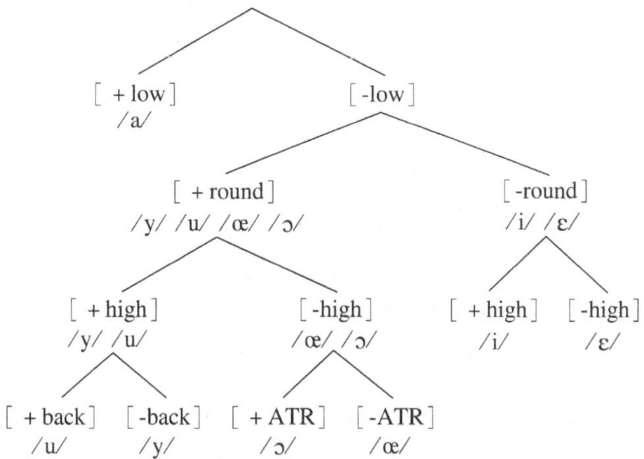

Diagram 6-3 Hierarchy of contrastive features of vowels in Fuzhou

In comparison of the contrastive hierarchies of vowels in Quanzhou and Fuzhou, it is clear that the vowels in two dialects are similar in the specification of the main parameter of vowel height, namely the feature [low]. This is in accord with the observation about the unmarkedness of the low vowel as discussed in Maddieson (1984).

But as indicated in the hierarchies of the two dialects, the vowel systems of Quanzhou and Fuzhou are noted for more differences than similarities: to begin with, two dialects bear specification of some contrastive features unique to their own systems, as follows:

Table 6-3 Specification of contrastive features of the simplex vowels in Quanzhou

	a	i	ɨ	u	e	ə	o	ɔ
[low]	+				-	-	-	-
[peripheral]		+	-	+	+	-	+	+
[ATR]							+	-
[high]		+	+	+	-	-	-	-
[back]		-		+	-		+	

Alongside of the specification of contrastive features of the simplex vowels in Quanzhou presented in Table 6-3, the specification of contrastive features of the vowels in Fuzhou is listed in Table 6-4, as follows:

Table 6-4 Specification of contrastive features of the vowels in Fuzhou

	a	i	y	u	ɛ	œ	ɔ
[low]	+				-	-	-
[round]		-	+	+	-	+	+
[high]		+	+	+	-	-	-
[back]			-	+			+

As seen in Table 6-3 and Table 6-4, the simplex vowel system of Quanzhou is different from that of Fuzhou in having the specification of the feature [Peripheral], which divides the vowel chart of Quanzhou into symmetrical pattern. In fact, the specification of [peripheral] can still be viewed as the division of the vowels from the main parameter of vowel such as [backness]. In contrast with Quanzhou, the vowel system of Fuzhou has the specification of parameters of the secondary articulation of vowels such as roundedness.

In addition to the difference in the specification of these contrastive features, what sets these two dialects apart is the sub-ranking of the contrastive features in these two dialects, as follows:

The ranking of the hierarchy of contrastive features of simplex vowels in Quanzhou:

[low] > [peripheral] > [high] > [ATR] > [back]

The ranking of the hierarchy of contrastive features of simplex vowels in Fuzhou:

[low] > [round] > [high] > [back]

It is remarkable that the hierarchies of contrastive features of vowels in Quanzhou and Fuzhou are different in their successive division algorithm. Apart from the low vowel which is cross-linguistically universal, the algorithms of Quanzhou and Fuzhou are distinctively different in that in Quanzhou the contrastive features of the main parameters of vowels such as height and backness are dominant in the successive division of the inventory. The dominance of the feature [high] over the feature [back] in Quanzhou highlights the biased importance of the height distinction in Quanzhou, which is reflected in the finals reduction is pervasive in Quanzhou tending to result in high vowels including both the front high vowel and the back high vowel as discussed. In contrast, in Fuzhou the parameter of the secondary parameter such as roundedness dominates the parameters of the main parameters such as height and backness. The ranking of the feature [round] over the feature [back] in Fuzhou highlights the predominance of rounding process over the assimilation of backness as discussed. Such distinctively different rankings and different specifications of contrastive features in two dialects account for different phonological behavior of the seemingly similar vowels in two dialects. Trubetzkoy (1969) proposes that which feature within a class pattern as unmarked can vary depending upon the system in which the feature occurs. Battistella (1990: 13 – 14), in a discussion of Jakobson's contributions to the understanding of markedness, compares the vowel systems of Turkish (/i, e, y œ, ɨ, a, u, o/) and Cayapa [Barbacoan, Ecuador] (/i, e, u, o/), commenting that the [i]'s in the two systems "differ in the function of the features that define them, even though they might be pronounced identically—the Turkish /i/ must be defined as high, non-back, and non-round, while the Cayapa /i/ is simply high and non-back". Using Battistella's features, one might expect different patternings in these languages with respect to [round], with it functioning actively in Turkish but not in Cyapa (Rice 2007: 86). Similarly, /u/ and /ɔ/ in Quanzhou and Fuzhou are different in the function of the feature [round] that defines them. Though these back vowels may pronounce identically, yet the Fuzhou /u/ and /ɔ/ are defined as rounded back vowels and the specification of [round] feature in these vowels render them to be active in triggering rounding assimilation. In contrast, for /u/ and /ɔ/ in Quanzhou, the feature [round] is a redundant feature implied by the feature of [+back], which may be responsible for why these back rounded vowels do not trigger rounding assimilation as the counterparts of Fuzhou.

Why does the same segments descended from Proto-Min display such distinct phonological behavior? Dreshera, Harveya & Oxford (2014) proposes the segmental reanalysis hypothesis: A segment may be reanalyzed as having a different contrastive status. Effectively, this means that a segment that was once contrastive because of a given feature can be reanalyzed to be contrastive for a separate one. Accordingly, it is suggested that it was the segmental reanalysis that played a key role in the divergence of Quanzhou and Fuzhou from the same Proto-Min, which resulted in such different typological characteristics. However, what triggers such segmental reanalysis? What motivates such different typological characteristics?

6.3 Comparison of the syllable markedness of finals in Quanzhou and Fuzhou

This section will focus on the comparison of the finals in Quanzhou and Fuzhou from the perspective of markedness of syllable structure. Since Min dialects are remarkably noted for their complexity of strata, it is difficult to have comparison in terms of simplex finals, complex finals individually, as it is quite common to find the correspondence between simplex finals and complex finals between different sub-dialects of Min. Therefore, the author will locate the comparison of finals in Quanzhou and Fuzhou within the framework of sixteen final groups of Middle Chinese, the cognates of which are abundant enough for the plausibility of the observation about the syllable markedness tendency about Quanzhou and Fuzhou, with the historical strata taken into consideration based on the related studies and the author's observation. The data on these rhyme groups about Fuzhou and Quanzhou are cited from Yuan (2010) and Zeng (2013).

A syllable is a string of segments grouped around one obligatory vowel or vowel-like (syllabic) element. According to Halle (1995), all levels of phonological representation may include organization into syllables. Sloan (1991) argues that syllabification occurs in two distinct stages: once at lexical level and then again at word level. In her analysis, syllabification processes assign nuclei, project syllables and incorporate onsets and codas at the lexical level. At this level, there is no epenthesis and they are no repairs. Pushing Sloan's idea a little further, the author proposes that syllable structure is underlyingly specified in lexical representations (See Vaux 2003). Languages differ in limited ways in their choices of syllable assignment. Different languages have different requirements for the preferred syllable structures. All languages permit CV syllables, but some disallow onsetless or closed syllables. As discussed above, the syllable structures of Quanzhou may include preglide, nuclear and coda which can be nasals of three different places of articulation or the obstruents of four types; in contrast, the syllable structures of Fuzhou may include preglide, nuclear, post-glide and coda which can only be the velar nasal and glottal stop, as follows:

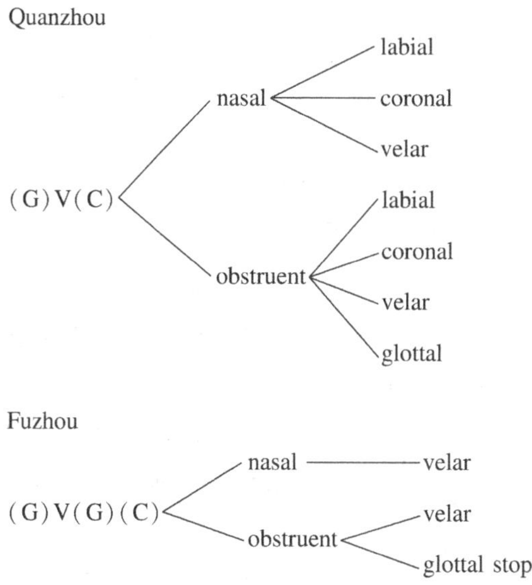

Diagram 6-4 Syllable structure of Quanzhou and Fuzhou

It is noticeable that the syllable structures in Quanzhou and Fuzhou are different in complexity of syllable structures as well as varieties of codas.

With respect to the markedness of syllables, there is a general agreement that CV syllables are unmarked with respect to syllable shape (e. g. Clements & Samuel 1983; Clements 1990; Rice 2007). On the basis of the syllable types observed in Maddieson (1984), Zhu (2013: 227) makes a summary about the markedness of syllables, as follows (Zhu 2013: 227):

(1) a. Cṽ > CV

b. CVC > CV

c. CGV > CV

d. CVm/n > CVŋ

e. CVp/t/k > CVʔ

f. CVV > CV

g. CVG > CGV

Such comparison of markedness of syllables covers the most syllable structures that are related to the syllable structures of Wu dialects. Yet such a markedness relationship of syllables can not account for the complex syllable structure such as GVGC in Fuzhou. Therefore, with the drastic case of superheavy final structure of Fuzhou taken into consideration, it is suggested to restate the markedness relationship of syllables as follows:

(2) Markedness Hierarchy of Syllable Structures

CGVG > CVG > CGV > CV > V/C

The following section will focus on the comparison of syllable structure types between Quanzhou and Fuzhou.

Chen Zhongmin (2013: 185) points out the corresponding relationship between Yu Final (虞韵) of Xiamen and that of Fuzhou as follows:

The strata correspondence of Yu Final between Xiamen and Fuzhou

(3) Xiamen	Fuzhou
iu	ieu
ɔ	uɔ
u	y(u)

According to the data of Quanzhou from Zeng (2013), and the data of Fuzhou from Yuan (2010), such a corresponding relationship of Yu Final as proposed in Chen Zhongmin (2013: 185) can also be found between Quanzhou and

Fuzhou. It is interesting to see that in the second strata in (3), [ɔ] which is the colloquial stratum (abbreviated as c) of Quanzhou finds its counterpart in [uɔ] which is the colloquial stratum of Fuzhou, as exemplified in (4):

(4)	Quanzhou	Yu Final, Yu She (虞韵)	Fuzhou	Yu Final, Yu She (虞韵)	Gloss
	$ɔ^{C}$	夫 $pɔ^{33}$	uo^{C}	夫 puo^{55}	husband
		斧 $pɔ^{55}$		斧 $p^{h}uo^{33}$	axe
		厨 $tɔ^{14}$		厨 tuo^{53}	kitchen
		雨 $hɔ^{22}$		雨 xuo^{242}	rain

Is such contrast of V versus GV between Quanzhou and Fuzhou a sporadic phenomenon or systematic phenomenon? This sub-section will show that the syllable structures in Quanzhou and Fuzhou find an unparalleled relationship which is reflected in that the cognates of Quanzhou and Fuzhou find their counterparts in different syllable structures.

6.3.1 (G)VX vs VGX

Lin & Wang (1992: 105) propose that while the maximal final is VX in most Chinese dialects, it can be larger in others, such as VVC (namely VGC in this book) in Fuzhou. Is the final form VGC a unique form of Fuzhou (or Eastern Min) or a final structure shared with Quanzhou? A comparison of cognates between sub-dialects of Min is as follows, which may bring some enlightening clue to this question:

(5)		East Min		Southern Min	
	Cognates	Fuzhou	Fuding	Quanzhou	Jieyang
		eiŋ/aiŋ	em/ɛm	iam	iam
	点 "dot"	teiŋ	tem	tiam	tiam
	店 "store"	taiŋ	tɛm	tiam	tiam
	念 "nag"	naiŋ	nɛm	liam	niam

It is observable that the cognates in Quanzhou display GVN structure while the same cognates in Fuzhou manifest VGN structure. Is the contrast of GVX (QZ) and VGX (FZ) a sporadic or systematic phenomenon?

With regard to the cognates on Fuzhou provided in Yuan (2010) and the cognates on Quanzhou offered by Zeng (2013), it is noted that the observation can also be found in the following cases:

Table 6-5 GVC of QZ vs VGC of FZ

Quanzhou	Rhyme	Fuzhou	Rhyme	Glossary
	Tian Final 添韵		Tian Final 添韵	
ũĩ/iam	店 tũĩ^{41}/tiam^{41}	aiŋ	店 taiŋ^{213}	store
	Xian Final 咸韵		Xian Final 咸韵	
iam	减 kiam^{55}	eiŋ	(减 keiŋ)	subtract
	Qia Final 洽韵		Qia Final 洽韵	
iap	夹 giap^{55}	eiʔ	夹 keiʔ/kieʔ^{33}	clip
	Ji Final 缉韵		Ji Final 缉韵	
iap	涩 siap^{55}	aiʔ	涩 saiʔ^{24}	tart
	Xie Final 屑韵		Xie Final 屑韵	
ueʔ	截 tsueʔ^{14}	eiʔ	截 tseiʔ^{5}	cut
	Deng Final 登韵	Fuzhou	Deng Final 登韵	
iəŋ^{L}	朋 piəŋ^{14} 灯 tiəŋ^{33} 等 tiəŋ^{55} 藤 tiəŋ^{14} 恒 hiəŋ^{14}	eiŋ	朋 peiŋ^{53} 灯 teiŋ^{55L} 等 teiŋ^{33L} 藤 teiŋ^{53L} 恒 xeiŋ^{53}	friend light wait vine persistent
	邓 tiəŋ^{41}	aiŋ	邓 taiŋ^{242} 赠 tsaiŋ^{242} 凳 taiŋ^{213}	surname present bench
	De Final 德韵		De Final 德韵	
iak at	默 biak^{14} 特 tiak^{14} 肋 liak^{55} 勒 liak^{55} 贼 at	eiʔ	默 meiʔ^{5} 特 teiʔ^{5} 肋 leiʔ^{5} 勒 leiʔ^{5} 贼 tsheiʔ^{5}	silent especial rib strangle thief

(continuous)

Quanzhou	Rhyme	Fuzhou	Rhyme	Glossary
	得 tiak^{55} 德 tiak^{55} 刻 k^{h}iak^{55} 克 k^{h}iat^{55L}	aiʔ	得 taiʔ^{24} 德 taiʔ^{24} 刻 k^{h}aiʔ^{24} 克 k^{h}aiʔ^{24}	get virtue carve unit of wight
	Zhi Final 职韵		Zhi Final 职韵	
iak^{L}	逼 piak^{55} 即 tsiak^{55} 息 siak^{55} 熄 siak^{55} 识 siak^{55} 式 siak^{55} 饰 siak^{55} 抑 iak^{55}	eiʔ	逼 peiʔ^{24} 即 tseiʔ^{24} 息 seiʔ^{24} 熄 seiʔ^{24} 识 seiʔ^{24} 式 seiʔ^{24} 饰 seiʔ^{24} 抑 eiʔ$^{24(L)}$	press namely breath extinguish recognize style decorate depress
	De Final 德韵		De Final 德韵	
iak	或 hiak^{14}	øyʔ	或 xøyʔ^{5}	or
	Geng Final 庚韵		Geng Final 庚韵	
iəŋ^{L}	猛 biəŋ^{55} 冷 liəŋ^{55} 澄 tiəŋ^{14} 牲 tsiəŋ^{33} 省 siəŋ^{55}	eiŋ	猛 meiŋ^{33L} 冷 leiŋ^{33} 澄 teiŋ^{242C} 牲 seiŋ^{55L} 省 seiŋ^{33L}	fierce cold limpid animal province
	孟 biəŋ^{41} 硬 giəŋ^{22}/ gĩ^{22C} 杏 hiəŋ^{22}	aiŋ	孟 maiŋ^{242} 硬 ŋaiŋ^{242} 杏 xaiŋ^{242}	surname hard apricot

In fact, on the basis of analysis of the cognates of sixteen rhymes of Fuzhou mainly from Yuan (2010) and of Quanzhou mainly from Zeng (2013), it is found that contrast of GVX (QZ) vs VGX (FZ) can be summarized in the following rhyme groups:

Table 6-6 Summary of contrast of GVX (QZ) vs VGX (FZ)

Finals	Quanzhou (GVX)	Fuzhou (VGX)
Xian Final 咸韵	iam	eiŋ
Qia Final 洽韵	iap	eiʔ/ieʔ
Tian Final 添韵	iam	eiŋ/ieŋ
	ũĩ/iam	eiŋ
Ji Final 缉韵	iap	aiʔ

(continuous)

Finals	**Quanzhou (GVX)**	**Fuzhou (VGX)**
Xie Final 屑韵	ueʔ	eiʔ
Deng Final 登韵	iəŋ	eiŋ/aiŋ
De Final 德韵	iak	eiʔ
Zhi Final 职韵	iak[L]	eiʔ
De Final 德韵	iak	øyʔ
Geng Final 庚韵	iəŋ[L]	eiŋ/aiŋ
Geng Final 耕韵	iəŋ[L]	eiŋ/aiŋ
Mo Final 陌韵	iak[L]	eiʔ/eiʔ
Mai Final 麦韵	iak[L]	eiʔ/aiʔ
Xi Final 昔韵	iak[L]	eiʔ
Mai Final 麦韵	iak/ueʔ	eiʔ
Zhong Final 钟韵	iəŋ[C]/aŋ[C]	øyŋ/œyŋ
Ge Final 戈韵	ua	uai
Hai Final 咍韵	ue/ui[C]	uei[C]
Jie Final 黠韵	uat ueʔ	eiʔ
Xie Final 屑韵	ueʔ	eiʔ

As is indicated, the contrast of GVX (QZ) and VGX (FZ) between Quanzhou and Fuzhou is a systematic phenomenon. In terms of syllable markedness, VGC is different from GVC in the position of glide, namely in GVC the glide is preceding the nuclear vowel while in VGC the glide occurs following the nuclear vowel. In contrast with the offglide in VGC which is often classified under the node of the rhyme, the preglide is noted for its unstable status. In some languages such as many sub-dialects of Min like Jianou (Beijing University 1989), the preglide is also classified under the node of the rhyme, which means such preglide is vocalic in essence; in some languages such as Squliq Atayal (Huang 2014), the preglide is labeled as belonging to initial, which implies such preglide is consonantal; even in some languages such as Mandarin, the preglide neither belongs to rhyme nor belongs to initial. The unstable status of the preglide due to whether preglide belonging to the nuclear or the initial may not only imply stronger tendency of the changes of syllable structures, but also may affect the weight of the syllable. In contrast, VGC is undoubtedly heavier than GVC since the offglide is usually labeled under the node of rhyme. Accordingly, it is reasonable to induce that Fuzhou prefers the syllable structure of more weight when compared with Quanzhou.

6.3.2 (G)V(X) vs GV(X)/VG(X)

The differences of syllable between Quanzhou and Fuzhou are not only manifested in the position of glide but also in the syllable types. It is observed that Quanzhou is often found to have more unmarked syllable structures compared with the more marked syllable structures found in Fuzhou, as follows (Wu 2010: 298):

(6)

Cognates	Eastern Min		Southern Min		Northern Min	
	Fuan	Fuzhou	Xiamen	Jieyang	Jianou	Jianyang
听 "listen"	t^hiaŋ	t^hiaŋ	t^hiã	t^hiã	t^hiaŋ	hiaŋ
惊 "scare"	kiaŋ	kiaŋ	kiã	kiã	kiaŋ	kiaŋ
命 "fate"	miaŋ	miaŋ	m	m	miaŋ	miaŋ
壁 "wall"	peʔ	pieʔ	piaʔ	piaʔ	pia	pia

As indicated, it is found that in contrast with GCX of Fuzhou as well as Fu'an, Xiamen and Jieyang of Southern Min have more less marked GV though V of Southern Min is a nasalized vowel. Can such markedness contrast between Fuzhou of Eastern Min and Xiamen of Southern Min can also be observed between Fuzhou and Quanzhou? A comparison of Qing Final 清韵 of Fuzhou and Quanzhou based on the cognates of Fuzhou in Yuan (2010) and Zeng (2013) indicate that such syllable markedness contrast can also be observed as follows:

Table 6-7 Examples of (G)V(X) (QZ) vs GV(X)/VG(X) (FZ) in Qing Final

Quanzhou	Qing Final 清韵	Fuzhou	Qing Final 清韵	Glossary
ĩã^{C}	饼 pĩã^{55}	iaŋ^{C}	饼 piaŋ^{33}	cookie
	名 bĩã^{14}		名 miaŋ^{53}	name
	精 tsĩã^{33}		精 tsiaŋ^{55}	proficient
	清 tshĩã^{33}		清 ts^{h}iaŋ^{55}	clear
	请 tshĩã^{55}		请 ts^{h}iaŋ^{33}	invite
	声 sĩã^{33}		声 siaŋ^{55}	voice
	成 sĩã^{14}		成 ts^{h}iaŋ^{53}	accomplish
	城 sĩã^{14}		城 ts^{h}iaŋ^{53}	city
	正 tsĩã^{41}		正 tsiaŋ^{213}	front
	圣 sĩã^{41}		圣 siaŋ^{213}	sacred
	赢 ĩã^{14}		赢 iaŋ^{52}	win
Quanzhou	**Qing Final 清韵**	**Fuzhou**	**Qing Final 清韵**	**Glossary**
ĩã^{C}	听 t^{h}ĩã^{33}	iaŋ^{C}	听 t^{h}iaŋ^{55C}	listen
	鼎 tĩã^{55}		鼎 tiaŋ^{33C}	tripod

As indicated, the GV structure in Quanzhou finds its counterpart in the GVC structure in Fuzhou. Is such difference as (G)V(X) (QZ) vs GV(G)(X) systematic phenomenon? On the basis of the observation of sixteen rhyme groups of Quanzhou according to the cognates of Quanzhou provided in Zeng (2013) and cognates of Fuzhou offered in Yuan (2010), it is found that such a syllable contrast can be found in more cases, as follows:

Table 6-8 Contrast of markedness of syllable structures of QZ and FZ

Finals	Quanzhou	Fuzhou	Syllable Contrast	
Tang Final I 唐韵	ɔŋ	ouŋ/auŋ	VN (QZ)	VGN (FZ)
Yang Final I 阳韵	ɔŋ	ouŋ/auŋ	VN	VGN
	ĩũ	ouŋ	GV	VGN
Tang Final II 合口唐韵	ɔŋ	uɔŋ	VN	GVN
Yang Final II 阳韵	ɔŋ^{L}	uɔŋ^{L}	VN	GVN
Duo Final I 铎韵	ɔk	ouʔ/auʔ	VC	VGC
Duo Final II 铎韵	ɔʔ/oʔ	uɔʔ	VC	GVC
Yao Final 药韵	ɔk/ak	uɔʔ	VC	GVC
Han Final 寒韵	ũã	iaŋ	GV	GVN
Shan Final 山韵	ũĩ	iaŋ	GV	GVN
Shan Final 删韵(closed)	ũĩ	uɔŋ	GV	GVN

It is noted that in contrast with GVX of Fuzhou, Quanzhou is noted to have more less marked syllable structures such as GV or VX, which is quite systematic for the rhyme groups of Quanzhou.

6.3.3 V/C vs GV(X)/VC

Through the comparison of sixteen rhyme groups of Quanzhou on the basis of Zeng (2013) and Fuzhou according to Yuan (2010), it is found that the syllable contrast between Quanzhou and Fuzhou can even be found in such contrast as V (QZ) vs GV (FZ), as follows:

Table 6-9 Xie She Ji Final 祭韵 of Quanzhou and Fuzhou

Quanzhou	Xie She (V) Ji Final 祭韵		Fuzhou	Xie She Ji Final 祭韵	Glossary
e	例 le^{41}	L	ie	例 lie^{242}	example
	厉 le^{41}			厉 lie^{242}	sever
	祭 tse^{41}			祭 tsie^{213}	offer a sacrifice to
	际 tse^{41}			际 tsie^{213}	border
	制 tse^{41}			制 tsie^{242}	make
	世 se^{41}			世 sie^{213}	generation
	势 se^{41}			势 sie^{242}	force
	誓 se^{41}			誓 sie^{242}	vow
	逝 se^{41}			逝 sie^{213}	elapse
	艺 ge^{41}			艺 ŋie^{242}	art

As indicated, for Ji Final 祭韵, regarding the literate forms, [e] of Quanzhou finds the counterpart in [ie] of Fuzhou for the cognates such as 例厉祭. Yuan (2010:97) proposes that [ie] of Fuzhou is composed of two strata, one of which is earlier than [ɛ] which can still be seen in some sporadic cases such as 弟 tie, 蹄 t^hie; the other of which can correspond to [e] of Xiamen (namely [e] of Quanzhou). But what accounts for the difference between Quanzhou and Fuzhou in [e] vs [ie]? With these finals in Ancient Chinese and Middle Chinese taken into consideration, it may offer some clues about such difference as follows:

(7) Cognates	Middle Chinese	Quanzhou	Fuzhou
例 "example"	liɛi	le^{41}	lie^{242}
厉 "strict"	liɛi	le^{41}	lie^{242}
祭 "sacrifice"	tsiɛi	tse^{41}	$tsie^{213}$
际 "international"	tsiɛi	tse^{41}	$tsie^{213}$
制 "make"	tɕiɛi	tse^{41}	$tsie^{242}$
世 "generation"	ɕiɛi	se^{41}	sie^{213}
势 "power"	ɕiɛi	se^{41}	sie^{242}
誓 "vow"	dʑiɛi	se^{41}	sie^{242}
逝 "elapse"	dʑiɛi	se^{41}	sie^{213}
艺 "art"	ŋiɛi	ge^{41}	ŋie^{242}

It is notable that comparatively speaking, [ie] of Fuzhou is more similar to Middle Chinese in retaining preglide [i], while [e] of Quanzhou is more unmarked in terms of syllable structures.

The syllable contrast of V versus GV between Quanzhou and Fuzhou can also be found in more rhyme groups based on the comparison of the cognates of Fuzhou provided in Yuan (2010) and the cognates of Zeng (2013), as follows:

Table 6-10 Correspondence of Zhi Final 止摄支韵 of Quanzhou and Fuzhou

Quanzhou	Zhi Final (I) 支韵	Fuzhou	Zhi Final (I) 支韵	Glossary
a	骑 k^ha^{14}	ia	骑 k^hia^{53}	ride
	倚 k^ha^{22}		奇 k^hia^{55}	strange
	寄 k^ha^{33}		倚 k^hia^{242}	lean on
i	披 p^hi^{33}	ie	披 pie^{55}	wrap
	避 pi^{41}		避 pie^{242}	evade
	篱 li^{14}		篱 lie^{53}	fence
	紫 tsi^{55}		紫 $tsie^{33}$	purple
	刺 ts^hi^{41}		刺 $tshie^{213\ C}$	thorn
	池 ti^{14}		池 tie^{53}	pool
	肢 tsi^{33}		肢 $tsie^{55}$	arm
	施 si^{33}		施 sie^{55}	bestow
	寄 ki^{41}		寄 kie^{213}	send by post
	骑 k^hi^{14}		骑 k^hie^{53L}	ride
	倚 i^{55}		倚 k^hie^{242L}	lean on
	椅 i^{55}		椅 ie^{33}	chair
	蚁 gi^{55}		蚁 ŋie^{53}	ant

(continuous)

Quanzhou	Geng Final 庚韵	Fuzhou	Geng Final 庚韵	Glossary
ĩ C	彭 phĩ 14 盲 bĩ 14 生 sĩ 33 牲 sĩ 33 粳 kĩ 55	aŋ	彭 phaŋ 53 盲 maŋ 53 生 saŋ 55C/seiŋ 55L 牲 saŋ 55C 粳 kaŋ 55C/ keiŋ 33L	surname blind give birth to livestock herb
Quanzhou	**Geng Final 庚韵**	**Fuzhou**	**Geng Final 庚韵**	**Glossary**
ĩ	平重 pĩ 14 坪 pĩ 14 柄 pĩ 41 病 pĩ 41 明	aŋ	平 phaŋ 53C 坪 paŋ 53C 柄 paŋ 213C 病 paŋ 242C 明 maŋ 53C	the same court handle illness bright
Quanzhou	**Qing Final 清韵**	**Fuzhou**	**Qing Final 清韵**	**Glossary**
ĩ	井 tsĩ 55 姓 sĩ 41	aŋ C	井 tsaŋ 33 姓 saŋ 213	well surname
Quanzhou	**Qing Final 青韵**	**Fuzhou**	**Qing Final 青韵**	**Glossary**
ĩ C	青 tshĩ 33 醒 tshĩ 55	aŋ C	青 tsʰaiŋ 55 醒 tsʰaiŋ 33	green awake

The markedness difference between Quanzhou and Fuzhou is found not only in more unmarked syllable structure, but also in more reduced segments, as follows:

Table 6-11 Comparison of Hai Final 咍韵 of Quanzhou and Fuzhou

Quanzhou	Hai Final, Xie She 咍韵	Fuzhou	Hai Final, Xie She 咍韵	Glosssary
ə C	胎 tʰə 33 代 tə 41 袋 tə 41	øy C œy C	胎 tʰøy 55 代 tœy 242 袋 tœy 242	fetus generation bag

It is clear that for the cognate of Hai Final 咍韵, there is a colloquial form [ə] of Quanzhou which finds its counterpart in [øy/œy] of Fuzhou. It is remarkable that while the cognates of Fuzhou are found to have VG structure, the cognates of Quanzhou have V structure and even the nuclear vowel is a relatively more unmarked vowel-schwa. Similar cases can be found as follows:

Table 6-12 [ə] of Quanzhou vs (G)V(G) of Fuzhou

Quanzhou	Zhi Final (I) 支韵	Fuzhou	Zhi Final 支韵	Glossary
$ə^C$	皮 $p^hə^{14}$	uei^C	皮 p^huei^{53}	skin
	糜 $bə^{14}$		糜 $muei^{53}$	plants
	被 $p^hə^{22}$		被 p^huei^{242}	quilt
	Zhi Final 支韵		Zhi Final 支韵	
ə	髓 $ts^hə^{55}$	øy	髓 $ts^høy^{33}$	marrow
	Wei Final 微韵		Wei Final 微韵	
ə	飞 $pə^{33}$	uei	飞 $puei^{55C}$	fly
	尾 $bə^{55}$		尾 $muei^{33}$	tail
	未 $bə^{41C}$		未 $muei^{242C}$	not
	Ge Final 戈韵		Ge Final 戈韵	
$ə^C$	果 $kə^{55}$	uei^C	果 $kuei^{33}$	fruit
	火 $hə^{55}$	(uoi 冯)	火 $xuei^{33}$	fire
	伙 $hə^{55}$		伙 $xuei^{33}$	bang
	粿 $kə^{55}$		馃 $kuei^{33}$	rice noodle
	坐 $tsə^{22}$	sœy	坐 $sœy^{242}$	sit
	螺 $lə^{14}$	øy	螺 $løy^{242}$	snail

Interestingly, there is another case about segmental reduction in Quanzhou which finds the correspondence of complex syllable structures in Fuzhou, indicated as follows:

Table 6-13 [ŋ] of Quanzhou vs (G)V(G)N of Fuzhou

Quanzhou	Huan Final 桓韵	Fuzhou	Huan Final 桓韵	Glossary
$ŋ^C$	酸 $sŋ^{33}$	ouŋ	酸 $souŋ^{55}$	sour
	断 $tŋ^{22}$	auŋ	断 $tauŋ^{242C}$	broken
	卵 $lŋ^{22}$		卵 $lauŋ^{242C}$	egg
	钻 $tsŋ^{41}$		钻 $tsauŋ^{213}$/钻 $tsouŋ^{33}$	drill
	蒜 $sŋ^{41}$	uɔŋ	蒜 $sauŋ^{213}$	garlic
	管 $kŋ^{33}$		管 $kuɔŋ^{33C}$	tube
	Shan Final 删韵		Shan Final 删韵	
$ŋ^C$	闩 ŋ	ouŋ	闩 $souŋ^{55}$	bolt

(continuous)

	仙韵 **Xian Final**		仙韵 **Xian Final**	
ŋ^C	串 tsʰŋ^41 穿 tsʰŋ^33 软 lŋ^55	øyŋ œyŋ	串 tsʰøyŋ^213C 穿 søyŋ^242 软 nœyŋ^213C	bunch wear soft
	Hun Final 魂韵		**Hun Final 魂韵**	
ŋ^C	顿 tŋ^41	ouŋ/auŋ	顿 tauŋ^213C	meal
	Wen Final 文韵		**Wen Final 文韵**	
ŋ^C	问 bŋ^41	uɔŋ	问 muɔŋ^213C	ask
	Yang Final 阳韵		**Yang Final 阳韵**	
ŋ^C	床 tsʰŋ^14	ouŋ	床 souŋ^53C	bed
	Yang Final 阳韵		**Yang Final 阳韵**	
ŋ^C	方 hŋ^33C	uŋ/ouŋ	方 puŋ^55C	
	Deng Final 登韵		**Deng Final 登韵**	
ŋ^C	等 tŋ^55 肯 kʰŋ^55	iŋ	等 tiŋ^33C 肯 kʰiŋ^33C	wait agree

As indicated, it is found that while Fuzhou still retains the (G)VN structure, the same cognates in Quanzhou are reduced to be the most unmarked syllable structure V and the nuclears of these cognates have all turned to be syllabic nasal [ŋ]. As discussed in the preceding section, the syllabic nasal in Quanzhou not only is rather active in being able to follow all kinds of initials, but can show up under all the tones, just similar to the independent status owned by the schwa of Quanzhou.

Before the discussion of this section is brought to a conclusion, it is necessary to ask a qucstion whether these segmentally reduced nuclears such as [ə] and [ŋ] are a remnant feature or an innovative characteristics? In this book, it is suggested the segmental reduction mignt be part of pervasive reduction both segmentally and syllabically found in Quanzhou. Here is one enlightening example that may give some clues (Zeng 2013: 91 –93, 114):

Table 6-14 Reduction both segmentally and syllabically in Quanzhou

Area	Zhi Final 髓 "marrow" 吹 "blow" 炊 "cook"	Wei Final 飞 "fly" 尾 "tail" 未 "not"	Yue Final 袜 "socks" 月 "moon"	Qi Final 讫 "end"
Quanzhou	ə	ə	əŋ	
Jinjiang	ə	ə	əʔ	ut
Shishi	e	e	eʔ	
Huian (Luocheng)	ə	ə	əʔ	
Hui'an (Congwu)	e	e	eʔ	it
Quangang	ue	ue	ue	
Nan'an	ə	ə	əʔ	ət
Anxi	ə	ə	əʔ	ut/ət
Xiamen	e	e	eʔ	
Tong'an	ə	ə	əʔ	
Yongchun	ə	ə	ə	

Zeng (2013: 91 – 93, 114) points out that for the cognates of Zhi Final such as 髓吹炊, the colloquial forms of Quanzhou and quite some sub-dialects of Southern Min such as Jinjiang, Huian is pronounced as [ə], which finds its counterpart in Xiamen as [e] and [ue] in Quangang. It is clear that among these sub-dialects of Southern Min there is a serial of rhyme forms such as [ue] – [e] – [ə]. Accordingly, it is suggested that [e] as well as [ə] is the result of further markedness reduction from [ue].

As indicated above, the syllable markedness contrast of Quanzhou and Fuzhou is consistent and pervasive across rhyme groups instead of sporadic observation.

6.4 Comparison of phonological changes of finals in Quanzhou and Fuzhou

As discussed, Quanzhou and Fuzhou are observed to undergo quite some noticeable phonological processes, such as vowel raising and segment merger of

Quanzhou and categorical rhyme alternation of Fuzhou and so on. This subsection is devoted to the comparison of such phonological processes in Quanzhou and Fuzhou.

6.4.1 Less marked final forms vs more marked final forms

Quanzhou is found to have undergone markedness reduction processes such as vowel raising and segment merger. As discussed, merger has two types: a conditioned merger applied only to restricted contexts, thus introducing a neutralization, and the other one which applies to all contexts, thus reducing the number of phonemes in the language (Trask 1996; Zhang Jisheng 2006: 80). The merger of Quanzhou which is a conditioned merger happens when middle vowels are the nuclear of rhymes, and results in markedness reduction such as from diphthongs to monothong or from CGVG to CGV. Such markedness reduction as the result of merger and raising is in contrast with systematic final alternation of Fuzhou which ushers in more sonorant and more marked final forms in the final syllable of prosodic words. As demonstrated, such syllable markedness contrast due to the related phonological processes is a systematic phenomenon for Quanzhou and Fuzhou.

6.4.2 Dissimilation vs assimilation

Phonotactics is the study of permissible and impermissible segment combinations in a language. As discussed, the phonological changes of Quanzhou and Fuzhou are noted to be related to phonotactics. It has often been noted that phonotactic principles appear to be gradient: lexical items can be more or less well-formed depending on the combinations they contain (Anttila 2008). What is interesting in Quanzhou and Fuzhou is that some categorical phonotactic phenomena are found in both dialects, which are remarkably in great contrast. It is well-noted that the parameter of roundedness plays an active role in Fuzhou, which is in contrast with Southern Min and Northern Min in which there are no obvious rounding processes, rounding assimilation influencing both the front vowels and the back vowels in Fuzhou. For such rounding assimilation, it is reasonable to suppose that in Fuzhou, there is a general filter * [-rounded] [+rounded] that works actively. Regarding whether such characteristics of Fuzhou is a remnant trait or an innovative feature, Chen Zeping (2010) compares the vowels preceding the 19th century and those of today, and finds that there are some following changes such as øŋ—øyŋ, aøŋ—oyŋ, ioŋ—yoŋ, which indicates the rounding assimilation alongside with diphthongization ever took place in the diachronic process in Fuzhou. Moreover, assimilation in Fuzhou is not limited to the feature of [round], but also extends to the feature [back], which is not found in Southern Min including Quanzhou. When the requirement of the agreement of such features as [round] and [back] can not be satisfied in Fuzhou, the minimum agreement of height may be a means to resort to. In contrast with assimilation of the finals of Fuzhou, it is observed that in Quanzhou the middle vowels are not allowed to co-exist with preglides that agree with them in terms of the features such as [round] or [back], due to which the following rhymes such as * -uɔ, * -uoŋ, * -uok disappear. Regarding dissimilation of Quanzhou, it is suggested that there is a co-occurrence restriction targeted at the middle vowel, namely * [α back][α back]. In fact, this restriction is also extended to the high vowel, which can be revised to be the violation of * [α Feature][α Feature] in segment clusters and such a violation should not be more than one. Such co-occurrence restriction can be explained from the perspective of the maximal contrast. It is supposed that the maximalization of contrast (which is driven by dissimilation) is highly ranked in Quanzhou, which requires that the sharing of features of the co-occuring segments can not be more than one, contrary to which the harmonic co-occurrence tendency of Fuzhou is supposed to be the need of ease of articulation.

6.4.3 Regressive assimilation vs progressive assimilation

Quanzhou and Fuzhou are both observed to go through assimilation across boundary which involve the coda of the preceding syllable and initial consonant of the following syllable. What is remarkable is that such assimilation of

Quanzhou is regressive assimilation which is noted for the place of articulation of the initial consonant of the following syllable assimilates that of the coda consonant of the preceding syllable while the concerned assimilation of Fuzhou is a progressive assimilation in which the manner of the initial consonant of the following syllable is assimilated by the coda of the preceding syllable. Regarding such assimilation involved in Quanzhou and Fuzhou, the two dialects are different not only in the direction of assimilation but also in the trigger of assimilation.

6.5 Summary

Comparatively speaking, Quanzhou and Fuzhou have displayed systematic differences both in terms of segments and syllable markedness. The phonological differences of the finals between Quanzhou and Fuzhou made through the above analysis can be summarized into the following 4 aspects:

a. Quanzhou is noted to have a symmetric vowel inventory which makes a maximal use of the two basic parameters of backness and height of vowels, while Fuzhou is remarkable in its imbalance distribution of its vowel inventory that has a strong bias towards the front vowels, which not only employs the basic vowel parameters such as backness and height but roundedness.

b. These two dialects are different in their requirement in sonority in that the simplex vowels in Fuzhou have greater sonority requirement than those of Quanzhou in excluding the lowest sonorant vowels such as /ə, ɯ/ in Quanzhou. With respect to vowel height, it is clear that the Quanzhou dialect tends to have mid-high vowels while the Fuzhou dialect tends to have mid-low vowels /ɛ/ and /œ/.

c. Quanzhou and Fuzhou are found to have a consistent markedness contrast in terms of syllable structure in that Quanzhou tends to show a less marked syllable structure while Fuzhou is observed to have a more marked syllable structure, which is pervasive across sixteen rhyme groups not only in literate forms but also in colloquial forms.

d. Quanzhou and Fuzhou are observed to undergo quite some noticeable phonological processes, such as vowel raising and segment merger of Quanzhou and categorical final alternation of Fuzhou. Quanzhou is also found to have undergone dissimilation in terms of rhymes and regressive assimilation between coda and initial, which is in contrast with assimilation with respect to finals as well as progressive assimilation between codas and initials in Fuzhou.

It is pointed out in this book that Quanzhou has displayed more traces of markedness reduction while Fuzhou showcases more characteristics of markedness preservation when observed from a comprehensive view. What leads to such distinct differences between Quanzhou and Fuzhou may be a conflict of ease of production and ease of perception: for these two dialects, different forces take the leading role, and model the different paths of the evolution of the respective phonological systems, resulting in the disparity observed syncronically. While just as it is proposed that the comparison of Southern Min and Eastern Min is a rather complicated issue which involves complex historic strata which is related to quite a number of mismatch of colloquial strata and literate strata regarding initials, finals as well as tones, hence it requires further studies of the related issues in the future.

Chapter 7

Tones of Quanzhou and Fuzhou

This chapter will concentrate on the analysis of the tone systems of Quanzhou and Fuzhou, after which the feature specifications for the tones will be introduced before a formal analysis of the tone sandhi processes of these two dialects is brought in. The focus will be on the comparison of the characteristics of the tone sandhi processes of Quanzhou and Fuzhou from the perspective of markedness.

7.1 Tone system of Quanzhou

In this section, I will present my analysis of the tonal inventory of Quanzhou and propose feature specifications for the tones in Quanzhou. I make an attempt to analyze the tone sandhi processes in Quanzhou under the framework of the markedness theory.

In Chinese linguistic literature tones are classified into yin and yang registers. Historically the yin tones occur in syllables with voiceless initial obstruents, and the yang tones occur in syllables with voiced initial obstruents. The voiced obstruents of Middle Chinese (ca. 600 A. D.) are seldom retained in modern dialects. Phonetically speaking, it is well known that voiceless consonants induce higher pitch in the following vowel, and voiced consonants induce lower pitch (see, for example, Halle & Stevens 1971; Maddieson 1974,

1978). The correlation between yin and yang on the one hand and the pitch of tone on the other can be seen in few cases such as the Wu dialect family (Bao 1999).

There are seven tones in Quanzhou dialect, as follows (Lin 1993):

(1)

Register	Ping	Shang	Qu	Ru
Yin	33	55	41	5
Yang	24	22		24

It is clear from (1) that seven tones of Quanzhou can be divided into yin register and yang register, except the merge of Qu, namely Departing Tone /41/. Bao Zhiming (1999: 10) points out that in the Southern Min dialect family, the situation between yin and yang and the pitch of tone is reversed, for example, in the Chaoyang dialect, and in many other Southern Min dialects spoken in southern Fujian Province and northern Guangdong Province, high-pitched tones are found in syllables with voiced initials, and low-pitched tones on syllables with voiceless initials (Wang 1967; Yue-Hashimoto 1986). But the tone in Quanzhou is a counterexample in which the yin/yang pattern of tone is still retained despite the fact that the contrast between the voiceless and voiced initials has disappeared. Yue-Hashimoto (1986) points out most Min dialects experienced the yin/yang split in the Even, Departing and Entering Tone, which is in line with many cross-linguistic evidences that Shang Tone (Rising Tone) is the most unstable from the diachronic perspective and it is merged to Qu Tone (namely Departing Tone) in many dialects such as the Wu dialect (Wu 2005). But the tone case in the Quanzhou dialect is interesting in that Qu Tone did not undergo the tone split as summarized by Yue-Hashimoto and Yu Aiqin but Shang Tone underwent the tone split, which is indicated as follows:

(2)

	Even	Rising	Departing	Entering
Quanzhou	33	55	41	5
	24	22	41	24

7.1.1 Tone specification of Quanzhou

The representation of tone has been probed widely (Yip 1980, 1989, 2002; Snider 1990; Duanmu 1990; Hyman 1993; Bao 1990a, 1990b, 1999). Most studies agree that a tone consists of two properties, register and contour. Bao (1999) argues that the register and the contour play different conceptual roles. The register node specifies the pitch level of the tone, whereas the contour node specifies how the pitch of the tone behaves over the temporal duration of the tone-bearing unit. These two components are encoded in the structure as sister nodes dominated by the tonal root node.

In this book, H, L, h and l are used to specify the internal structure of tone. These symbols have the following meanings:

H = [+stiff] ([+upper])
L = [-stiff] ([-upper])
h = [-slack] ([+raised])
l = [+slack] ([-raised])

The features [stiff] and [slack] are equivalent to [upper] and [raised] as proposed by Yip (1980, 1989), Bao (1999).

In the specification of tone features in Quanzhou tone, there is a question about the specification of mid-tone. The mid-level tone in three-tone system can be specified either as [+upper, -raised], or [-upper, +raised], depending on how the middle tone behaves: whether it patterns like a high tone or a low tone in either undergoing or conditioning a sandhi rule (Chen 2000: 55). In Quanzhou, 33 is specified as a high tone, which may make it better suit the pattern of tones in Quanzhou which is still clear in its division of yin register and yang register. Therefore, the tones of Quanzhou are specified as follows:

(3)

Register	Ping	Shang	Qu	Ru
Low	H. l	H. h	H. hl	H. h
Low	L. lh	L. l		L. lh

7.1.2 Tone sandhi of Quanzhou

Tone sandhi refers to tonal alternation conditioned by adjacent tones or by the prosodic or morphosyntactic position in which the tone occurs (Yue-Hashimoto 1987; Zhang Jie 2007: 259 - 302). Tone sandhi is quite common across China. Different dialects vary greatly in the complexity of their tone sandhi patterns, from Cantonese and many other northern dialects that have relatively few sandhi changes to Min in which virtually any tonal combinations will trigger sandhi (Zhang Jie 2014a, 2014b). In Quanzhou, tone sandhi almost involves most tones, except Yinping and Yangshang, as follows:

(4) Register	Ping (Even)	Shang (Rising)	Qu (Going)	Ru (Entering)
Yin (High)	33	55→24	41→55	5→24
Yang (Low)	24→22	22	41→22	24→22

In (4), the tones preceding arrow are the citation tones and the tones following arrow are the sandhi tones. As indicated, all the tones of Quanzhou are noted to undergo the process of tone sandhi, except Yinping 33 and Yangqu 22 which are not involved in the tone sandhi.

According to the tone feature specification discussed above, the tone sandhi processes in Quanzhou can be formulized as follows:

(5) Yin Register	H. l	H. h→L. lh	H. hl→H. h	H. h→L. lh
Yang Register	L. lh→L. l	L. l	H. hl→L. l	L. lh→ L. l

It is remarkable that the tones of yang register in the second row of (5) all tend to result in L. l; the two of three tones of yin register which undergo the tone sandhi processes also lead to tones in low register as indicated in H. h → L. lh and H. h → L. lh. Such tendency of tone sandhi of Quanzhou will be further addressed in the following section.

The synchronic analysis of the "tone circle" pattern in Xiamen or other related dialects such as Taiwanese can be seen in Wang (1967), Hsieh (2005), Barrie (2006), and Lin (2019). Yet in literature, there is little analysis about the tone sandhi of Quanzhou. Tone sandhi in Quanzhou is right-dominant, in which it is the final syllable in the sandhi domain that preserves its tone while non-final syllables undergo sandhi. Right-dominant sandhi often involves default insertion and paradigmatic neutralization of non-final tones (Zhang Jie 2007). But this is not the case in Quanzhou. In fact, the tone sandhi in Quanzhou is noted for that the mapping between the base tone and the sandhi tone is context free to the extent that tone A is always replaced by tone B, regardless of what tone precedes or follows, similar to that of Xiamen, which is described as random and arbitrary substitution of one tone for another without apparent articulatory, perceptual, or functional motivation. Chen (2000) proposes that the tone sandhi in Xiamen, which is not triggered by functional factor, nor phonetic factor, is deemed as paradigmatic substitution. The Quanzhou dialect, which is the main origin of Xiamen, is also a case of paradigmatic substitution, or replacement. Replacement is distinguished from dissimilation in terms of such parameter as context: replacement is not context-sensitive, whereas dissimilation is sensitive to neighbouring tones (Bao 1999: 202). The tone semi-circle in Quanzhou is a context-insensitive replacement. Hyman and Schuh's (1974) universal tone rules summarized in Bao (1999) indicate that replacement mainly involves tone register replacement. And replacement in Quanzhou involves not only register replacement but also pitch replacement, as follows:

(6) a. L. lh → L. l
b. H. h → L. lh
c. H. hl → L. l

There are three observations about the tone sandhi changes in Quanzhou: in the first change, it involves the change from the complex tone [lh] to [l]; in the second case, it includes two changes, the first is from H register to L register, and the second is from [h] to [lh]; the third displays two changes, the first is from H register to L register, and the second is from /hl/ to /l/. Despite that substitution is a good summary of the characteristics of tone sandhi in Quanzhou, it still needs to account for the principles hidden under the bewildering surface manifestations.

7.1.3 Markedness of tone and tone sandhi in Quanzhou

In the Southern Min dialect of Taiwan the output of a tone shift is often identical to another input, and some of the tone shifts change the register but retain the contour, while others alter the contour but preserve the register. Thus the mappings of tones can not be described by markedness. The Quanzhou dialect has close affinity with the Southern Min dialect of Taiwan. Different from the tone chain shift in Taiwan, the tone sandhi in Quanzhou is a semi-circle, which involves the alternation of contour and register in two cases and deals with the change of contour in the rest two cases. Is it possible to account for the tone sandhi in Quanzhou from the perspective of markedness? In this book, it is proposed that the tone sandhi in Quanzhou can be accounted for within the framework of the markedness theory.

As for the question of whether there is a general way to determine tonal markedness in two-height systems as a whole, an old (and intuitive) view is that H is universally marked and L unmarked (Pulleyblank 1986, 2004: 415). At the first sight, this hypothesis appears to be contradicted in privative systems, where the specific tone is presumably also the marked value, such as the distinction between "high-marked" (/H/ vs Ø) and "low-marked" (/L/ vs Ø) tone systems in Athabaskan (Hargus & Rice 2005: 11 – 17, cited from Hyman 2011). In equipollent systems, where both tones are "activated", hence necessarily specified, there are two possible approaches: (i) universal markedness, whereby H = marked and L unmarked (cf. De Lacy 2002a: 28); (ii) language-specific markedness: H is marked in (most) languages, L in others. Recognizing these two possibilities, Maddieson (1978: 341) distinguishes possible (marked-H, marked-L) vs probable (marked-H) systems: "It may be that high tones are more frequently marked because an upward deflection of pitch is naturally salient against an overall downward intonational contour than a downward deflection. Falling intonations seem to be the most frequent in speech." (Maddieson 1978: 342n) Yip (2001: 315) proposes Minimize Articulatory Effort (MINARTICEFF) to account for the markedness of tones, which includes three principles as follows:

a. Contour tones are more marked than level tones: ∗CONTOUR.

b. Rising tones are more marked than falling tones: ∗RISE >> ∗FALL.

c. High tones are more marked than low tones: ∗H >> ∗L.

Based on the markedness theory, it is proposed that the change from lh to l in (1) is a markedness reduction due to its avoiding the violation of ∗CONTOUR; the change from H. hl – L. l in (3) is a double markedness reduction in that it not only transfers from the high register to the low register, but also reduces the contour hl to the level tone l. What seems to be contradictory is the change in (2). The change in (2) embodies two steps, namely the transfer from the high register to the low register, accompanied by the pitch change from h to lh. How to account for such contradictory effect? It is clear that the first step of change in (3) is a typical markedness reduction, the following step from h to lh seems to be contradictory. For such contradiction, I propose to employ the Principle of Priority put forward in Wilson (2001: 177) to account for such seeming discrepancy. This principle is first intended to account for the priority of the more harmonic pair, which states that let C be any constraint, and let f > x and g > y be any two harmonic orderings asserted by C. If "f" is more harmonic than "g", according to the hierarchy (i.e. if the highest-ranked constraint that prefers one of the candidates over the other favours f), then "f > x" takes priority over "g > y" when adding both of them to the cumulative harmonic ordering. It is suggested to revise this principle as follows, namely let C be any constraint, and let "f" and "g" be any two successive phonological changes. If "f" is more harmonic than "g" according to hierarchy, then the change result of "f" takes priority over the change result of "g". According to this principle, the change from high register to low register in the first step of change in (2) takes priority over the change result from hh to lh in the low register in the second step. Hence, as a whole, the change from H. h -L. lh as a whole is a markedness reduction. This is in accord with the assumption that register and pitch play different roles in languages: in some languages register plays a more important role such as the Shaoxing dialect while in some other languages pitch exerts more influence such as the New Chongming dialect, and in some other languages both register and pitch are active (Zhu 2013: 131). Accordingly, it is proposed that in the Quanzhou dialect, register has a greater say. This is in line with the observation that the markedness reduction in the Quanzhou dialect is mainly reflected in adopting low register as the markedness reduction result.

7.2 Tone system of Fuzhou

7.2.1 Tones of Fuzhou

The literature about the tonal transcription of Fuzhou dialect includes Wright (1983), Yip (1980), Chan (1985), Chen (1998), and Chan (1998). There are inconsequential differences in tonal transcription among the published sources. Synchronically, there are seven tones in the Fuzhou dialect, which are arranged according to the traditional, tonal categories of Ping "level", Shang "ascending, rising", Qu "departing" and Ru "entering".

(7) Register	Ping (I)	Shang (II)	Qu (III)	Ru (IV)
(a) Yin (High)	55	33	213	24
(b) Yang (Low)	53		242	5

(7) is an indication of the tone inventory of Fuzhou. To have a clear understanding of this tone inventory, tones from Ping to Ru are marked with (I) to (IV), which are further divided into yin register or yang register which are marked with (a) and (b) respectively. In the Fuzhou dialect, there are two complex tones, namely 213 and 242, which only occur in the final position and

turn to simple tones in non-final syllables. Ru Tones differ from the other tones in that these syllables end in a glottal stop. As a result, although the toneme-assignment is identical, the syllables bearing these underlying tones are distinguished by their syllable structure. For this reason I do not include them in the discussion.

7.2.2 Tone sandhi of Fuzhou

The following table is about the tone sandhi of Fuzhou:

(8)

1st syllable	2nd syllable			
	55	53 / 5	33	213/ 242/ 24
55 213/242/24	55	55	53	53
53 5	55	33	33	21
33 24	21	21	35	55

(8) indicates the tone sandhi processes of bi-syllabic words of Fuzhou. The tones in the first collumn represent the tones that appear in the non-final position while the tones in the first row stand for the tones in the final position. It seems that the tone sandhi of Fuzhou is a quite complicated process. Zhang Jie (2014) proposes that the tone sandhi nuetralization of the base tones in Fuzhou seem largely arbitrary.

As indicated above, in the tone sandhi of Fuzhou, seven citation tones on the surface turn to five sandhi tones as the result of the tone sandhi process, such as [55], [53], [33], [21], and [35]. Among the five sandhi tones, the first three tones are the same as the citation tones, with the last two as the new results of the tone sandhi process. The high rising sandhi tone /35/ never contrasts with the low, rising /24/, and is consequently not given phonemic status.

There is one obvious observation about the tone sandhi of Fuzhou:

regardless of whatever the tonal alternation is, it is always the tone on the left that undergoes tone sandhi and the tone on the right that preserves its underlying tone. Bao (2004: 880) points out that the retention of the lexical tone is often associated with prosodic prominence. In the literature, languages that tend to maintain the identity of the rightmost tone while allowing tones in other positions to change are referred to as right prominent languages; languages that tend to maintain the identity of the leftmost tone while allowing tones in other positions to change are referred to as left prominent languages (Chen 2000; Hyman & VanBik 2004; Lin 2004). The right-prominent tone sandhi pattern is quite common cross-linguistically such as Mandarin, Southern Min dialect, Tijian dialect, and Sixian Hakka dialect. Similarly, the Fuzhou dialect is also a right prominent language, in which the rightmost (final) syllable keeps the contrast of all lexical tones, while the non-final syllable only has five tones after neutralization. The neutralization of tones in Fuzhou leads to reduction of contrasts instead of complete disappearing (Chen 2000), which is unlike the tone sandhi of Trique which is a right-prominent tone language, in which the tones of non-final position undergo the process of neutralization, even the deletion of tones. What is the motivation for the final syllable to keep all the contrasts of lexical tones?

7.2.3 Internal structure of tones in Fuzhou

Phonologically, pitch height needs to be taken into account if it serves to contrast two tones of the same pitch shape in the same environment. Besides, one more distinctive feature is needed to be posited in the tonal phonology of Fuzhou, namely register: [High] register yields high tone, and [Low] register yields low tone (Chan 1985). The high and low registers are represented as Hr and Lr, which are the register level. h and l are the tone features that are dominated by contour. Hence, [55] can be specified as [H. h], and [53] as [H. hl].

Here is one question about the specification of [213] and [242]. What are the underlying forms of these two tones? How to specify these tones? The choice of the underlying tones are based on several factors. Two important ones are: firstly, the pitch height and pitch contour of the tones in mono-syllabic words (i.e. in isolation forms), and secondly, the behavior of these tones in other contexts. Chan (1985:119) proposes that on the terminal syllable of a tone sandhi span, tone IIIa (namely 213) may be accompanied by an initial drop in pitch. Nonetheless, this tone behaves as though it is initially low, patterning with other tones with an initial L-toneme, namely tones IIIb (namely 242) ([lhl]) and IVa (namely 24)([l(h)]). It is note-worthy that Yuan (1960) has [213] as the citation tone for tone IIIa, and he also gives a simple rising tone [13] as a phonetic variant. Thus, the initial drop in pitch is not significant, so that the tone should be treated as underlyingly ([lh]). At the same time, in preterminal position in a tone sandhi span, tone IIIa behaves identically to tone Ia (namely 55) ([h]); that is, it behaves as if it is tone Ia. The assignment of [lh] then suggests the deletion of the initial l-toneme in preterminal position as one of the early tone sandhi rules. Therefore, tone IIIa is treated as having [213] as the basic citation form, and is assigned the underlying [lh], ignoring the initial dip in the citation form, which fits the distributional facts. The behavior of tone IIIa in preterminal position in tone sandhi context is also found in tone IIIb ([lhl]) and some cases of tone IVa (namely those with underlying [lh]). Here the author adopts the suggestion of Chan (1985) by specifying the underlying form of [213] as [L. lh] and [242] as [L. hl].

As for the specification of [33], it can be specified with [H. l] or [L. h]. The intermediacy of [33] can be resolved by examining the sandhi behavior of the middle tone. Which specification is chosen depends on its phonological behavior and its patterning. Since the behavior of [33] in tone sandhi does not pattern with two high tones such as [55] and [53], it is suggested to specify [33] as [L. h]. More details will be seen in the following section. When it comes to the specification of [21], it seems reasonable to specify it as [L. hl]. While considered from the whole perspective, it is found that [21] pattern with [55] and [33] as the most frequent tone sandhi results. Since [55] and [33] are specified as the level tone, it is more reasonable to represent [21] as [L.l], which makes it more conformable to [55] and [33] as the tone sandhi results. Furthermore, the specification of [21] as [L.l] allows the production of [213] and [242] by linking a floating [h] tone to the underlying specification [L.l], as follows:

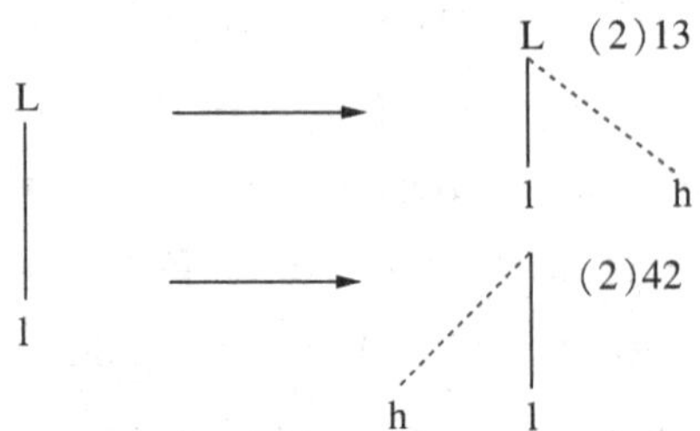

Diagram 7-1 Production of [213] and [242] on the basis of L.l [21]

Accordingly, the lexical tones and the derived tones in Fuzhou are represented as follows:

(9)

1st syllable	2nd syllable			
	H. h	H. hl	L. h	L. l
H. h/L. l	H. h	H. h	H. hl	H. hl
H. hl	H. h	H. l	H. l	L. l
L. h/L. l	L. l	L. l	H. lh	H. h

It is clear from (9) that in the tone sandhi of Fuzhou the level tones and contour tones display similar tone sandhi results, for example both [H. h] and [H. hl] can result in [H. h] when followed by [H. h]. And the tone sandhi results have the tendency of being reduced to be level tones, either as [55] (H. h), [33] (H. l) or [11] (L. l) (namely[21]), with only three exceptional cases. Furthermore, the high level tone 55 (H. h) is the most frequent tone sandhi result compared with the other two level tones. Why are so many level tones chosen as the tone sandhi results? What is responsible for such tone sandhi results?

7.2.4 Markedness of tone and tone sandhi in Fuzhou

With regard to the markedness of tones, Yip (2001: 315) uses Minimize Articulatory Effort (MINARTICEFF) to account for the different markedness of different tones as follows:

a. Contour tones are more marked than level tones: * CONTOUR.

b. Rising tones are more marked than falling tones: * RISE >> * FALL.

The markedness of tones not only is related to the markedness of tones themselves, but also is concerned with the prosodic positions in which they occur. There is one observation about the preference of different prosodic positions for tones. De Lacy (2002) shows that in a prosodic head position, H is preferred over M, which in turn is preferred over L. On the other hand, in a prosoidc non-head position, the tonal preference is the reverse: L is preferred over M, which in turn is preferred over H.

As mentioned above, the Fuzhou dialect, like Mandarin, Southern Min dialect, Tijian dialect, and Sixian Hakka dialect, is a right prominent language, and the rightmost (final) syllable retains all the contrast of the lexical tones, while the non-final syllable only has five tones after neutralization, mostly the level tones. The only two complex tones in Fuzhou such as [213] and [242] can only occur in the final position in Fuzhou, which turn to [55] or [53] in non-final position. Based on such characteristics, Chan (1985) proposes the Fuzhou dialect is an iambic language.

On the basis of the above prosodic theory and the markedness theory, the markedness aspects about the tone sandhi phenomenon of Fuzhou will be analyzed from the following three perspectives.

Firstly, when H tones appear in the non-head position and Low tones occur in the final position, which is listed as follows (the first column is the citation tone, and the first line is the tone in the final syllable):

(10)

1st syllable	2nd syllable			
	H. h	H. hl/H. h	L. h	L. l
H. h	---	---	H. hl	H. hl
H. hl	---	---	H. l	L. hl

As indicated in (11), the pitch or the register of high tone in the non-final position will lower as follows:

(11) H. h →H. hl/____L. h/L. hl

H. hl→H. l/_____L. h

H. hl→L. hl/____L. hl

As is shown in these three cases where the non-final syllables are H tones while the final syllables are L tones, the first syllable turns to a falling tone or a low tone. This process is not complete neutralization, as it is obvious that there is a tendency to preserve the comparative distinctness in the tone sandhi results. But there is no doubt that when the high marked H tone appears in the non-final syllable, the tone sandhi result chooses to be less marked by lowering H tone or changing high tone to low tone to better meet the requirement of the prosodic preference. Linguists have also observed that in tone languages, greater effort is needed to produce a rising tone than a falling tone, which accounts for the frequency of falling tones found in tone sandhi contexts, while rising tones in such positions are much rarer. Typically, the extent of pitch range covered by a low rising contour is less than that for a high falling contour (Chan 1985: 121). In fact, the similar case of the preference of low tone in the non-prominent position in Fuzhou can also be found in the phonological process of word splitting in Fuzhou in which the tones of the final syllables maintain the underlying tones, while the first syllable tones such as Yinqu ([213]), Yangqu ([242]) and Yinru ([24]) change to be [21], and [53] as well as [5] turn to [33] as follows (Chen Zeping 1998: 112):

(12)	吊 tau^{213}	→	ta^{21} lau^{213}	卷 kuoŋ^{33}	→	kuo^{33} luoŋ^{33}
	塌 t^{h}aʔ^{24}	→	t^{h}a^{21} laʔ^{24}	缠 tieŋ^{53}	→	tie^{33} lieŋ^{53}
	腆 t^{h}aiŋ^{213}	→	t^{h}a^{21} laiŋ^{213}	跳 t^{h}iu^{213}	→	t^{h}iu^{21} liu^{213}
	勾 kau^{55}	→	ka^{55} lau^{55}	夹 keiʔ^{24}	→	ke^{33} leiʔ^{24}

The similar case can also be found in the reduplication result of nouns and verbs in Fuzhou, which further backs up the unmarked status of L tone as well as falling tone in the non-head position. Such change from high tone to high falling tone in non-prominent position can also be found in the Wenzhou dialect of Wu, which is adjacent to Fuzhou.

There is one case such as 55 → 53/_33, namely H. h →H. hl/____L. h, which seems to be contradictory to choose the level tone as the tone sandhi result. It may be considered as an assimilation of the offset of [55] to the onset of the second tone [33], which results in [53], as suggested in Zhang Jie (2014). This is compatible with the assimilation pervasive both segmentally and suprasegmentally observed in Fuzhou.

Secondly, when the non-final position and the final position both have H tones, such as the following cases:

(13)		
	H. h	H. hl
H. h	H. h	H. h
H. hl	H. h	L. h

As is clear in (13), for the two adjacent high tones, the high tones in the non-final syllable turn to level tone in tone sandhi. This case is less marked than the first case where the non-final syllable is H tone while the final syllable is L tone. For the unmarkedness of high level tone, although it seems to be contradictory to the view that H tone is more marked, it is proposed here that in these tone sandhi results, what counts more is the level tone instead of register. In different languages, tone contour and register play different roles. As is clear in Fuzhou tone sandhi, the first available choice is thc tone contour in the process of reducing markedness. Only secondly does one need to consider the overall pitch register. A similar example of reduction to level tones can also be found in the Southern Wu dialect Wuyi, whose tonal inventory has six tones: 24, 213, 53, 31, 55, and 13, and in which the final syllable of a disyllabic word always preserves the original tone; but in non-final positions, tone sandhi neutralizes the inventory to two tones 55 and 11 (Zhang Jie 2007: 259 – 302).

Thirdly, when the two L tones occur in the final syllable and the non-final syllable, the tone sandhi results are as follows:

(14)

	L. h	L. l
L. l	H. hl	H. hl
L. h	H. lh	H. h

It seems that the tone sandhi results of two adjacent low tones turn to be more marked than before. In many Asian tone languages, there is evidence that two adjacent identical contours are not allowed, especially in Chinese (Yip 1989, 2002; Bao 1999; Chen 2000; Zhang Jisheng 2006). Chen (2001: 106) proposes that two identical tones may not abut each other (a fairly common manifestation of the Obligatory Contour Principle or OCP); consequently, they must undergo a dissimilatory process. For example, the Tianjin dialect not only bars adjacent identical tones, and it also disallows partially identical sequences of tone segments. In particular, it prohibits the sequence of two successive low tones. When such a sequence arises, it undergoes a common process called tonal absorption, which has its analogs in many West African languages. What is interesting in Fuzhou is that two adjacent identical low tones are not allowed irrespective of their contour. When two low level tones co-occur in one disyllabic compound or phrasal expression, the tone of the left-hand syllable change to be a tone of high register. The low tone is unmarked in the non-head position, but it is more marked in the head position according to De Lacy (1999, 2002). It has been observed that the unmarked element is more common and more stable, and it is also perceptually less salient (Rice 2007).

Hence, in the tone sandhi of Fuzhou dialect, when the tone of the first syllable and the second syllable are both L tone, bigger differences are produced to increase contrasts and enhance perceptability.

7.2.5 Characteristics of Fuzhou tone sandhi

Zhang Jie (2014) proposes that the tone sandhi nuetralization of the base tones in Fuzhou seem largely arbitrary: although the changes in 44 may be considered as assimilation of the offset of 44 to the onset of the second tone (e.g. 44→53/_2), no such motivation can be found for the behavior of 212 or 242. The sandhi tones of 53 and 32 also seem largely arbitrary phonetically: tonal assimilation and contour reduction may account for the change from 53 to 44 before 44, but not other changes. Why is the tone sandhi of Fuzhou so complicated? What is the typological characteristics of Fuzhou tone sandhi? However, tone sandhi is a kind of operation of sound change.

Clements (1989) lists eight "elementary operations", which can be presented as follows:

(15) Elementary Operations

a. Spread X

b. Delink X

c. Insert X

d. Delete X

e. Break X

f. Fuse X, Y

g. Permute X, Y

h. Map X to Y

As indicated in the above discussion, in the Fuzhou tone sandhi, most tone sandhi involves spreading and delinking of some tone features. Consider the following examples:

(16) a. [55] + [213/242/24]→[53] + [213/242/24]
([H. h] + [L. lh/L. hl]→[H. hl] + [L. lh/L. hl])
b. [53] + [55]→[55] + [55]
([H. hl] + [H. h]→[H. h] + [H. h])
c. [53] + [33]→[33] + [33]
([H. hl] + [L. h]→[L. h] + [L. h])
d. [53] + [213/242/24]→[21] + [213/242/24]
([H. hl] + [L. lh /L. hl]→[L. l] + [L. lh /L. hl])

The contour formation in the above examples occurs on the first tone and is made possible by spreading a [h] feature from the following syllable and delinking [l], as shown in Diagram 7-2, or spreading of register as well as tone as in Diagram 7-3, or spreading of tone contour as in Diagram 7-4:

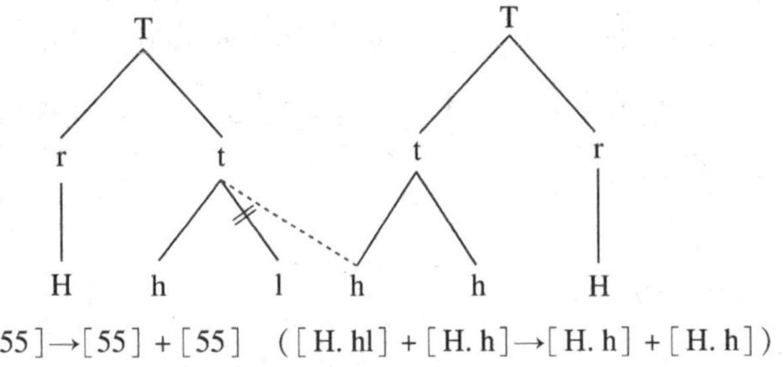

[53] + [55]→[55] + [55] ([H. hl] + [H. h]→[H. h] + [H. h])

Diagram 7-2 Delinking [l] and spreading [h] from the following syllable

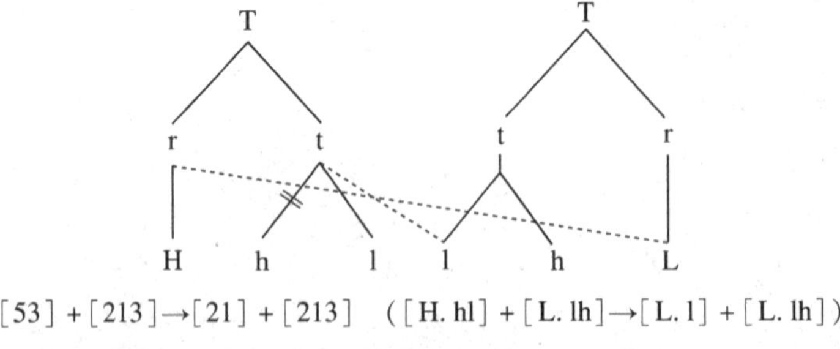

[53] + [213]→[21] + [213] ([H. hl] + [L. lh]→[L. l] + [L. lh])

Diagram 7-3 Spreading of register as well as tone

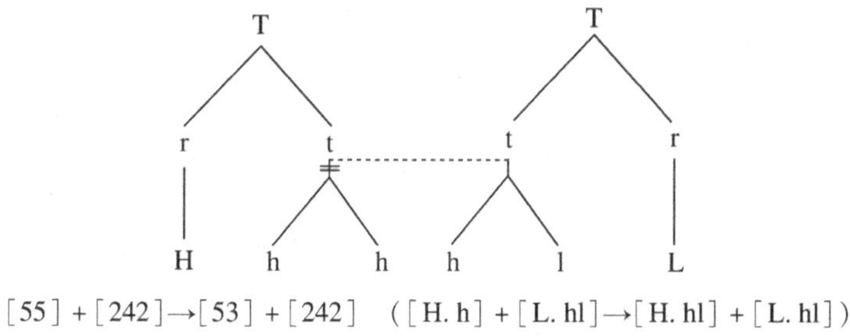

[55] + [242]→[53] + [242] ([H. h] + [L. hl]→[H. hl] + [L. hl])

Diagram 7-4 Spreading of tone contour

Articularily speaking, assimilation is often preferred to dissimilation in utterances, because assimilation serves to make sequences of articulatory gestures easier to produce, while dissimilation makes sequences that sound alike more unlike (Zhang Jisheng 2006: 211). Bao (1999: 174) proposes four types of assimilation in tone sandhi: tone assimilation, register assimilation, contour assimilation, and feature assimilation. As is shown in the above examples, there are quite a number of feature assimilation, as in the case of 55 + 33, and 55 + 213/242/24 and tone assimilation, as in the case of 213/242/24 + 55. Chen (2000: 79) puts forward that it is worth noting that contour assimilation is quite rare. Yet quite a number of contour assimilation cases can be found in Fuzhou tone sandhi such as the tone sandhi results of 53 + 55/ 33/ 213, 242, 24.

Along with the above cases, there are some cases which are obviously not the results of assimilation, as follows:

(17) Exceptional Examples

55 + 33→53 + 33	H. h + L. h→H. hl + L. h
53 + 53→33 + 53	H. hl + H. hl→L. h + H. hl
33 + 55→21 + 55	L. h + H. h→L. l + H. h
33 + 33→35 + 33	L. h + L. h→H. lh + L. h
33 + 213/242/24→55 + 213/242/24	L. h + L. l→H. h + L. l

What characteristics do these cases have in common? What category should these cases be put into? Bao (1999: 202) summarizes the universal tone rules in Hyman and Schuh's (1974) as follows:

(18)

Category	Types of Tone Sandhi Definition
1. Tone Shifting	Shifting of register, contour and tone
2. Dissimilation	An underlying tone changes to the opposite of the tone of an adjacent syllable.
3. Replacement	An underlying tone is replaced by another.
4. Displacement	A tone is realized on syllables away from its original syllable.
5. Downstep	Tones are realized with lower pitch than that of preceding tones within the same tone group.
6. Copying	A toneless syllable receives a copy of the tone of an adjacent syllable.
7. Polarization	A toneless syllable receives the opposite of the tone of an adjacent syllable.

Which category should the cases in (17) be included in (18)? Are they the converse of assimilation, namely dissimilation? Or should they be labeled under the category of replacement? Both dissimilation and replacement may involve the register, the contour, or the entire tone. Replacement is not easily distinguishable from instances of assimilation (tone shifting) or dissimilation. Yet context provides a clue: replacement is not context-sensitive, whereas assimilation and dissimilation, for example, are sensitive to neighbouring tones. Given this characterization, the Min Circle, the deictic expressions in Kejia, and the tone-derived verbs or nouns in classical Chinese are included in the category of tone replacement (Bao 1999: 202). As in these cases of Fuzhou, the tones of the first syllables change irrespective of the register and contour of the tones of the following syllables, as follows:

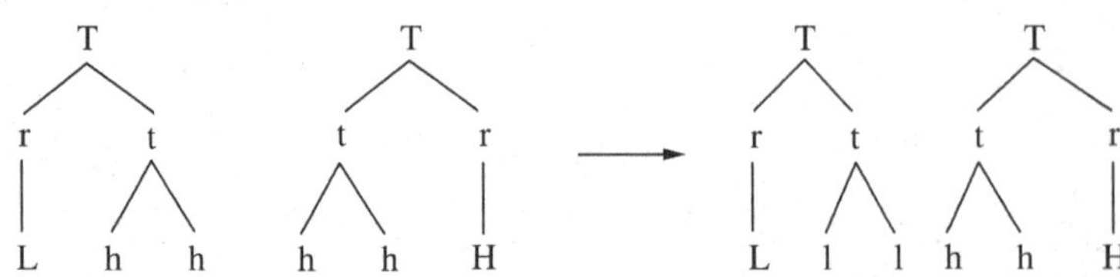

Diagram 7-5 Change irrespective of the register and contour of following tone

In this example, two high tone features under the tone node of the first syllable turn to be two low tone features, which is neither register dissimilation nor contour dissimilation. The tone of the first syllable changes with no influence from the second syllable. Accordingly, it is better to classify these cases under the category of replacement.

In the co-existence of assimilation and replacement in Fuzhou, it is obvious that tones under assimilation are a bit more than those under replacement, as indicated in (19):

(19)

	H. h	H. hl	L. h	L. l
H. h	H. h (A)	H. h (R)	H. hl (R)	H. hl (A)
H. hl	H. h (A)	L. h (R)	L. h (A)	L. l (A)
L. h	L. l (R)	L. l (R)	H. lh (R)	H. h (R)
L. l	H. h (A)	H. h (A)	H. hl (R)	H. hl (R)

Here it is suggested that despite the complexity of tone sandhi in Fuzhou, the arbitrariness of tone sandhi on the surface should not be arbitrary if viewed from the whole language system. As discussed in the above section, a large part of tones in tone sandhi undergo the influence of assimilation, leading to tone sandhi results closer to the tones of the following syllables in terms of feature, contour or even the whole tones. But it is clear that there are still some cases of replacement. Why did they not go through assimilation? This question can not be answered without the comprehensive perspective of Proto-Min. As discussed in the section of Quanzhou tone sandhi, it is put forward that the tone sandhi of Quanzhou is dominantly replacement similar to the Southern Min circle as discussed in literature. As an important branch of Proto-Min, the replacement in Fuzhou tone sandhi may be the relics of Proto-Min, which are left behind intact in the assimilation force that once worked so pervasively in the Fuzhou dialect either on segmental and suprasegmental levels. Then why are these replacement relics untouched in the assimilation? Wang (1983) discusses the assimilation in Middle Chinese, which assimilated the nuclear vowel [a] to [e], changing 野 from [ia] to [ie], 斜 from [ɕia] to [ɕie], leaving behind the cognates 家 as [tɕie], 吓 as [ɕie] without being assimilated. Wang Li proposed that only conditional sound changes can account for it, namely the assimilation rule worked during the time of *Zhong Yuan Yin Yun*, then it stopped, leaving some cognates untouched. Therefore, it is suggested that assimilation that once worked on segmental level also exerted influence upon the suprasegmental level. But the process of assimilation came to a halt before it brought all the tones under its influence. This may account for the reason for the complexity of tone sandhi of Fuzhou synchronically.

7.3 Comparison of tones between Quanzhou and Fuzhou

The comparison of tone systems of Quanzhou and Fuzhou may involve the perspectives of citation tones, and tone sandhi processes. In terms of citation tones, what is important is not only the pitch and register of tones, but also the patterning of the tones in the related systems. Zhu (2013: 230) puts forward that for a tone system, more tone contrasts, more marked for a tone system; more complex tones, more marked for a system (Yip 2002); more tone sandhi rules, more marked a system. As discussed, in the tone system of Quanzhou, there are seven tones in the Quanzhou dialect, as follows (Lin 1993):

Table 7-1 Tone patterning of Quanzhou

	Register	Ping	Shang	Qu	Ru
Quanzhou	Yin (High)	33	55	41	5
	Yang (Low)	24	22		24

Table 7-2 Tone patterning of Fuzhou

	Register	Ping	Shang	Qu	Ru
Fuzhou	Yin (High)	55	33	213	24
	Yang (Low)	53		242	5

It is noted that on the surface there are five tone contrasts in both Quanzhou and Fuzhou, which makes it impossible to judge the markedness of tone system only from the perspective of tone contrasts on the surface. But it is noticeable that the

Fuzhou tone system has complex tones which are not found in Quanzhou. Due to such observation, it may be more enlightening to delve into the tone sandhi processes of the two dialects to bring about their uniqueness.

Table 7-3 Tone sandhi of Quanzhou

	Register	Ping (Even)	Shang (Rising)	Qu (Going)	Ru (Entering)
Quanzhou	Yin (High)	33	55→24	41→55	5→24
	Yang (Low)	24→22	22	41→22	24→22

Table 7-4 Tone sandhi of bisyllabic words of Fuzhou

1st syllable	2nd syllable			
	55	53/5	33	213/242/24
55 213/242/24	55	55	53	53
53 5	55	33	33	21
33 24	21	21	35	55

The tone sandhi processes in Quanzhou and Fuzhou are the same in that they are the right dominant tone sandhi type, which means that in the tone sandhi process it is usually the left tone of a sandhi unit that undergoes the tone sandhi process. They are also similar in that the tone sandhi results in the two dialects tend to choose the level tones as the tone sandhi results. The two dialects differ in that in Quanzhou the low level tone is more preferred as the tone sandhi result while all the original yang (low) register tones choose 22 as the sandhi result; in contrast, the level tones chosen as the tone sandhi results in Fuzhou range from the high level tone 55 to the middle level tone 33, to the low level tone 21 (specified as low + low, namely 11 as discussed), which implies that despite the fact that the neutralization is also a mainstream in the tone sandhi of Fuzhou, the tone system of Fuzhou still prefers to maintain more tone contrasts in its tone sandhi results. But what is more important for tone sandhi processes of these two dialects lies in the typological characteristics reflected. As discussed, the tone sandhi process in Quanzhou, which is a contextually-free tone sandhi, is under no influence of the adjacent tone, and the tone sandhi result is part of the original tone inventory, without bringing about new tone contrasts, due to which the tone sandhi in Quanzhou is labeled under the type of replacement as mentioned in Bao (1999). In contrast, the tone sandhi in Fuzhou which is contextually sensitive is more affected by the adjacent tone in the tone sandhi and the tone sandhi processes involve more types either in the form of assimilation which is the dominant process or in the form of replacement which is deemed as the remnant of the gradient process of assimilation. On the basis of such observation, it is suggested that the tone system in Fuzhou is more marked either in owning more complex tones on the surface or in the preservation of more contrasts in the tone sandhi process as well as involving more types of tone sandhi processes such as assimilation as well as replacement. While the tone system in Quanzhou is less marked in the reduction of tone contrasts in its tone sandhi process. The difference between Quanzhou and Fuzhou in the suprasegmental perspective is the result of the conflict of markedness mechanisms.

7.4 Summary

The tone systems of Quanzhou and Fuzhou are not only different in the exact specification of tones but also different in tone sandhi complexity and types despite the fact that both two dialects belong to the right-dominant type. The disparity of the tone systems as well as the tone sandhi processes of Quanzhou and Fuzhou is summarized as follows:

a. The specification of tones is not the same in both dialects. In the Fuzhou dialect, there are two complex tones, namely 213 and 242, which only occur in the final position and turn to simple tones in the non-final syllable, which is not found in Quanzhou.

b. The unmarked tones in two dialects are also not the same as in Quanzhou the low level tone is more preferred which finds its countrpart in Fuzhou ranging from the high level tone 55 to the middle level tone 33, to the low level tone 21, which implies that despite the fact that the neutralization is also a mainstream in the tone sandhi of Fuzhou, the tone system of Fuzhou still prefers to maintain more tone contrasts in its tone sandhi results.

c. The tone sandhi of Quanzhou is a typical case of replacement which is not related to the tone sandhi context. In contrast, the tone sandhi of Fuzhou, while retaining some cases of replacement, also exhibits remarkable cases of assimilation involving either register or contour or both these two factors, which is similar to the case of Wenzhou.

Chapter 8

Conclusion

This book is devoted to present a detailed analysis of the phonology of Quanzhou and Fuzhou followed by the comparison of the markedness of the phonological systems of these two dialects, which includes (i) the inventories of the initial consonants and finals of Quanzhou and Fuzhou, (ii) the markedness of the initial consonants and simplex vowels of Quanzhou and Fuzhou, (iii) the hierarchies of the contrastive features of initial consonants and simplex vowels in Quanzhou and Fuzhou, (iv) the syllable structures of Quanzhou and Fuzhou, (v) the colloquial and literate systems of the two dialects, and (vi) the tone systems of the two dialects. The most significant conclusions drawn from the analysis is that cross-linguistically speaking, Southern Min and Eastern Min have evolved to manifest quite different phonological characteristics in terms of segmental and suprasegmental perspective under the influence of different mechanisms. The main research procedures include: firstly, the phonological systems of Quanzhou and Fuzhou are analyzed under the guidance of the markedness theory and the theory of hierarchy of contrastive features. Secondly, the markedness of Quanzhou and Fuzhou are compared with an aim to account for the differences between these two dialects observed synchroncially. The main findings include: Quanzhou is a showcase of more markedness reduction which is not only manifested in the initial changes, the final changes but also reflected in the neutralization of tones; in contrast, Fuzhou reflects more markedness preservation in having more marked initials, retaining more marked simplex vowels and finals, manifesting more marked syllable structures, and displaying more complicated tone sandhi. The following section will offer a report on general conclusions with respect to the findings concerning the observation about the phonological differences about Quanzhou and Fuzhou.

8.1 Main findings

8.1.1 Main phonological characteristics of Quanzhou

In the diachronic development of Quanzhou phonology, there is a remarkable tendency of markedness reduction in terms of debuccalization of initials, reduction of finals to be less marked finals such as schwa and syllabic nasal, simplification of syllable structures and neutralization of tone sandhi results.

(1) With respect to consonants, regarding PoA, the Quanzhou initial system contains most unmarked glottal fricative, which in many cases is the reduction result of nasal initials. With respect to MoA, Quanzhou not only contains the contrast between aspiration and unaspiration but also manifests the alternation between the nasal initials and the voiced initials due to the process of denasalization. In terms of finals, the Quanzhou vowel system contains five most unmarked peripheral simplex vowels as well as two non-low central vowels.

The hierarchy of the contrastive features of initial consonants in Quanzhou is manifested as [nasal] > [strident] > [continuant]; [Labial], [Dorsal] > [Coronal]. The dominance of MoA over PoA in Quanzhou is a reflection of the tendency of retaining MoA while neutralizing PoA in the phonological process of regressive assimilation of Quanzhou. The classification of Labial and Dorsal under the natural class distinct from Coronal also finds evidence in the changes of finals following these three places of articulation. The hierarchy of the contrastive features of simplex vowels of Quanzhou is [low] > [peripheral] > [high] > [ATR] > [back], which highlights the employment of two main parameters such as [back] and [high] in the construction of simplex vowel inventory of Quanzhou as well as in forming the contrast between the peripheral vowels and the non-peripheral vowels.

(2) In terms of syllable structure, Quanzhou displays more unmarked syllable structures compared with Fuzhou, which is interestingly reflected in that when Fuzhou retains offglide, Quanzhou tends to show up with preglide in the same cognates, when Fuzhou manifests pre-glide, Quanzhou turns to have no glide, which is even furthered by the segmental reduction to be central vowel or syllabic consonant. Regarding the markedness tendency of syllables of Quanzhou, the literate and colloquial systems also provide profound evidence. Such markedness reduction tendency of Quanzhou is attested to be systematic phenomenon instead of sporadic cases.

(3) Regarding the phonological processes, Quanzhou is found to have manifested such processes as dissimilation, merge, regressive assimilation, which is related to markedness in some way.

(4) With respect to tone, Quanzhou contains no complex tones and its tone sandhi is noted for replacement with no reference to context, and the tone sandhi results of yang register all leveled to be the same low level tone.

8.1.2 Main phonological characteristics of Fuzhou

The phonological system of Fuzhou is noted for maintaining more marked elements in its diachronic development, which is manifested in the phonological process of categorical transformation of initials, the final alternation, and in its tone system. In the categorical transformation of initials of Fuzhou, the contrasts of underlying initials are neutralized to usher new contrasts. In terms of finals, the simplex vowel inventory of Fuzhou retains more marked rounded vowels as well as remarkable contrasts of front vowels. The final system of Fuzhou containing more marked diphthongs is more complicated by its unique rhyme alternation.

(1) For the initial consonants of Fuzhou, in terms of PoA, Fuzhou consonant system contains more sonorant velar fricatives and velar nasal initials; regarding MoA, the initials of Fuzhou retain the contrast between aspiration and

unaspiration. The initials of Fuzhou are remarkably noted for the categorical transformation which renders the contrasts of underlying consonants to be replaced by the new contrasts of surface consonants. With regard to the simplex vowel system, Fuzhou is noted for its rich and systematic distribution of front vowels which are contrasted in [round] and [high]. The phonology system of Fuzhou displays the systematic preference for the more sonorant finals, which is also attested in the final alternation process triggered by the lengthening of the final syllable which brings about more sonorant finals.

The observation about the initial consonant inventory as well as the vowel inventory and the analysis of the diachronic as well as synchronic sound changes of Fuzhou bring about the hierarchy of the contrastive features of initial consonants and simplex vowels of Fuzhou. It is found that in the hierarchy of the contrastive features of initial consonants of Fuzhou, PoA is dominant over MoA, which is a reflection of the observation that the places of consonants tend to be preserved while the manners of consonants are prone to be changed in the related phonological process such as the categorical transformation. In the sub-ranking of PoA, [Dorsal] dominates [Labial] that outranks [Coronal], which mirrors the different markedness reduction in the process of categorical transformation of initials of these places of articulation in Fuzhou; in the ranking of MoA, [nasal] dominates [strident] that outranks [continuant], which indicates the great markedness of nasal consonants that is responsible for them being the trigger of systematic progressive assimilation. Through the observation of simplex vowels, it is found that the hierarchy of the contrastive features of vowels is [low] > [round] > [high] > [back], which indicates the active role played by roundedness feature in the rounding assimilation in Fuzhou. Accordingly, it is reasonable to state that the unique hierarchies of contrastive features of Fuzhou provide a good account for the phonological uniqueness of this dialect.

(2) Regarding syllable structures, Fuzhou is noted for having marked syllable structure containing preglide as well as offglide such as GVG. The markedness of Fuzhou syllable structures is part of the preference for more weightier elements in Fuzhou phonological system. Besides, the diphthongs of

Fuzhou are noted to have a remarkable assimilation especially in terms of [round] as well as [backness] feature. Such markedness tendency of Fuzhou is also attested to be a systematic phenomenon rather than sporadic cases.

(3) With respect to the phonological processes, Fuzhou is remarkably noted even among the Chinese dialects for its categorical transformation of the initials of Fuzhou and the final alternation, which can still be observed synchronically. Besides, Fuzhou is also noted to manifest an assimilation tendency which may have been a result of diachronic evolution. All these phonological processes lend a proof to the active role of assimilation in the evolution of Fuzhou.

(4) In terms of the tone system of Fuzhou, the tone sandhi of Fuzhou manifests both assimilation and replacement, the former of which is considered to be an innovation of Fuzhou, and the latter of which is suggested to be the remnant of Proto-Min similar to Southern Min.

8.1.3 Markedness differences and the characteristics of Southern Min and Eastern Min

Based on the analysis of the inventories of initial consonants and finals in Quanzhou and Fuzhou, the numbers and contents of contrasts, the phonological performances of the contrastive features, the hierarchies of contrastive features of Quanzhou and Fuzhou, it is found that Quanzhou and Fuzhou have manifested a systematic phonological difference. It is observed that Quanzhou has more tendencies of markedness reduction in terms of the segmental and suprasegmental perspective while Fuzhou is remarkable in retaining more marked elements both segmentally and suprasegmentally. The different numbers and contents of contrastive features may exert different influence upon the related phonological systems. The more contrastive features, the larger inventory may be and more complex segments may surface up in the system. Furthermore, more complicated features may trigger more sound changes. Such markedness differences of Quanzhou and Fuzhou are partly due to the influence of the principles of markedness preservation, markedness reduction, and markedness conflation.

According to the above discussion, the differences between markedness and phonological characteristics of Quanzhou and Fuzhou may be summarized as follows:

(1) In terms of the inventory of the initial consonants, Quanzhou and Fuzhou have the same contrasts except that the fricative in Quanzhou is glottal fricative while the fricative in Fuzhou is velar fricative. But on the surface, Fuzhou is noted to have new contrasts different from the underlying contrasts brought about by sound changes though restricted in the non-initial syllables, which ushers in more marked consonants such as [β] and [ns]. In contrast in the case of Quanzhou, the underlying contrasts are the same with the surface contrasts and there is a more unmarked consonant on the surface, for example, the glottal fricative which is the reduction result of the corresponding nasal initials. From the perspective of simplex vowel inventory, Fuzhou is more marked in having more marked simplex vowels and more contrastive features which are responsible for the related sound changes in Fuzhou. Furthermore, Fuzhou is noted to have more front vowels and rounded vowels, which leads to asymmetric vowel pattern in Fuzhou, while Quanzhou has a more symmetric vowel pattern, including five most common vowels added by non-low two central vowels. This provides a good evidence to the hypothesis that the systematic contrast shifts may result in differences of dialects.

Table 8-1 Markedness comparison of the consonants and vowels as well as sound changes in Quanzhou and Fuzhou

		Quanzhou	Fuzhou
Initial Consonants	Before the related sound changes	p, p^h; t, t^h; k, k^h s, ts, ts^h, h m, n, ŋ	p, p^h; t, t^h; k, k^h s, ts, ts^h, x m, n, ŋ
	After the related sound changes	• [h] as the result of reduction • The same contrasts with the underlying	• [β] and [ns] as the result of categorical transformation • Many new contrasts different from the underlying
Simplex Vowels	Underlying	Totally eight vowels: /i, u, e, o, ɔ, ɨ, ə, a/, including five most common peripheral vowels and two central vowels.	Totally seven vowels: /i, y, u, ɔ, ɛ, œ, a/, with more marked rounded vowels such as /y, œ/.

(2) The ranking of hierarchies of contrastive features of the initial consonants of the two dialects are quite different in that in Quanzhou MoA outranks PoA while in Fuzhou PoA dominates MoA, in addition to which, the sub-ranking in PoA are also distinct in Quanzhou in that Coronal is unmarked with respect to Labial as well as Dorsal, in contrast in Fuzhou Dorsal is more marked than Labial which is more marked than Coronal. Regarding the hierarchies of contrastive features of the simplex vowels of the two dialects, it is found that Fuzhou employs one more feature such as [round] than Quanzhou which is observed to have fuller employment of such parameter as height. Such a disparity between Quanzhou and Fuzhou provides a good answer to the hypothesis that the unique hierarchies of contrastive features provide a good account for the phonological differences of these two dialects.

Table 8-2 Markedness comparison of hierarchies of the contrastive features in Quanzhou and Fuzhou

		Quanzhou	**Fuzhou**
Hierarchy	consonant	I MoA [nasal] > [strident] > [continuant]	I PoA [Dorsal] > [Labial] > [Coronal]
		II PoA [Labial], [Dorsal] > [Coronal]	II MoA [nasal] > [strident] > [continuant]
	vowel	[low] > [peripheral] > [high] > [ATR] > [back]	[low] > [round] > [high] > [back]

(3) From the perspective of syllable structure, Quanzhou displays more tendency of syllable markedness reduction even segmental reduction while containing more coda contrasts, in contrast Fuzhou tends to retain more marked and more complex syllable structures accompanied with the merging of coda contrasts to be only the velar nasal and glottal stop. In addition, in Quanzhou preglide is preferred when the nuclear vowel is the middle vowel, which finds their counterparts in Fuzhou in offglide. The markedness tendency and contrast finds more profound evidence in the literate and colloquial systems of these two dialects. Such markedness differences between Quanzhou and Fuzhou have been

attested to be a quite systematic phenomenon.

Table 8-3 Markedness comparison of syllable structures of Quazhou and Fuzhou

Syllable Structures		Quanzhou	Fuzhou
Open Syllable	$V_{mid}G$		√
	GVG		√
	Nasalized V	√	
Closed Syllable	Multi-contrasts in coda	√	
	Uni-contrast in coda		√

Under the influence of different mechanisms, Quanzhou and Fuzhou undergo a number of sound changes, which shape the phonological system of Quanzhou to show more markedness reduction characteristics and the phonological system of Fuzhou to manifest more markedness preservation traces.

Table 8-4 Markedness comparison of sound changes of Quazhou and Fuzhou

	Types		Quanzhou	Fuzhou
Sound Changes	initial	denasalization	√	
		regressive assimilation	√	
		categorical transformation		√
		correlation between initials and rhymes		√
	final	final alternation		√
		vowel rising	√	
		segment merger	√	
		assimilation		√
		dissimilation	√	
	tone	tone sandhi	replacement	assimilation + replacement

In this book, the phonology of Quanzhou and Fuzhou is analyzed under the framework of the markedness theory, the theory of the hierarchy of contrastive features, and the typology theory. It is found that cross-linguistically speaking, Quanzhou and Fuzhou which though descended from the same Proto-Min have evolved in divergent directions to manifest rather different phonological systems, which may be responsible for so many suggestions on dividing Southern Min and Eastern Min into two different dialect groups. The cases of Quanzhou and Fuzhou provide evidence to the cross-linguistic observation that different dialects/languages with similar-looking inventories may actually differ in their feature ordering, and hence in the relative scopes of contrastive features. The case of Quanzhou and Fuzhou is also a good example for the argument that the dialects descending from the same Proto-dialect may evolve to bear systematic markedness differences. It is observed that phonologically speaking, Southern Min with Quanzhou as representative and Eastern Min with Fuzhou as representative have evolved to be dialects with systematically different phonological characteristics.

8.2 Limitations and suggestions for further study

8.2.1 Limitations

With an aim to analyze the phonological characteristics of Southern Min and Eastern Min from the perspecitve of markedness, two typical dialects such as Quanzhou and Fuzhou are chosen as the subjects of analysis in this book. Despite the fact that these two dialects indeed bear the most typical characteristics of Southern Min and Eastern Min, the same typical characterists can not be guaranteed to exist in all other sub-dialects of Southern Min and Eastern Min. The phonological characteristics which have remarkably manifested in Quanzhou and Fuzhou may not be found to be systematic and categorical in the other sub-dialects of Southern Min and Eastern Min. More comprehensive description and comparison of the other sub-dialects of Southern Min and Eastern Min is needed in viewing such different typological evolution processes within these two areas. The different phonological characteristics observed in Quanzhou and Fuzhou can be better verified with more related data available. Moreover, for the motivation for such phonological differences, this book probes into this issue from the perspective of language-internal factors such as assimilation and dissimilation; for the external factors, this book only mentions the possible influence from Southern Wu, such as Wenzhou whose phonetic parameters of vowels are quite similar to those of Fuzhou whose are quite different from those of Quanzhou. Whether the language contact has played a role in shaping the phonological characteristics of Southern Min and Eastern Min and how much influence the language contact has exerted in such evolution need more attention in understanding the phonological differences of Southern Min and Eastern Min.

8.2.2 Suggestions for further study

Due to deficit data or lack of more background information, some issues listed in the book require further study. The phonological study of Southern Min and Eastern Min is a quite interesting issue, which covers a large number of related topics. Even within Southern Min as well as Eastern Min themselves, how the phonological characteristics are manifested is also a quite attractive issue worthy further probing. For example, in Southern Min which is composed of Quanzhou accent, Zhangzhou accent and Xiamen accent, how are the systematic markedness reduction chararcteristics found in Quanzhou manifested in the other sub-dialects of Southern Min? This question not only needs more phonetic and phonological investigation, but also requires other approaches. This book is just a beginner, which starts a wonderful journey into the exploration of the variety of Min.

References

Akinlabi, A. *Tonal Underspecification and Yoruba Tones.* PhD dissertation. Nigeria: University of Ibadan, 1985.

Anttila, Arto. Gradient phonotactics and the complexity hypothesis. *Natural Language & Linguistic Theory*, 2008, 26 (4): 695 – 729.

Archangeli, Diana. *Underspecification in Yawelmani Phonology and Morphology.* PhD dissertation. Bosfon: MIT, 1984.

Archangeli, Diana. Aspects of underspecification theory. *Phonology*, 1988 (5): 183 – 208.

Ashton, Ethel O. *Swahili Grammar (Including Intonation).* London: Longmans, Green & Co., 1944.

Avanesov, R. I. *Russkoe Literaturnoe Proiznoshenie.* Moscow: Prosveshchenie, 1972.

Avery, Peter & Rice, Keren. Segment structure and coronal underspecification. *Phonology*, 1989 (6): 179 – 200, 195.

Bagemihl, Bruce. The crossing constraint and "backwards languages". *NLLT*, 7: 481 – 549, 1989.

Battistella, Edwin. *Markedness: The Evaluative Superstructure of Language.* Albany: State University of New York Press, 1990.

Bao, Zhiming. Fan-Qie languages and reduplication. *Linguistic Inquiry*, 1990a (21): 317 – 350.

Bao, Zhiming. *On the Nature of Tone.* PhD dissertation. Boston: MIT, 1990b.

Bao, Zhiming. *The Generative Phonology and Its Application.* Beijing: Chinese

Social and Scientific Press, 1997.

Bao, Zhiming. *The Structure of Tone*. New York, Oxford: OUP, 1999.

Bao, Zhiming. Sub-syllabic processes and the Southern Min syllable. In Debao Xu (ed.), *Chinese Phonology in Generative Grammar*. NewYork: Academic Press, 95 - 116, 2000.

Bao, Zhiming. Accentualism in Chinese. *Language and Linguistics*, 2004 (5): 863 - 889.

Barnes, Jonathan. *Positional Neutralization: A Phonologization Approach to Typological Patterns*. PhD dissertation. Berkeley: University of California, 2002.

Barries, Michael. Tone circles and contrast preservation. *Linguistic Inquiry*, 2006, 37 (1): 131 - 141.

Bauer, Laurie. Contrast in language and linguistics. *Journal of English Linguistics*, 2008 (36): 93 - 98.

Beckman, Jill N. *Positional Faithfulness*. PhD dissertation. Amherst: University of Massachusetts, 1997.

Bell, A. Syllabic consonants. In J. Greenberg (ed.), *Universals of Human Language* (*Volume* 2): *Phonology*. Stanford: Stanford University Press, 153 - 201, 1978.

Bernhardt, Barbara & Joseph, Stemberger. *Handbook of Phonological Development from the Perspective of Constraint-Based Non-linear Phonology*. San Diego: Academic Press, 1998.

Bloomfield, Leonard. *Language*. New York: Holt, 1933.

Browman, C. P. & Goldstein, L. "Targetless" schwa: An articulatory analysis. In J. Kingston & M. E. Beckman (eds.), *Papers in Laboratory Phonology II. Gesture, Segment, Prosody*. Cambridge: Cambridge University Press, 26 - 56, 1992.

Burquest, Donald A. & David, L. Payne. *Phonological Analysis: A Functional Approach*. Dallas, TX: Summer Institute of Linguistics, 1993.

Bybee, Joan. Markedness: Iconicity, economy and frequency. In Jae Jung Song (ed.), *The Oxford Handbook of Linguistic Typology*. Oxford:

Oxford University Press, 134, 2010.

Cai, Guomei. *The Study of Puxian Dialect.* PhD dissertation. Fuzhou: Fujian Normal University, 2006.

Cai, Sujuan. The tone sandhi of Southern Min and the hypothesis of choice of lexical alternative. *Modern Linguistics*, 2002 (4): 18 –25.

Cao, Fengfu. The changes of diminutives of *Hui Yin Miao Wu*. *Language and Linguistics*, 2012, 13 (2): 221 –246.

Causley, Trisha. *Complexity and Markedness in Optimality Theory.* PhD dissertation. Toronto: University of Toronto, 1999.

Chan, Lee Lily. *Fuzhou Tone Sandhi.* PhD dissertation. San Diego: University of California, 1998.

Chan, Marjorie. *Fuzhou Phonology: A Non-linear Analysis of Tone and Stress.* PhD dissertation. Washington: University of Washington, 1985.

Chan, Marjorie. On the final glottal stop in Fuzhou. In Scott Delancey & Russell S. Tomlin (eds.), *Proceedings of the First Annual Meeting of the Pacific Linguistics Conference.* Eugene: University of Oregon, 54 –68, 1985.

Chan, Marjorie. Prelinked and floating glottal stops in Fuzhou Chinese. *Canadian Journal of Linguistics*, 1990 (35): 331 –349.

Chan, Marjorie. Fuzhou glottal stop: Floating segment or correlation of close contact? In Wang Jialing & Norval Smith (eds.), *Studies in Chinese Phonology*. Berlin: Mouton de Gruyter, 275 –289, 1996.

Chao, Yuanren. *Studies in the Modern Wu-Dialects*. Peking: Tsing Hua College Research Institute, 1928.

Chao, Yuanren. The non-uniqueness of phonemic solutions of phonetic systems. *Bulletin of the Institute of History and Philology*, *Academic Sinica*, 1934 (4): 363.

Chao, Yuanren. *Mandarin Primer*. Harvard: Harvard University Press, 1948.

Chao, Yuanren. The contrastive aspects of the Wu dialects. *Language*, 1967 (43): 1, 92 –101.

Chen, Baoxian. The tone sandhi of Xinqiao, Zhangping, Fujian. *Dialect*, 2010 (2): 171 –175.

Chen, Matthew Y. Cross-dialectal comparison: A case study and some theoretical considerations. *Journal of Chinese Linguistics*, 1973, 1 (1): 38 -63.

Chen, Matthew Y. An areal study of nasalization in Chinese. *Journal of Chinese Linguistics*, 1975, 3 (1): 16 -59.

Chen, Matthew Y. The syntax of Xiamen tone sandhi. *Phonology Yearbook*, 1987 (4): 109 -150.

Chen, Matthew Y. *Tone Sandhi: Patterns Across Chinese Dialects*. Cambridge: Cambridge University Press, 2000.

Chen, Matthew Y. *Tone Sandhi: Patterns Across Chinese Dialects*. Beijing: Foreign Language Teaching and Research Publishing House, 2001.

Chen, Shujuan. The new sound changes of Southern Min of Taiwan. *Language and Linguistics*, 2010, 11 (2): 425 -468.

Chen, Zhangtai & Li, Rulong. *The Study of Min Dialects*. Beijing: Yu Wen Press, 1983.

Chen, Qin. The categorical transformation of onsets of Pinghu Gutian. *Minjiang College Journal*, 2006 (6): 93 -97.

Chen, Zhongmin. On stratum of Yu rhyme of Min: The stratum analysis and comparison methods. *Bulletin of Language Studies*, 2012 (9): 6 -26.

Chen, Zhongmin. *The Study of the Phonetic History of Chinese Dialects as Well as the Analysis of the Historic Strata*. Shanghai: Zhongxi Book Company, 2013.

Chen, Zeping. *The Study of Fuzhou Dialect*. Fuzhou: Fujian People Press, 1998.

Chen, Zeping. Some literature for the study of Fuzhou used by the preachers of the 19th century. *Journal of Fujian Normal University*, 2003 (3): 34 -38.

Chen, Zeping. *Fuzhou Dialect since the 19th Century*. Fuzhou: Fujian People Press, 2010.

Chen, Xiaoqi. The phonological changes of Yongfu, Zhangping, Southern Min. *Qinghua University Journal*, 2010 (4): 73 -120.

Chen, Zeping. The OT analysis of the categorical transformation of onsets of Eastern Min. *Journal of Fujian Normal University (Philosophy and Social*

Sciences Edition), 2013 (5): 108 – 117.

Cheon, Sang Yee. Glides as consonants in Korean. *Language Research*, 2002, 38 (2), 619 – 645.

Chung, Raung-fu. *The Segmental Phonology of Southern Min in Taiwan*. Taipei: The Crane Publishing Co., Ltd, 1996.

Chung, Raung-fu. The preglide of Southern Min of Taiwan. *Studies of Chinese Languages*, 1997 (4): 289 – 294.

Chomsky, N. & Halle, M. *The Sound Pattern of English*. New York: Harper and Row, 1968.

Christopher, R. Green, et al. On the role of margin phonotactics in colloquial Bamana complex syllables. *Nat Lang Linguist Theory*, 2014 (32): 499 – 536.

Clements, G. N. The geometry of phonological features. *Phonology Yearbook*, 1985 (2): 223 – 252.

Clements, G. N. The role of the sonority cycle in core syllabification. In J. Kingston & Mary E. Beckman (eds.), *Papers in Laboratory Phonology I: Between the Grammar and Physics of Speech*. Cambridge: CUP, 283 – 333, 1990.

Clements, G. N. Place of articulation in consonants and vowels: A unified theory. *Working Papers of the Cornell Phonetics Laboratory*. Ithaca: Cornell University, 77 – 123, 1991.

Clements, G. N. Affricates as non-contoured stops. In O. Fujimura, et al. (eds.), *Item, Order in Language and Speech*. Prague: Charles University Press, 271 – 299, 1999.

Clements, G. N. Feature economy in sound systems. *Phonology*, 2003 (20): 287 – 333.

Clements, G. N. & Samuel, J. Keyser. *CV Phonology. A Generative Theory of the Syllable*. Cambridge: MIT Press, 1983.

Crosswhite, Katherine. *Vowel Reduction in Optimality Theory*. New York: Routledge, 2001.

Crothers, John. *Typology and Universals of Vowel Systems*. Stanford: Stanford

University Press, 1978.

Dai, Ligang. *The Stratum of Min and Its Evolution*. PhD dissertation. Shanghai: Fudan University, 2005.

Dai, Ligang. The spreading of Fuzhou within Puxian dialects. *Shangrao College Journal*, 2006 (2): 98 - 101.

Dai, Ligang. Diachronic strata analysis in dialectology: A critical review of the theories, methods and difficulties. *Contemporary Linguistics*, 2007 (1): 14 - 25.

Dai, Ligang. The rhyme alternation of Fu'an. *Studies of Chinese Languages*, 2008 (3): 216 - 227.

Dai, Ligang. The reason for exceptions of the categorical transformation of onsets of Fuzhou. *Dialect*, 2010 (3): 230 - 236.

De Lacy, Paul. Markedness in prominent positions. In Ora Matushansky, et al. (eds.), *HUMIT 2000: MITWPL 40*. Cambridge, MA: MIT Working Papers in Linguistics, 53 - 66, 2000.

De Lacy, Paul. *The Formal Expression of Markedness*. PhD dissertation. Amherst: University of Massachusetts, 2002.

De Lacy, Paul. *Markedness: Reduction and Preservation in Phonology*. Cambridge: Cambridge University Press, 2006.

De Lacy, Paul. *The Cambridge Handbook of Phonology*. Cambridge: Cambridge University Press, 2007.

Deng, Xiangzhang. *The Phonetic Analysis of Northern Min and Central Min*. PhD dissertation. Xiamen: Xiamen University, 2007.

Ding, Bangxin. The conditions for dividing Chinese dialect groups. The proceedings for the celebration of 80-year-old of Mr Li Fanggui. *Qinghua University Journal*, 1982, 14 (1, 2): 257 - 273, 169 - 170.

Ding, Bangxin. *The Collection of Papers of Ding Bangxin*. Beijing: The Commercial Press, 1998.

Dong, Xinsheng. The phonology of Hui Yin Miao Wu and its changes. Dissertation for Master Degree. Xiamen: Xiamen University, 2006.

Dresher, B. Elan. Child phonology, learnability, and phonological theory. In

Tej Bhatia & William C. Ritchie (eds.), *Handbook of Language Acquisition*. New York: Academic Press, 299 – 346, 1998.

Dresher, B. Elan. Contrast and asymmetries in inventories. In A.-M. di Sciullo (ed.), *Asymmetry in Grammar: Morphology, Phonology, Acquisition*. Amsterdam: John Benjamins, 239 – 257, 2003a.

Dresher, B. Elan. The contrastive hierarchy in phonology. In D. C. Hall (ed.), *Toronto Working Papers in Linguistics*. Toronto: University of Toronto, 47 – 62, 2003b.

Dresher, B. Elan. *The Contrastive Hierarchy in Phonology*. Cambridge: Cambridge University Press, 2009.

Dresher, B. Elan & Hulst, Harry van der. Head-dependent asymmetries in phonology: Complexity and visibility. *Phonology*, 1998 (15): 317 – 352.

Dresher, B. Elan & Zhang, Xi. Contrast in Manchu vowel systems. In Carsten Naher (ed.), *Proceedings of the First International Conference on Manchu-Tungus Studies II: Trends in Tungusic and Siberian Linguistics*. Wiesbaden: Harrassowitz, 23 – 43, 2004.

Dreshera, B. Elan, Harveya, Christopher & Oxford, Will. Contrast shift as a type of diachronic change. In Hsin-Lun Huang, Ethan Poole & Amanda Rysling (eds.), *Proceedings of NELS 43*. Amherst, Massachusetts: GLSA, 103 – 116, 2014.

Dressler, Wolfgang U. Markedness and naturalness in phonology: The case of natural phonology. In Olga Tomic (ed.), *Markedness in Synchrony and Diachrony*. New York: Mouton de Gruyter, 111 – 120, 1989.

Du, Jialun. The stratum analysis of the ancient voiced onsets of Min. *Language and Linguistics*, 2013, 14 (2): 409 – 456.

Du, Jialun. *The Diachronic Strata Analysis of Min Phonology*. Taipei: Zhongxi Book Company, 2014.

Duanmu, San. *A Formal Study of Syllable, Tone, Stress and Domain in Chinese Languages*. PhD dissertation. Boston: MIT, 1990a.

Duanmu, San. On the fixed syllabic structures of Chinese languages. *Proceedings of the 1989 Western Conference on Linguistics*. Fresno: California State University, 1990b.

Duanmu, San. *The Phonology of Standard Chinese*. Oxford: Oxford University Press, 2007.

Duke, Daniel & Martin, Marieke. Pharyngealized vowels in Kwasio (Bantu A80): A case of devoicing? Paper presented at the 6th World Congress on African linguistics, August 2009.

Du, Xiaoping. The historical stratum reflected in the words bearing [- m] coda. *Ancient Chinese Research*, 2006 (1): 17 - 20.

Fallon, Paul D. *The Synchronic and Diachronic Phonology of Ejectives*. New York: Routledge, 2002.

Feng, Aizhen. *A Study of the Fuqing Dialect*. Beijing: Social Sciences Academic Press, 1993.

Feng, Aizhen. *Fuzhou Dialect Dictionary*. Nanjing: Jiangsu Education Press, 1998.

Flemming, Edward. Contrast and perceptual distinctiveness. In Bruce Hayes, Robert Kirchner & Donca Steriade (eds.), *Phonetically Based Phonology*. Cambridge: Cambridge University Press, 232 - 276, 2005.

Glover, Justin. An OT account of dorsal consonant alternation in Kranichfeld German. Paper presented at the 15th mid-continental workshop on Phonology, Indiana University, October 2009.

Gordon, Matthew. *Phonological Typology*. Oxford: Oxford University Press, 2016.

Gouskova, Maria. *Deriving Economy: Syncope in Optimality Theory*. PhD dissertation. Amherst: The University of Massachusetts, 2003.

Greenberg, J. H. *Language Universals, with Special Reference to Feature Hierarchies*. Mouton: The Hague, 1966.

Greenberg, J. H. Research on language universals. *Annual Review of Anthropology*, 1975 (4): 75 - 94

Greenberg J. H. *Universals of Human Language: Method and Theory*. Stanford: Stanford University Press, 1978.

Gudschinsky, Sarah C., Harold, Popovich & Frances, Popovich. Native reaction and phonetic similarity in Maxakali phonology. *Language*, 1970 (46): 77 – 88.

Gussenhoven, Carlos & Haike, Jacobs. *Understanding Phonology*. Beijing: Foreign Language Teaching and Research Press, 2001.

Gussenhoven, Carlos & Haike, Jacobs. *Understanding Phonology*. London: Hodder Education, 2011.

Hall, Daniel Currie. *The Role and Representation of Contrast in Phonological Theory*. PhD dissertation. Toronto: University of Toronto, 2007.

Hall, T. A. The status of diachronic buccalizations in Germanic. *Beitröge zur Geschichte der Deutschen Sprache und Literatur*, 2011, 133 (3): 389 – 410.

Hall, T. A. Middle high German [rs] > [r] as height dissimilation. *J Comp German Linguistics*, 2008 (11): 213 – 248.

Halle, Morris. *The Sound Pattern of Russian: A Linguistic and Acoustical Investigation*. The Hague: Mouton, 1959.

Halle, Morris. On markedness. In Proceedings of the 6th International Congress of Phonetic. *Sciences*. Prague: Academia, 61 – 71, 1970.

Halle, Morris. Feature geometry and feature spreading. *LI*, 1995 (26): 1 – 46.

Halle, Morris & Vergnaud, J.-R. Three dimensional phonology. *Journal of Linguistic Research*, 1980 (1): 83 – 105.

Halle, M. & Steven, K. *A Note on Laryngeal Features*. Berlin / New York: Mouton de Gruyter, 1971.

Hargus, Sharon & Rice, Keren. *Athabaskan Prosody*. Amsterdam & Philadelphia: John Benjamins Publishing Company, 2005.

Harris, John. *English Sound Structure*. Oxford: Blackwell, 1994.

Hayes, Bruce. Compensatory lengthening in moraic phonology. *Linguistic Inquiry*, 1989 (20): 253 – 306.

Hayes, Bruce, et al. *Phonetically Based Phonology*. Cambridge: Cambridge University Press, 2004.

He, Da'an. *Rules and Direction—The Rhyme Structures in the Evolution Process*. Beijing: Beijing University Press, 2004.

Hong, Weiren. The types of phonological evolution in Southern Min. *Sheng Yun Lun Ye*, 1999 (8): 403 - 440.

Hong, Weiren. The breakdown and glide formation of the marked vowel of Southern Min. *Sheng Yun Lun Ye*, 2001 (10): 243 - 273.

Hong, Weiren. The collapse of the schwa of Quanzhou accent in Taiwan as well as its markedness. *Chinese Social Linguistics*, 2003 (1): 34 - 51.

Hooper, J. B. *An Introduction to Natural Generative Phonology*. New York: Academic Press, 1976.

Howie, J. M. *An Acoustic Study of Mandarin Tones and Vowels*. London: CUP, 1976.

Hsieh, F.-F. Tonal chain-shifts as anti-neutralization-induced tone sandhi. In S. Arunachalam, et al. (eds.), *Proceedings of the 28th Annual Penn Linguistics Colloquium, University of Pennsylvania Working Papers in Linguistics*. Philadelphia: Penn Linguistics Circle, 99 - 112, 2005.

Hsu, Hui-Chuan. A sonority model of syllable contraction in Taiwanese Southern Min. *Journal of East Asian Linguistics*, 2003, 12 (4), 349 - 377.

Hsu, Hui-chuan. Compositional structure of /iu/ and /ui/ in Taiwanese Southern Min revisited. *Language and Linguistics*, 2004, 5 (4): 1003 - 1018.

Hu, Fang. On the phonetic characteristics of [mb] [ŋg] [nd] of Amoy. *Dialect*, 2005 (1): 11 - 19.

Huang, Diancheng & Li, Rulong. *Fujian Dialects*. Beijing: Fangzhi Publishing House, 1998.

Huang, Hui-chuan J. Phonological patterning of prevocalic glides in Squliq Atayal. *Language and Linguistics*, 2014, 15 (6): 801 - 824.

Hume, Elizabeth. Coronal consonant, front vowels parallels in Maltese. *Natural Language and Linguistic Theory*, 1996, 14 (1): 163 - 203.

Hume, Elizabeth. Language specific. Markedness: The case of place of articulation. *Studies in Phonetics, Phonology and Morphology*, 2003 (9): 295 - 310.

Hume, Elizabeth & Tserdanelis, Georgios. Labial unmarkedness in Sri Lankan Portuguese Creole. *Phonology*, 2002 (19): 441 - 458.

Hyman, Larry M. *A Theory of Phonological Weight.* Dordrecht: Foris, 1985.

Hyman, Larry M. Register tones and tonal geometry. In Hary van der Hust & Keith Snider (eds.), *The Phonology of Tone: The Representation of Tonal Register.* Dordrecht: Foris, 1993: 75 – 108.

Hyman, Larry M. & Russell, G. Schuh. Universals of tone rules: Evidence from West Africa. *Linguistic Inquiry*, 1974 (5): 81 – 115.

Hyman, Larry M. & Schuh, Russell G. Universals of tone rules: Evidence from West Africa. *Linguistic Inquiry*, 1974 (5): 81 – 115.

Hyman, Larry M. & VanBik, Kenneth. Output problems in Hakha Lai-or: What's (not) Chinese about directional tone sandhi? *Language and Linguistics*, 2004, 5 (4): 821 – 861.

Iverson, Gregory K. On the category supralaryngeal. *Phonology*, 1989 (2): 285 – 303.

Jakobson, Roman. The phonemic and grammatical aspects of language in their interrelations. In Roman Jakobson (ed.), *Selected Writings II.* The Hague: Mouton, 103 – 14, 1949.

Jakobson, Roman. *Child Language, Aphasia, and Phonological Universals.* The Hague: Mouton, 1968.

Jakobson, Roman. *Six Lectures on Sound and Meaning.* Cambridge, MA: MIT Press, 1978.

Jakobson, Roman & Halle, Morris. *Fundamentals of Language.* The Hague: Mouton, 1956.

Jakobson, Roman & Lotz, John. Notes on the French phonemic pattern. *Word*, 1949 (5): 151 – 158.

Jones, Daniel. *An Outline of English Phonetics (9th edition).* Cambridge: CUP, 1975.

Jun, Jongho. *Perceptual and Articulatory Factors in Place Assimilation: An Optimality Theoretic Approach.* PhD dissertation. Los Angeles: University of California, 1995.

Jun, Jongho. Place assimilation is not the result of gestural overlap: Evidence from Korean and English. *Phonology*, 1996 (13): 377 – 407.

Jun, Jongho. Place assimilation. In Bruce Hayes, Robert Kirchner & Donca Steriade (eds), *Phonetically Based Phonology*. Cambridge: Cambridge University Press, 58 – 86, 2004.

Kaplan, Lawrence D. *Phonological Issues in North Alaskan Inupiaq*. Fairbanks, AK: Alaska Native Language Center, 1981.

Katamba, F. X. *An Introduction to Phonology*. Longman: Katamba, 1989.

Kaye, J. & De la Syllabicit. In F. Dell, D. Hirst & J.-R. Vergnaud (eds.), *Forme sonore du langage*. Paris: Hermann, 123 – 159, 1984.

Kean, M.-L. *The Theory of Markedness in Generative Grammar.* PhD dissertation. Boston: MIT, 1975.

Kehrein, W. *Phonological Representation and Phonetic Phrasing: Affricates and Laryngeals.* Tübingen: Niemeyer, 2002.

Kenneth, Hurlstone Jackson. *A Historical Phonology of Breton*. Dublin: Dublin Institute for Advanced Studies, 1967.

Kiparsky, Paul. Lexical morphology and phonology. In the Linguistic Society of Korea (ed.), *Linguistics in the Morning Calm*. Seoul: Hanshin, 3 – 91, 1982.

Kiparsky, Paul. Some consequences of lexical phonology. *Phonology Yearbook*, 1985 (2): 85 – 138, 1985.

LaCharité, D. *The Internal Structure of Affricates.* PhD dissertation. Ottawa: University of Ottawa, 1993.

Ladefoged, Peter. *Preliminaries to Linguistic Phonetics*. Chicago: University of Chicago, 1971.

Ladefoged, Peter. *A Course in Phonetics*. New York: Harcourt Brace Jovanovich, 1982.

Ladefoged, Peter & Maddieson, Ian. *The Sounds of the World's Languages*. Oxford: Blackwell Publishing Ltd, 1996.

Lan, Ruchun. *Fu'an City Chronicles*. Beijing: China Local Records Publishing House, 1999.

Levi, S. V. Phonemic vs derived glides. *Lingua*, 2008, 118: 1956 – 1978.

Li, Paul Jen-Kui. A secret language in Taiwanese. *Journal of Chinese Linguis-*

tics, 1985 (13): 91 - 121.

Li, Paul Jen-Kui. *An Analysis of the Syllable-Final Glottal Stop in Southern Min.* Bulletin of the Institute of History and Philology, Academic Sinica 60, 487 - 492, 1989.

Li, Rulong. On the present forms of the voiced onsets of Middle Chinese in Min. *Studies in Language and Linguistics*, 1985 (1): 143 - 153.

Li, Rulong. The constraints of the categorical transformation of onsets of Fuzhou. *Xiamen University Journal*, 2000 (1): 123 - 130.

Li, Rulong, etc. *Fujian Dialects.* Beijing: Dialect Publishing House, 1998.

Liang, Yuzhang. L-words in the Fuzhou dialect. *Dialect*, 1982 (1): 39 - 48.

Lijencrants, J. & Lindbom, B. Numeric simulation of vowel quality systems: The role of perceptual contrast. *Language*, 1972 (48): 839 - 862.

Li, Rong. On the division of Chinese dialects. *Dialect*, 1989 (4): 3 - 21.

Lin, Hansheng. *The Lexicon and Grammar Study of Eastern Min.* Kunming: Kunming University Press, 2002.

Lin, Huishan. *Directionality in Tone Sandhi and the Effect of Identity Preservation.* PhD dissertation. Taipei: Tsing Hua University, 2004.

Lin, Liantong. *A Survey of the Dialect in Quanzhou City.* Beijing: Social Sciences Academic Press, 1993.

Lin, Qing. The sound change of rhymes bearing the old nasal codas of Chaozhou dialect. *Jinan Journal (Philosophy and Social Sciences)*, 2013 (9): 155 - 164.

Lin, Qing. *The Diachrony of Tone Sandhi: Evidence from Southern Min Chinese.* Beijing: Peking University Press & Springe Nature, 2019.

Lin, Tao & Wang, Lijia. *A Course in Phonetics.* Beijing: Peking University Press, 1992.

Lin, Yen-Hwei. Nasal segments in Taiwanese secret languages. *Arizona Phonology Conference*, 1988 (1): 60 - 74.

Lin, Yen-Hwei. *Autosegmental Treatment of Segmental Processes in Chinese Phonology.* PhD dissertation. Austin: University of Texas, 1989.

Lin, Yen-Hwei. Mid vowel assimilation across Mandarin dialects. *Journal of*

East Asian Linguistics, 2002, 11 (4): 303 - 347.

Lindblom, B. Experiments in sound structure. Paper read at the Eighth International Congress of Phonetic Sciences, Leeds, 1975.

Liu, Lunxing. *Fundamental Course of Chinese Phonology*. Beijing: China Society and Science Publishing House, 2001.

Lombardi, Linda. *Laryngeal Features and Laryngeal Neutralization*. PhD dissertation. Amherst: University of Massachusetts, 1991.

Lombardi, Linda. Coronal epenthesis and markedness. *Phonology*, 2002 (19): 219 - 251.

Luo, Changpei. *Xiamen Phonology*. Beijing: Science Press, 1956.

Luo, Mingqiong. *Chinese Syllable Structure: An X-Bar Approach*. PhD dissertation. Shanghai: Shanghai International Studies University, 2014.

Ma, Chongqi. The comparative studies of the rhyme books of Southern Min of Chinese Mainland. *The Journal of Fujian Normal University*, 2002 (2): 102 - 107.

McCarthy, John J. Feature geometry and dependency: A review. *Phonetica*, 1988 (43): 45.

McCarthy, John J. & Taub, Alison. Review of Paradis & Prunet. *Phonology*, 1992, 9 (2): 363 - 370.

Mackenzie, S. Similarity and contrast in consonant harmony systems. In Chiara Frigeni, Manami Hirayama & Sara Mackenzie (eds.), *Toronto Working Papers in Linguistics (Special Issue on Similarity in Phonology)*. Toronto: University of Toronto, 169 - 182, 2005.

Mackenzie, S. *Contrast and Similarity in Consonant Harmony Systems*. PhD dissertation. Toronto: University of Toronto, 2009.

Maddieson, Ian. A note on tone and consonants. *UCLA Working Papers in Phonetics*, 1974, 27: 18 - 27.

Maddieson, Ian. Universal of tone. In J. H. Greenberg (ed.), *Universals of Human Languages*. Stanford: Stanford University Press, 335 - 366, 1978.

Maddieson, Ian. *Patterns of Sound*. Cambridge: Cambridge University Press, 1984.

Maddieson, Ian. Phonetic universals. In William Hardcastle & John Laver (eds.), *The Handbook of Phonetic Sciences*. Oxford: Blackwell Publishers, 619 - 639, 1997.

Michaud, Alexis. Monosyllabicization: Patterns of evolution in Asian languages. In Nicole Nau, Thomas Stolz & Cornelia Stroh (eds.), *Monosyllables: From Phonology to Typology*. Berlin: Akademie Verlag, 2012.

Mohanan, K. P. On syllabicity. *Linguistics*, 1979 (1): 182 - 194.

Mohanan, K. P. Fields of attraction in phonology. In J. Goldsmith (ed.), *The Last Phonological Rule*. Chicago: University of Chicago Press, 61 - 117, 1993.

Morris, Halle. Feature geometry and feature spreading. *Linguistic Inquiry*, 1995, 26 (1): 1 - 46.

Nearey, Terrance Michael. *Phonetic Feature Systems of Vowels*. Indiana: Bloomington: University Linguistics Club, 1978.

Nie, Yujuan. *The Phonetic Study of Taining Dialect*. PhD dissertation. Fuzhou: Fujian Normal University, 2012.

Norman, Jerry. Tonal development in Min. *Journal of Chinese Linguistics*, 1973, 1 (2): 222 - 238.

Norman, Jerry. Chronological strata in the Min dialects. *Dialect*, 1979, 4: 268 - 273.

Norman, Jerry. The proto-Min finals. Proceedings of the First International Conference on Sinology: Section on Linguistics and Paleography. Taipei: Academia Sinica, 35 - 73, 1981.

Norman, Jerry. On Chinese dialects from the perspective of rhymes. *Dialect*, 2006 (1): 6 - 15.

Ohala, John J. The phonetics of nasal phonology: Theorems and data. In M. K. Huffman & R. A. Krakow (eds.), *Nasals, Nasalization, and the Velum*. San Diego, CA: Academic Press, 225 - 249, 1993.

Oostendorp, Marc van, et al. *The Blackwell Companion to Phonology*. Oxford: Blackwell Publishing Ltd, 2011.

Padgett, Jaye. Glides, vowels and features. *Lingua*, 2008, 118: 1937 - 1955.

Padgett, Jaye. Consonant-vowel place feature interactions. In M. C. Van Oostendorp, E. Hume Ewen & K. Rice (eds.), *The Blackwell Companion to Phonology*. Malden, MA: Wiley-Blackwell, 1761 - 1786, 2011.

Pan, Wuyun. *Chinese Historical Phonology*. Shanghai: Shanghai Education Press, 2000.

Paradis, Carole & Prunet, Jean-Francois. *Phonetics and Phonology*. San Diego: Academic Press, 1991a.

Paradis, Carole & Prunet, Jean-Francois. Asymmetry and visibility in consonant articulations. In Carole Paradis & Jean-Francois Prunet (eds.), *The Special Status of Coronals: Internal and External Evidence. Phonetics and Phonology 2*. San Diego: Academic Press, 1 - 28, 1991b.

Peng, Jianguo, et al. The historical study of Hunan dialects. *Hunan Social Science*, 2008 (1): 162 - 168.

Prince, Alan & Smolensky, Paul. *Optimality Theory: Constraint Interaction in Generative Grammar*. Oxford: Blackwell, 2004.

Pulleyblank, Edwin. *Middle Chinese: A Study in Historical Phonology*. Vancouver: The University of British Columbia Press, 1984.

Pulleyblank, Douglas. *Tone in Lexical Phonology*. Dordrecht: D. Reidel, 1986.

Pulleyblank, Douglas. A note on tonal markedness in Yoruba. *Phonology*, 2004, 21: 409 - 425.

Rachel, Walker. *Vowel Patterns in Language*. Cambridge: Cambridge University Press, 2011.

Reh, Mechthild. *Anywa Language: Description and Internal Reconstruction*. Cologne: Ruddiger Koppe, 1996.

Rice, Keren. Default variability: The coronal-velar relationship. *Natural Language and Linguistic Theory*, 1996, 14 (3): 493 - 543.

Rice, Keren. Featural markedness in phonology: Variation. *GLOT*, 1999, 4 (7): 3 - 6.

Rice, Keren. Markedness in phonology. In Paul de Lacy (ed.), *The Cambridge Handbook of Phonology*. Cambridge: Cambridge University Press, 79 - 98, 2007.

Rice, Keren & Avery, Peter. On the relationship between laterality and coronality. In Carole Paradis & Jean-Francois Prunet (eds.), *The Special Status of Coronals: Internal and External Evidence: Phonetics and Phonology*. San Diego: Academic Press, 101 - 123, 1991.

Rose, Sharon. Coronality and vocalic underspecification. In Carrie Dyck (ed.), *TWPL 12.2*. Toronto: University of Toronto, 155 - 176, 1993.

Rubach, J. Affricates as strident stops in Polish. *Linguistic Inquiry*, 1994 (25): 119 - 143.

Ruhlen, Merritt. Nasal vowels. *Working Papers on Language Universals*, 1973 (12): 1 - 36.

Sagey, Elizabeth C. The representation of features and relations in non-linear phonology. PhD dissertation. Boston: MIT, 1986.

Schane, Sanford A. The fundamentals of particle phonology. *Phonology Yearbook*, 1984 (1): 129 - 155.

Sezer, Egin. The alternation in Turkish. In George N. Clements (ed.), *Harvard Studies in Phonology*. Bloomington: IULC Publications, 354 - 382, 1981.

Shen, Zhongwei. Syllabic nasals in Chinese dialects. *Bulletin of Chinese Linguistics*, 2006, 1 (1): 81 - 108.

Shi, Xiujuan. *The Vowel Pattern of Chinese Dialects*. Beijing: Chinese Social and Scientific Press, 2010.

Sloan, K. *Syllables and Templates: Evidence from Southern Sierra Miwok*. Boston: MIT, 1991.

Smith, Jennifer. *Phonological Augmentation in Prominent Positions*. PhD dissertation. Amherst: University of Massachusetts, 2002.

Snider, Keith L. Tonal upstep in Krachi: Evidence for a register tier. *Language*, 1990, 66: 453 - 474.

Stampe, David. *How I Spent My Summer Vacation*. PhD dissertation. Chicago: University of Chicago, 1972.

Steriade, Donca. *Vowel Tiers and Geminate Blockage*. Boston: MIT, 1987a.

Steriade, Donca. Redundant values. In A. Bosch & E. Schiller (eds.), *Paras-*

ession on Autosegmental and Metrical Phonology. Chicago: University of Chicago, 339 – 362, 1987b.

Steriade, Donca. Locality conditions and feature geometry. *NELS*, 1987c (17): 595 – 617.

Stevens, Kenneth. On the quantal nature of speech. *Journal of Phonetics*, 1986 (17): 3 – 45.

Tang, Zuofan. *The Course for Chinese Phonology*. Beijing: Peking University Press, 2013.

Torre, Erik Jan van der. *Dutch Sonorants: The Role of Place of Articulation in Phonotactics*. Utrecht: LOT, 2003.

Trask, R. L. *A Dictionary of Phonetics and Phonology*. London: Routledge, 1996.

Trigo, Lauren. *On the Phonological Deviation and Behavior of Nasal Glides*. PhD dissertation. Boston: MIT, 1988.

Trubetzkoy, N. S. *Principles of Phonology*. Berkley: University of California Press, 1969.

Tucker, Archibald. *A Grammar of Kenya Luo (Dholuo)*. Cologne: Ruddiger Koppe, 1994.

Vaux, Bert. Syllabification in Armenian, universal grammar and the lexicon. *Linguistic Inquiry*, 2003, 34 (1): 91 – 125.

Walker, Rachel. A vowel feature hierarchy for contrastive specification. In Carrie Dyck (ed.), *Toronto Working Papers in Linguistics* (Special Issue on Complexity in Phonological Representations). Toronto: University of Toronto, 179 – 197, 1993.

Wang, Li. *The Phonology of Chinese*. Beijing: Zhonghua Book Company, 1963.

Wang, Li. The conditioned sound changes of Chinese phonetic history. *Studies in Language and Linguistics*, 1983 (1): 5 – 9.

Wang, Li. *History of Chinese Phonology*. Beijing: China Society and Science Publishing House, 1985.

Wang, Shuangcheng. *The Phonetic Study of Anduo Tibetan*. Shanghai:

Zhongxi Publishing House, 2012.

Wang, William S.-Y. Phonological features of tone. *IJAL*, 1967, 33 (2): 93 – 105.

Waugh, Linda. Markedness and phonological systems. In W. Wolck & Paul L. Garvin (eds.), *The Fifth LACUS Forum*. Columbia, SC: Hornbeam Press, 155 – 165, 1979.

Weijer, Jeroen M. van de. *Segmental Structure and Complex Segments*. PhD dissertation. Tübingen: Max Niemeyer Verlag, 1994.

Wilson, Colin. Consonant cluster neutralisation and targeted constraints. *Phonology*, 2001, 18 (1): 147 – 197.

Wright, Martha S. A metrical approach to tone sandhi in Chinese dialects. PhD dissertation. Amherst, MA: University of Massachusetts, 1983.

Wu, Qingran. The OT analysis of tone sandhi of Fu'an. Master dissertation. Xi'an: Shaanxi Normal University, 2009.

Wu, Ruiwen. *On Three Strata of the Fourth Grade Rhymes of Min*. Shanghai: Shanghai Education Press, 2002.

Wu, Ruiwen. *A Comparative Study of the Phonologies of Wu and Min*. PhD dissertation. Taipei: Zhengzhi University, 2005.

Wu, Ruiwen. The reconstruction of the rhyme *y in Proto-Min as well as the related questions. *Language & Linguistics*, 2009 (2): 205 – 237.

Wu, Ruiwen. On the evolution and strata of Kaikouhu of Geng She in common Min dialect. *Language and Linguistics*, 2010, 11 (2): 297 – 334.

Wu, Ruiwen. On the reconstruction of Qi rhyme of Jiangdong dialects of Nanchao Period from the perspective of comparison of Min. *Oriental Linguistics*, 2014 (14): 60 – 80.

Xu, Tongqiang. *Historical Linguistics*. Beijing: The Commercial Press, 1991.

Xu, Tongqiang. The principles of the phonological non-linear structures and the phonetic history. *Minority Languages of China*, 1996 (6): 1 – 10.

Yang, Xiufang. *On the Differentiation of Literary and Colloquial Strata of Southern Min*. PhD dissertation. Taipei: Taiwan University, 1982.

Yang, Xiufang. *The Grammar of Taiwan Southern Min*. Taipei: Da An Publishing House, 1991.

Yang, Yifan. *A Diachronic Phonological Study of Zi Rhyme Change in Northern Henan Province*. Dissertation for Master Degree. Shanghai: ECNU, 2015.

Ye, Xiaofeng. *The Typological Research of Chinese Dialects*. PhD dissertation. Shanghai: Fudan Univeristy, 2011.

Yip, Moira. *The Tonal Phonology of Chinese*. PhD dissertation. Boston: MIT, 1980.

Yip, Moira. Contour tones. *Phonology*, 1989 (6): 149 – 174.

Yip, Moira. Morpheme-level features: Chaoyang syllable structure and nasalization. Proceedings of the Sixth North-American Conference on Chinese Linguistics. Los Angeles: University of Southern California, 1994.

Yip, Moira. Lexical optimization in languages without alternations. In J. Durand & B. Laks (eds.), *Current Trends in Phonology: Models and Methods*. Salford: University of Salford publications, 757 – 788, 1996.

Yip, Moira. Tonal features, tonal inventories and phonetic targets. *UCL Working Papers in Linguistics*, 2001 (13): 303 – 329.

Yip, Moira. *Tone*. Cambridge: Cambridge University Press, 2002.

Yuan, Bixia. *The Historical Strata of Finals in the Eastern Min Dialects*. PhD dissertation. Hangzhou: Zhejiang University, 2010.

Yuan, Bixia, et al. On the initial assimilations of Eastern Min dialects in Fujian Province. *Dialect*, 2013 (1): 52 – 67.

Yuan, Jiahua. *A Study of Chinese Dialects*. Beijing: Language Reform Press, 1960.

Yuan, Jiahua, et al. *An Introduction to Chinese Dialects*. Beijing: Language Reform Press, 1989.

Yue-Hashimoto, Anne. Tonal flip-flop in Chinese dialects. *Journal of Chinese Linguistics*, 1986 (14): 161 – 182.

Yue-Hashimoto, Anne. Tone sandhi across Chinese dialects. In Chinese Language Society of Hong Kong (ed.), *Wang Li Memorial Volumes*. Hong Kong: Joint Publishing Co, 445 – 474, 1987.

Zec, Draga. *Sonority Constraints on Prosodic Structure*. PhD dissertation.

Stanford: Stanford University, 1988.

Zec, Draga. *Sonority Constraints on Syllable Structure*. Cambridge: Cambridge University Press, 1995.

Zeng, Nanyi. *The Comparison Study of Phonologies of Quanzhou and Xiamen*. PhD dissertation. Beijing: Peking University, 2013.

Zeng, Nanyi. Three possibilities of the extinction of the difference of literary and colloquial strata with Sucuo Anhai of Jinjiang as an example. *Bulletin of Language Studies*, 2014 (2): 233 –241.

Zeng, Rongrong. *The Study of Southern Min of Dongtou of Southern Zhengjiang*. Dissertation for Master Degree. Guangzhou: Jinan University, 2008.

Zhan, Bohui. *Chinese Dialects and the Dialect Investigation*. Wuhan: Education Publishing House of Hubei, 1991.

Zhang, Guangyu. On the formation of Min. *Zhong Guo Yu Wen*, 1996 (1): 16 – 26.

Zhang, Guangyu. The disappearing stages of the rounded preglides of Chinese dialects. *Studies of the Chinese Language*, 2006 (4): 346 –358.

Zhang, Guangyu. On Min dialects: From the phonological perspective. *Studies in Language and Linguistics*, 2011 (1): 96 –105.

Zhang, Guangyu. The nasalization of Chinese dialects. *Studies in Language and Linguistics*, 2012 (2): 17 –28.

Zhang, Jie. *The Effects of Duration and Sonority on Contour Tone Distribution-Typological Survey and Formal Analysis*. PhD dissertation. Los Angeles: UCLA, 2001.

Zhang, Jie. A directional asymmetry in Chinese tone sandhi systems. *Journal of East Asian Linguist*, 2007 (16): 259 –302.

Zhang, Jie. Tones, tonal phonology, and tone sandhi. In C.-T. James Huang, Y.-H. Audrey Li & Andrew Simpson (eds.), *The Handbook of Chinese Linguistics*. Oxford: Wiley-Blackwell, 443 –464, 2014a.

Zhang, Jie. The productivity of tone sandhi in Chinese dialects and its theoretical analysis. *Contemporary Linguistics*, 2014b, 16 (3): 273 –287.

Zhang, Jingfen. *The Historical Comparison and Phonetic Reconstruction of South-*

ern Min. Dissertation for Master Degree. Beijing: Peking University, 2013.

Zhang, Jisheng. *The Phonology of Shaoxing Chinese.* Utrecht: LOT, 2006.

Zhang, Jisheng. The phonological motivation for the evolution of Chinese codas. *Studies of the Chinese Language*, 2007 (4): 291 – 297.

Zhang, Kun. On the comparison of Min dialects. *Studies in Language and Linguistics*, 1985 (1): 111 – 142.

Zhang, Kun. On the comparison of Min dialects again. *Studies in Language and Linguistics*, 1991 (1): 95 – 119.

Zhang, Xi. *Vowel Systems of the Manchu-Tungus Languages of China.* PhD dissertation. Toronto: University of Toronto, 1996.

Zhang, Yanfen. *The Types of Nasal Codas of Middle Chinese in Modern Chinese.* PhD dissertation. Jinan: Shandong University, 2009.

Zhang, Zhenxing. The division of Min sub-dialects. *Dialect*, 1985 (3): 13 – 22.

Zhang, Z. X. *Notes on the Southern Min Dialect in Taiwan.* Fuzhou: Fujian People's Press, 1983.

Zheng, Weina. The distribution of obstruent codas of Southern Min as well as the possible reasons. *Shangtou University Journal (Humanities & Social Sciences)*, 2012 (1): 53 – 59.

Zhengzhang, Shangfang. *Old Chinese Phonology*. Shanghai: Shanghai Education Publishing House, 2003.

Zhengzhang, Shangfang. *Wenzhou Dialect*. Beijing: Chinese Publishing Company, 2008.

Zhou, Cangji. The division of Southern Min dialects of Fujian. *Studies in Language and Linguistics*, 1986 (2): 73 – 88.

Zhu, Titi. The rhyme changes of Quanzhou dialect reflected in the rhyme use of Liyuan Opera. *Jinggangshan University Journal*, 2012, 33 (6): 99 – 104.

Zhu, Yiner. *A Phonological Investigation of the Asymmetrical Mutual Intelligibility Between Northern and Southern Wu Dialects.* PhD dissertation. Shanghai: East China Normal University, 2013.